Contents

Contributors vii

Preface xi

Overview

1 Introducing Competition into Regulated Industries
Dieter Helm and Tim Jenkinson 1

2 Regulation, Competition, and the Structure of Prices
John Vickers 23

3 Network Industries
Michael Klein 40

The UK Experience

4 The Electricity Industry in England and Wales
Richard Green and David M. Newbery 77

5 The UK Gas Industry
Catherine Waddams Price 108

6 Telecommunications
Mark Armstrong 132

7 The Water Industry
Simon Cowan 160

8 The Rail Industry
W. P. Bradshaw 175

The Regulators' Perspective

 9 The Generation and Supply of Electricity:
    The British Experience
    S. C. Littlechild   193

10 Regulating Telecommunications
    Fod Barnes   213

11 Competition in the Water and Sewerage Industry
    I. C. R. Byatt   234

12 Competition in the Rail Industry:
    The Regulatory Perspective
    John Swift   247

Bibliography   263

Index   273

Contributors

Mark Armstrong
Mark Armstrong is a Fellow of Nuffield College, Oxford, and formerly Professor of Economic Policy, University of Southampton. His research interests include the economics of price discrimination, regulation and competition policy.

Fod Barnes
Fod Barnes is Policy Adviser to the Director General of Telecommunications, a position he has held since 1989. He is an expert in the economic and social regulation of utilities, including the problems associated with the introduction of competition to previously monopolistic markets. Prior to that he was Head of Public Affairs at the National Consumer Council.

I. C. R. Byatt
Ian Byatt became the first Director General of Water Services in 1989. His previous post was Deputy Chief Economic Adviser to the Treasury (1978–89). He joined the Civil Service in 1967 and his career there included spells at the Ministry of Housing and Local Government and the Department of the Environment, before he joined the Treasury. He is a member of the Council of Management of the National Institute of Economic and Social Research and an Honorary Fellow of the Chartered Institution of Water and Environmental Management.

W. P. Bradshaw
Bill Bradshaw is a senior research fellow at Wolfson College, Oxford. He held senior executive posts in British Rail before moving into academic life. Throughout the last Parliament he was Special Adviser to the Transport Select Committee.

Simon Cowan
Simon Cowan is a lecturer at Oxford University and Wigmore Fellow in Economics at Worcester College, Oxford. He is the author, with Mark Armstrong and John Vickers, of *Regulatory Reform: Economic Analysis*

and British Experience, published in 1994 by the MIT Press, and is Managing Editor of *Oxford Economic Papers*.

Richard Green

Richard Green is a Senior Research Officer in the Department of Applied Economics, University of Cambridge, and Director of Studies in Economics at Fitzwilliam College, Cambridge. His work on the electricity industry has included a year on secondment to the Office of Electricity Regulation.

Dieter Helm

Dieter Helm is Fellow in Economics at New College, Oxford, and a director of Oxford Economic Research Associates. He is a member of the Department of Trade and Industry's energy advisory panel and chairman of the Department of the Environment, Transport and the Regions' academic panel. He is an Associate Editor of the *Oxford Review of Economic Policy*.

Tim Jenkinson

Tim Jenkinson is a lecturer at Oxford University and Fellow in Economics at Keble College. He is also a Research Fellow of the Centre for Economic Policy Research in London, Managing Editor of the *Oxford Review of Economic Policy*, and a member of the editorial board of *Oxford Economic Papers*.

Michael Klein

Michael Klein became Chief Economist at Shell International in 1997. Previously, he held posts at the World Bank and in the economics department of the OECD, returning to the World Bank in 1993 to manage its advisory group on Private Participation in Infrastructure. In the latter position, he worked on market structure, regulation, and financing issues in the telecommunications, energy, transport, and water sectors.

S. C. Littlechild

Stephen Littlechild is Director General of Electricity Supply. Previously, he was Professor of Commerce and Head of the Department of Industrial Economics and Business Studies at the University of Birmingham. He advised on the regulatory regime for British Telecom and the water industry, and was a member of the Monopolies and Mergers Commission for 6 years.

David M. Newbery

David Newbery has been Director of the Department of Applied Economics and Professor of Applied Economics at the University of Cambridge since 1988. He is a Fellow of the Centre for Economic Policy Research, of the Econometric Society and of the British Academy. He is currently a member of the Monopolies and Mergers Commission and on the academic panel of the Department of the Environment, Transport and the Regions.

John Swift

John Swift holds the joint posts of Rail Regulator and International Rail Regulator, heading the Office of the Rail Regulator, which was designated under the 1993 Railways Act. He has been a Queen's Counsel since 1981 and, when at the Bar, specialized in the field of competition law.

John Vickers

John Vickers is Drummond Professor of Political Economy at Oxford University and a Fellow of All Souls College. He has also held visiting positions at Harvard, Princeton, and the London Business School. His books include *Privatization: An Economic Analysis* (with George Yarrow, 1988) and *Regulatory Reform: Economic Analysis and British Experience* (with Mark Armstrong and Simon Cowan, 1994). He was a member of the Hansard Commission on the regulation of privatised utilities, and he is an advisor to Oftel.

Catherine Waddams Price

Catherine Waddams Price became Director of the Centre for Management under Regulation at the University of Warwick in October 1995, following 16 years in the Economics Department of the University of Leicester. Her research has centred on privatization and regulation of utilities, and particularly the effect on tariff rebalancing and consequent distributional implications. She is a member of the Office of Gas Regulation Panel of Economic Experts.

Preface

DIETER HELM and TIM JENKINSON

The transfer of much of the state's productive assets to the private sector in Britain in the 1980s and early 1990s had profound effects on the role of the state in the economy. It changed the incentives of firms, with civil servants and ministers replaced by shareholders and financial institutions as the instruments of control.

Although at the outset this was very much an afterthought, privatization also forced the government to develop its new role as regulator of the privatized utilities. It posed two distinct but related problems—how to regulate monopoly, and how to introduce competition.

The successful introduction of competition, it was envisaged, should reduce the need for detailed regulation. According to this blueprint, regulation would concentrate on those activities that are, for technological reasons, 'natural monopolies'. By stripping out potentially competitive activities—such as the provision of train services, electricity generation, or gas supply—and exposing them to competition, the remaining regulated activities—such as the railway track network or electricity and gas transmission and distribution—should be easier to regulate. The focus of such regulation would be to provide incentives to increase efficiency and to make sure all competitors had 'fair' access to the natural monopoly services.

A significant part of this restructuring has, indeed, taken place in the UK. However, the promotion of competition has turned out to be altogether more complex than the architects of privatization imagined. Indeed, to a considerable degree, the politicians handed over the difficult issues to the new breed of high-profile regulators, notionally 'independent' from government. These individuals (with the exception of the water regulator) were given the duty to promote, secure, or otherwise enable competition, to be achieved by a mixture of exhortation, voluntary agreements, licence amendments, and references to the Monopolies and Mergers Commission (MMC).

In telecommunications, the initial duopoly established at the time of BT's privatization has given way to a more open market in which competitors exist in all market segments. Regulation of final prices has now, to a considerable extent, withered away, with only the smallest households being protected by a price cap determined by the regulator. In electricity, the regulator has forced through plant divestment and encouraged new entry into generation. The opening up of the electricity supply market is due to start in 1998, although the regulator will continue to set a price-cap for domestic consumers for the next few years. In gas, competition in the industrial market and, recently, the domestic gas supply market has been established, although the complex issues involved have resulted in three separate investigations by the MMC in recent years. In water and railways, competition has been somewhat lower on the agenda, largely because of the particular circumstances of these industries. The water regulator does not have an explicit duty to promote competition, and the scope within the water industry is, in any case, limited. In rail, the Conservative government that effected the privatization 'moderated' competition in order to get the train-operator franchises sold.

Although it will be some time before definitive conclusions can be made about the British experiments in introducing competition, enough time has elapsed to draw some preliminary lessons from the British experience. In many industries Britain was the first to experiment with competition on a significant scale, and especially so in telecoms, electricity, and gas. In consequence, it has also been at the forefront of those grappling with the regulatory, social, and political consequences.

This book draws on that experience, providing not only commentary and analysis of what has happened, and proposals to take matters forward, but also a set of examples to enable other countries better to design their own competition policies—to avoid the mistakes and to build on the successes.

The volume falls into three parts. The first chapters analyse the general issues that arise when competition is introduced into utility industries. Dieter Helm and Tim Jenkinson consider the important transitional and structural issues encountered. John Vickers analyses the theoretical issues raised for the appropriate structure of prices in regulated industries. Michael Klein draws on a wealth of international experience to provide an overview of the main issues confronting policy-makers when competition is introduced into network industries.

The second part of the volume focuses on the UK experience in specific industries. Richard Green and David Newbery consider the problems encountered in the electricity industry, in particular those caused by the structure of the generation market. Catherine Waddams

Price focuses on the gas industry and provides evidence of the response of domestic consumers to the introduction of competition. Mark Armstrong assesses the rationale for the pro-competition policies pursued in telecommunications, which have even extended to encouraging competition in the local loop. Simon Cowan considers the various forms competition could take in the water industry, and the effects such competition would have on the structure of tariffs. Finally, Bill Bradshaw considers the impact, on both competition and the extent of public subsidies, of the fundamental restructuring of railways that has recently been completed.

The final chapters present the perspectives of the regulators. In such a highly personalized regulatory system as that in the UK, where regulators are given general duties and wide-ranging powers to amend licences subject to an MMC appeal, there is very considerable scope for personal interpretations of competition and the best means to promote it. These chapters, therefore, provide not only an insight into the specific industries, but also, when compared and contrasted, a powerful example of the different ways in which discretion has been exercised.

Wherever possible, we have endeavoured to avoid the trap of time-dependency. This volume is not designed to be simply an account of the historical and current events, which will lose its impact as time unfolds. No doubt new and surprising events will yield more information about the promotion of competition. Nevertheless, the evidence from experience of the first decade of competition policy — during and after privatization — stands as a concrete example to other countries which are now embarking on this course. The Scandinavians were better able to design their electricity markets because the Pool established in England and Wales provided a working example of one sort of model. Similarly, the Germans have been able to predict some of the consequences of competition in the gas industry on long-term contracts, and hence supply security, by observing the impact on British Gas of the introduction of competition in first industrial and then domestic markets. The United States, too — in telecoms and electricity — has begun to fashion its policies in the light of British experience. This volume is intended as much to inform this international audience as to address the outstanding agenda for the introduction of competition in the UK privatized industries.

Finally, thanks are due to James Martin and Andrew Schuller at Oxford University Press and, in particular, to Alison Gomm, our production editor.

Overview

1

Introducing Competition into Regulated Industries

DIETER HELM AND TIM JENKINSON*

1. Introduction

For most of the post-war period it has been a conventional wisdom that the market failures in the utility industries were so great as to merit state ownership, vertical integration, and monopoly. State ownership 're-solved' the conflict of interests between the private and public good; vertical integration ensured that customers bore the risk of upstream sunk investments; and monopoly prevented the destructive competition which was widely thought to have pervaded the industries in the 1920s and 1930s.

For a variety of reasons—some ideological, some budgetary and some grounded in economics—state ownership was abandoned as the preferred option in the 1980s. In Britain, assets with a current market value in excess of £100 billion[1] have been transferred to the private sector in the course of the extensive privatization programme.

As privatization got under way, the merits of vertical integration and monopoly were increasingly questioned, and the possibility of introducing competition actively considered. In the early 1980s, Mercury was created as a competitor to British Telecom (BT). For certain companies in the state sector, the 1980 Competition Act abandoned the statutory monopoly, the 1982 Oil and Gas (Enterprise) Act limited British Gas's vertical integration into the North Sea, and the 1983 Energy Act provided for private purchase tariffs and network access in the electricity industry.

From these early tentative steps, bolder plans emerged, leading eventually to the idea of retail customer choice for all gas and electricity

* Respectively, New College and Keble College, University of Oxford.

[1] It is increasingly difficult to estimate the market value of privatized companies as a result of the large number of takeovers that have occurred. However, Jenkinson and Mayer (1994) estimated that in July 1992, before the recent takeover wave, the market capitalization of the listed privatized companies was over £80 billion. Subsequent privatizations and general stock-market movements suggest that this figure would now be over £100 billion.

customers, the arrival of cable to rival BT, and even plans to introduce competition into the supply of water. The electricity and (eventually) the gas industries have been broken up, and the railways have been split along vertical and horizontal lines.

The concept of supply competition has caught on in Europe and the USA. Following the Single European Act in 1987, and the programme for completing the internal market by 1 January 1993, the European Commission turned its attentions to the utility sectors, with initiatives in telecoms, energy, and postal services. Draft directives in these areas have had a difficult history, but the general direction of European utility policy is now well-established as a process of gradually prising open the utility markets. In the USA the 1996 Telecoms Act further liberalized the telecommunications market, while the 1992 Energy Act and the subsequent order 888 by the Federal Energy Regulatory Commission (FERC, 1996) provided for the transition to a more competitive electricity supply market, at least at the wholesale level. Numerous other countries have also begun the process of introducing competition, notably New Zealand, Chile, Australia, and Sweden.

As with privatization, the idea of competition has driven politicians frequently to embrace policies without sufficient attention to the details of implementation. The simple political rhetoric extolling the virtues of competition belies the complexities in its application. Too often the public debate fails to distinguish the different kinds of competition and the particular characteristics of each industry. Competition is not an end in itself, but rather a means to higher economic welfare. Its applicability to particular circumstances depends upon the relevant costs and benefits. While there are frequently considerable gains, regulated monopoly may in some circumstances be preferable. Even where competition is both feasible and desirable, the transitional arrangements may have profound effects on the type and degree of competition that emerges, and the political acceptability of the outcome.

In this chapter, a number of these complexities are considered. In section 2, we discuss the types of competition and the necessary conditions which must be met to make competition work. In section 3, the transitional issues are considered, including the problem of stranded assets, the impact of technology, and cross-subsidies. Finally, in section 4, we examine the regulatory implications. Contrary to the views of some of the early exponents of competition, there is little evidence (and little reason to imagine) that as competition rises, regulation will 'wither away'.

2. The Structure of Competitive Markets

In order to design a policy to introduce competition, there are a number of conceptual issues which need to be addressed. The utilities comprise different elements, each of which displays different kinds of market failure. All utilities contain networks, and most of these have significant elements of natural monopoly. Access to the network is essential for producers to get their products to customers. It follows that not all parts of utilities are open to production and supply competition, though there may be other kinds of competition which can be applied to the core network.

Thus, we need to distinguish the different kinds of competition which can be applied to utilities and the underlying structural components to which these may be appropriate. We also need to consider the linkages between stages of production, and therefore the forms and degrees of vertical integration which maximize efficiency.

(a) *Types of Competition*

When the advocates of competition discuss utilities, they typically distinguish between natural monopoly and potentially competitive activities, and focus on the latter. This distinction is useful, and we return to it below. The competition they have in mind is *output* (or commodity) *competition*, and the traditional models of competitive markets are used to elicit the conditions under which it can be promoted.

Within the domain of output competition, a number of distinctions can be made. These focus on two dimensions: *the definition of the output* and *the time period*. In the utility sector, the boundaries between production and transmission, and between supply and distribution are uncertain. For example, in the electricity industry, generation of electricity is a fairly well-defined activity, but the boundary between generation and the related dispatch and Pool activities is not. In addition, electricity generation provides not only the commodity itself, but the stand-by capacity which ensures that, whatever time of day we turn on a light, the power is instantly available.

Downstream, at the customer interface, there are a variety of services which lie on the boundary between supply and distribution. Customers buy electricity with associated services, such as meter reading, energy advice, credit facilities, and payment options. If competition is confined to the commodity (which is, after all, homogeneous), it focuses on purchasing strategy, financial risk management, and marketing, and, as such, may be highly competitive with small margins. Financial failures of suppliers are quite possible and mechanisms have to be put in place to deal with customers stranded by a failed supplier. If, however, the other services are added in, supply competition is a much broader activity.

The strategy many policy-makers and regulators have adopted is to begin with the core supply activities, and gradually extend competition to the ancillary services. There is much to commend this approach, as we discuss in section 3 below. However, in a number of utilities, a prior decision has been made to widen the initial definition of outputs. In gas, for example, supply is given a wide scope, to include social obligations. The consequence has been a form of quasi-franchise competition.[2]

Turning to the second dimension of output competition, the time period, very little economic activity is governed purely by spot transactions, even where there are spot markets. Competition also arises in contract markets and between vertically integrated firms. Economic theory suggests that the term structure of contracts will be determined in part by the project characteristics of upstream production and the lives of associated infrastructure assets. Again, the electricity industry provides a good example. Virtually all new entrants' combined-cycle gas-turbine power stations (CCGTs), built by independent power producers (IPPs), were based upon 10–15-year power purchase contracts with regional electricity companies (Helm, 1994a).

These time-period distinctions matter in designing policies to promote competition. Regulators have considerable control over the structure of contracts with final customers. If these customers are inhibited in signing long-term contracts with suppliers, risks cannot be assigned downstream. This will influence the type and amount of upstream investment. Similarly, if all electricity has to be dispatched through the Pool, and bilateral contracting outside the Pool is prohibited, then the structure of investment will be affected. (These issues are discussed further in section 3(a) below.)

Output competition is not the only option in the utilities. Competition can also be applied to *inputs*. The usual mechanism is competitive tendering, whereby the utility is required to test its own production costs against the market. The uses of such mechanisms stretch from the reduction of the core areas of natural monopoly, through to a mechanism for overcoming the informational asymmetries between utilities and regulators when prices are set at periodic reviews.

It is not surprising that competitive tendering has been used most extensively as a regulatory tool in the water industry, where the scope for output competition is limited and, therefore, the pressure on costs to

---

[2] In the pilot phases of domestic gas competition, participants were required to designate supply areas which contained a balanced socio-economic range of domestic customers. See the chapter by Catherine Waddams Price in this volume.

prevent the loss of market share is very weak. Although the theory of price-cap regulation stresses the incentives created to minimize costs, the severity of the problems associated with defining the starting cost base for periods, and the frequent inter-period interventions have reduced these incentives.[3] The role of input competition has been further refined in the case of multi-utilities (notably Hyder, United Utilities, and ScottishPower) where the creation of facilities management companies, providing services to a number of utilities, has brought additional cost-allocation problems.

Most utilities operate under licences. These are granted for a period of time, and they can be open to competitive bidding. The competition in this case is for a monopoly right and, in theory, bidding should transfer the potential monopoly rent to customers or government. Such *franchise competition* has been applied most extensively in the railway privatization, where train-operating companies were required to provide a minimum standard of service, and then to bid for the right to a 7-year (or in some cases longer) monopoly. Where subsidies are involved, the bids were aimed at minimizing the Treasury contribution (see Bill Bradshaw's chapter in this volume).

The final form of competition is provided by the *capital market*. Competing sets of owners and managers can take over the assets and licences of utilities and, given a price cap, attempt to reduce costs to maximize profits. Indeed, Professor Stephen Littlechild (now Director General of Electricity Supply) placed very considerable faith in this form of competition, arguing, for example, that the capital market pressure could be relied upon to play a significant role in the water industry in enforcing efficiency (Littlechild, 1988). Such competition has, however, been limited in many privatized utilities by golden shares put in place by government[4] and regulatory and political uncertainty as to references to the Monopolies and Mergers Commission (MMC) and subsequent decisions. Nevertheless, following the expiry of golden shares in the regional electricity companies and water companies in 1995, a large number of takeovers occurred, ironically mainly by US utilities whose claimed inefficiencies (as a result of the rate-of-return regulation) had been the main motive for adopting the superior price-cap incentives.[5]

[3] See Helm and Rajah (1994) for a discussion of the erosion of these incentives in the water industry.

[4] See Jenkinson and Ljungqvist (1996, ch. 7) for a discussion of golden shares and the conflicting objectives often faced by governments in conducting a privatization programme.

[5] See Beesley and Littlechild (1989) for a critique of US regulation. It has been suggested that the difference between US and UK costs of capital in utilities in part explains the valuation differences.

These various types of competition — outputs, inputs, franchises, and takeovers — set in various time horizons provide a much more complex set of considerations for the design of competition initiatives. As we shall see below, politicians have rarely paid much attention to these distinctions, preferring a crude catch-all concept.

(b) *Separating Out the Natural Monopoly*

While the previous section noted that input and output competition has, to a considerable extent, blurred the definition of what activities we would expect the operator of a set of natural monopoly assets to perform, it is still clear that it is typically the networks of pipes, wires, and rails that constitute the natural monopoly assets. A clear trend in UK regulatory policy has been to attempt to separate the operation (and increasingly the ownership) of these assets from the upstream or downstream activities (where competition may be possible). Some have seen this separation as a necessary condition for the development of competition.

Early privatizations, such as BT and British Gas, maintained horizontally and vertically integrated monopolies having *de jure* or *de facto* franchise areas that consisted of most UK customers. In such integrated businesses, definitions of costs for the various vertical stages of the businesses were ill-defined and, as a result, cross-subsidies were rife.[6] Indeed, in many of the early privatizations there was no proper cost allocation between the various businesses, let alone a realistic set of transfer prices.

As governments attempted to introduce competition into the sectors, it became apparent that cross-subsidization might well stifle entry, with new entrants potentially being at a competitive disadvantage to the integrated incumbent, who was able to cross-subsidize the competitive part of the business with profits from the natural monopoly element. There were also fears that if the network operator also operated in one of the potentially competitive upstream or downstream markets (such as generation or supply) they would be tempted to favour their associated business over competitors, whether in quality of service or in the prices charged for using the system. Even where such anti-competitive conduct did not, in fact, take place, the expectation that it *might* provided a powerful entry deterrent.

These concerns led, in the case of the gas industry, to the MMC (1993*a*) recommending that *prior to the introduction of competition* British Gas should be split up, with the operation of the pipeline network being the responsibility of a separate company, legally distinct from both the

[6] In addition to cost uncertainties, a further cause of cross-subsidy was deliberate social policy. This is discussed more extensively in section 3(b) below.

upstream exploration and the downstream supply business. The government rejected this recommendation. Accounting separation between the pipeline business and the other parts of British Gas was introduced, and the company itself eventually chose, in 1997, to split itself into two separate legal entities, BG plc and Centrica. However, from a regulatory perspective, the way the company was split was not ideal: the pipeline business was bundled together with most of the upstream exploration and production business (BG plc), while the downstream supply business was bundled together with the servicing company and the large Morecambe gas field (Centrica). The reasons for including a gas field with the supply company revolve around the impact of the introduction of competition on existing contracts (essentially a serious contracting problem was internalized within one company) and the need to make Centrica financially viable. We return to this issue of 'stranded contracts' in section 3(a).

In the later privatizations of electricity (see chapter 4 by Richard Green and David Newbery in this volume) and rail (as discussed by Bradshaw, chapter 8), attempts were made to introduce vertical separation between ownership of the network assets and the other markets into which competition was to be introduced. In the case of rail, the vertical separation has gone to its logical extreme, with the rail network being operated by Railtrack (which is barred from running train services), and train-operating companies competing for the right to run particular services and leasing trains from separate rolling-stock companies. In the electricity supply industry, two networks exist: the high voltage transmission network (operated by the National Grid Company) and the local distribution networks operated by the regional electricity companies. The latter, however, are also involved in the supply of electricity to the final households and many have also made significant investments in electricity generation. The logic of separating out the natural monopoly suggests that separation of the distribution businesses from the supply and generation businesses is likely to become an issue in the near future.

The encouragement of entry and competition is clearly one important motivation for separating out the natural monopoly. However, a further justification for such a policy is that it improves the information upon which regulators make their decisions. While 'ring-fence' accounting of regulated assets is possible, the task of regulators would certainly become easier if all data — both accounting and market-related, such as share prices, credit ratings, and dividends — referred solely to the regulated company. This issue has become especially important as utilities have diversified into unregulated businesses, or have been acquired by other companies.

By mid-1997, for example, 11 of the 12 original UK regional electricity companies (privatized in 1990) had been taken over. The majority have been acquired by US utilities keen to diversify overseas. Some have been acquired by water companies to form 'multi-utilities'. One (Manweb) has been acquired by the vertically integrated ScottishPower. Another (Eastern Electricity, later the Eastern Group) was acquired by Hanson and has since been spun off into an integrated energy company (the Energy Group), after acquiring divested coal generation assets from National Power and PowerGen. The Energy Group was then subject to a bid by the US utility, PacifiCorp. This last bid was referred, by the new Labour government, to the MMC, despite the fact that the original takeover by Hanson was not subjected to MMC scrutiny. Water companies, themselves protected to a considerable extent from takeover, have also been acquisitive, moving into both unregulated businesses (such as waste management) and other regulated sectors (for example, North West Water acquired its local electricity distribution company, Norweb, and renamed the merged group United Utilities, while Welsh Water similarly acquired SWALEC and became Hyder).

While accounting information on the core regulated company has been retained (and in some cases ring-fencing has been reinforced) such acquisitions inevitably raise questions about abuses of transfer pricing and cross-subsidy, as well as denying the regulator potentially valuable market information about the performance of the regulated companies.

These regulatory concerns motivate the calls for the separate listing of the core utility businesses (see, for example, Byatt, 1997; Jenkinson and Mayer, 1997) that have, so far, been vigorously opposed by the companies themselves. On the one hand, separate listing represents one substantive way in which the information flowing to regulators could be improved, and is, in many ways, the logical extension of the policy to separate out the core natural monopoly from the potentially competitive businesses. On the other, it can be argued that changes in the underlying cost structure dictate a more market-based approach.

(c) *Vertical Integration and Contracts*

When utilities face no competition for final customers they are able to enter into all sorts of contracts—for supply, fuel, assets, and services—with very limited risk, provided they are allowed to pass on the costs to final customers. In the case of vertically integrated monopolies many of these contracts are internalized within the firm and may not even be formally defined. The utility may be able to cross-subsidize between customers, and invest in assets that may not be economic (or are too risky) since it can earn supernormal returns on other assets to compensate.

Two important characteristics of utility industries are the relatively long asset lives and the fact that a large proportion of the investment is sunk, with few alternative uses. Given these asset characteristics it is quite rational for companies to want to sign long-term contracts with customers in order to reduce the risk of investing. In particular, long-term contracts may be needed in order to prevent the hold-up problem (see Williamson, 1985; Lyons, 1996) whereby customers may act opportunistically, once the investment has been sunk, and renegotiate terms to their own advantage. A lack of competition in large parts of the final market essentially allowed such long-term contracts to be written.

When the core natural monopoly is separated (either legally or by ring-fencing) from the upstream and downstream businesses, contracts are typically put in place between companies at different vertical positions in the production chain. These contracts reproduce many of the characteristics of vertical ownership. Before privatization they were frequently put in place by the government. For example, in the case of the UK electricity industry, the generators were required to sign contracts with coal suppliers which were linked to 'back-to-back' contracts to sell power on to regional electricity companies. The regional electricity companies in turn had a monopoly franchise in their domestic markets which guaranteed a market for the final electricity. The (high) cost of coal was thus passed down the contract chain to the final consumer with few risks to any of the parties concerned. Arguably, the industry was more vertically integrated in the early years after privatization than before, despite the vertical separation of formal ownership.

Similarly, British Gas could enter into long-term gas supply contracts with North Sea producers to meet its supply obligations in the expectation that it would continue to have a monopoly franchise over the residential market into which the gas could be sold. Of course, such expectations have, in the event, been overly optimistic, and we explore in the next section the implications of unanticipated changes in policy on the incumbent and potential entrants.

Hence, franchise markets for the final product provide an end point in the contracting chain. Even if there is extensive vertical separation of the various parts of the chain, the existence of a monopoly market into which the product can ultimately be sold allows long-term contracts to be written between firms at various stages of production. Competition for final customers undermines this chain. Thus, in introducing competition, a significant shift in risk allocation takes place. It is to the problems of this transition that we now turn.

3. The Transition to Competitive Markets

The design of a competitive market will vary from industry to industry, according to the kinds of market failure identified. However, design is only a necessary condition for a competition policy for the utilities. It is practically impossible instantaneously to translate a monopolistic, state-owned industry into a competitive one. Although there may be much debate concerning a relatively fast versus a slower transition, in the UK all the main transitions have taken at least 7 years to liberalize formally, and all will, in practice, take more than a decade to complete.

There are several reasons why transitions are complex. Some of these are primarily distributional, related to the property rights the affected parties hold at privatization. Those held by producers may give rise to stranded assets. Consumers, too, have typically experienced widespread cross-subsidies in the state sector, and the unwinding of these under competition creates losers as well as winners. In addition, there are important technical constraints on the form and speed of the transition. We now consider each of these constraints in turn.

(a) *Contracting Problems*

In the previous section we argued that the introduction of competition can have significant implications for the whole vertical chain of contracts in utility industries. In the absence of such contracts (or even if they are written, because they are likely to be of a much shorter duration) uncertainty is increased. This increased uncertainty has two major implications. First, the required rates of return to investment are likely to increase. Since many investments in the utility sector are partially, or completely, irreversible, increased uncertainty is likely to result in higher required rates of return for investment. As Dixit and Pindyck (1994) show, when the capital stock can be adjusted upwards by investment, but cannot be adjusted downwards other than through depreciation, expansion today may leave the firm with surplus assets over a prolonged period should future conditions turn out to be less favourable than currently expected. By *not* investing today, the firm retains an *option* to expand later, should investment indeed be warranted. This option is more valuable as uncertainty increases, and the loss of the option can be considered an important part of the cost of investing. While it is difficult to value such options, this approach suggests that increased uncertainty is likely to increase significantly the cost of capital and hence the 'hurdle rates' that firms use to evaluate investment projects. Ultimately, of course, the effect of an increase in the cost of capital is likely to be borne by the consumer in the form of higher prices.

Second, the increased level of uncertainty helps to explain the general desire to reintegrate vertically in some sectors, such as electricity. It is well known that there are potential benefits and costs from such integration. If the upstream is not competitive then vertical integration can be welfare-enhancing under certain circumstances (see Waterson, 1996). On the other hand, vertical integration may act as a barrier to entry and lead to foreclosure problems. In the UK, the Conservative government lacked consistency in its treatment of vertical reintegration, waving through some early vertical takeovers, and allowing Eastern Group (an electricity distribution and supply company) to acquire a substantial amount of generating capacity from PowerGen and National Power, while blocking bids by the latter two companies to acquire regional distribution and supply companies themselves.[7] The Labour government's position is yet to be defined, but it has referred the first bid to occur since it took office — by PacifiCorp for the Energy Group (which now owns Eastern Group) — to the MMC on regulatory grounds.

In theory, there are solutions to these contracting problems. Markets can develop to replace the long-term implicit or explicit contracts that previously existed. In theory, once spot markets develop, derivative markets should soon follow, such as options and futures markets. It should, in principle, be possible to spread risks and transact in such markets, just like any other competitive industry.

However, in practice, the emergence of such markets is not spontaneous or straightforward. In the case of electricity, it is necessary to define precisely what the market refers to. A megawatt-hour of electricity produced at 5 p.m. is worth much more than one produced at 3 a.m., and one produced in the summer is worth less than one produced in the winter. Electricity is not storable[8] and so such issues matter. In addition, there are concerns related to market power in the Pool. A forward market in electricity (the Electricity Forward Agreement, or EFA) has existed for some while, but is not yet sufficiently developed or liquid to replace longer-term contracts between firms. Gas markets are even less developed. While a sizeable proportion of gas is traded in bilateral deals,[9] the first formal physical gas spot market was only introduced at the end of January 1997 by the International Petroleum Exchange. The contracts traded are for delivery of physical natural gas to a notional point in the

---

[7] See MMC (1996a,b). In this case the government went against the majority recommendation of the MMC.

[8] The pumped storage facilities in North Wales, now owned by First Hydro, owned in turn by Edison Mission Energy, are an exception.

[9] Typically for delivery to the beach-head, although also for delivery to a notional point in the gas pipeline network.

pipeline network, and are typically for a duration of 1 month. So far, volumes have been extremely small, although the market prices have already started to be used as reference points for longer-term gas supply contracts. [10]

Thus, although markets can be used, in theory, to hedge many of the risks introduced by competition, to date the development of such spot, forward, and derivative markets has been inadequate to solve such problems. Furthermore, it is unlikely that these problems will be solved in the short to medium term, and the traditional risk-spreading mechanism — vertical integration — is likely to remain a substantive objective of firms in utility markets for some time to come.

The introduction of competition not only makes it more difficult to write new contracts but can also result in existing contracts being *stranded*. This is especially a problem when there is a change in policy regarding the introduction of competition.

For example, in the 1980s and early 1990s British Gas had signed a portfolio of long-term contracts with upstream gas producers (including its own exploration and production division) in the expectation that it would retain a monopoly over residential (although not industrial) gas supply. During its investigation into the gas industry in 1993, the MMC considered how competition should be introduced and concluded that such competition should be phased in cautiously with most residential customers being offered a choice of supplier by 2002 (see Waddams Price, chapter 5, in this volume). In the event, in exchange for rejecting the MMC's recommendation for structural break-up (discussed above), the government chose to ignore this caution and announced that the market would be completely liberalized by 1998 (in line with electricity).

Of course, had British Gas anticipated such a policy change, its optimal portfolio of supply contracts would, in all likelihood, have looked very different. It would have known that, after 1998, it would be exposed to substantial price risk, as there would no longer be a guaranteed market for its contracted supplies. Hence, it is unlikely that British Gas would have agreed to contracts extending beyond 1998 that were not referenced, in some way, on the post-1998 spot price of gas. This is especially important as many gas supply contracts are of the 'take-or-pay' variety, specifying both price and quantity.

In the event, the stranded contracts problem for British Gas resulting from the change in government policy has been exacerbated by the large falls in the spot price of gas in the run-up to liberalization. British Gas

[10] There is also the 'flexibility mechanism' introduced recently to allow the pipeline operator to balance the demands on the system with the overall supply of gas. However, although this system generates a spot price for buying and selling additional gas, it is not intended to act as a formalized mass market for gas trading.

entered the new competitive era with a portfolio of supply contracts committing it to purchase gas at an average of around 20p per therm, while gas could in 1995 (when new entrants were first entering into supply contracts) be bought for as little as 8–10p per therm. The gas spot price has since recovered somewhat—to around 14p per therm in early 1997—but is still well below the price British Gas is committed to pay. New entrants, unencumbered with such contracts, are thus able to enter the market and undercut the incumbent with ease. While such stranded contracts certainly make entry easier and may further the cause of reducing the incumbent's market share (as discussed below), they result in large distributional issues that governments should take into account.

Such problems are not isolated. There have been enormous problems of stranded assets and contracts in US energy markets as states have sought to introduce competition in supply. There are similarly large problems for many European utilities as the European Union progressively moves towards creating integrated networks and encouraging competition in utilities.[11]

Such problems can be dealt with much more easily under public ownership as the government can effectively write off any losses and decide on their distribution (for example, as between the general taxpayer or consumers of the product). However, when the contracts are between private-sector companies, the allocation of contract losses is a matter for negotiation between the parties concerned. Of course, the government could step in and cover such losses by imposing a levy on all competitive suppliers (as with the Fossil-fuel Levy in the UK to contribute towards nuclear costs), or recover costs through the transmission system charges (as has happened in the US transition (see FERC, 1996). In the case of gas in the UK, no such intervention has been forthcoming. In the absence of such action, the cost of the stranded contracts inevitably ends up being borne in part by the shareholders of the incumbent.

It is worth stressing that while stranded assets and contracts resulting from changes in government policy are (or should be) a major distributional issue, their existence will greatly encourage entry. For example, the ease with which rival UK gas suppliers have entered the market probably has less to do with their superior efficiency compared to British Gas than with their ability to write contracts based upon the current (low) market price of gas. It would be quite wrong to think of the large price

[11] The long delay in the Directive to liberalize the European Union electricity market (finally agreed in a watered-down form in December 1996) can be in part explained by the potential stranding of France's nuclear power stations, and of both nuclear and coal power stations in Germany. Objections to the draft gas Directive have focused on the problem of signing new long-term gas supply contracts.

reductions on offer in the pilot areas of the UK residential gas market already open to competition as simply reflecting the impact of increased competition on efficiency.[12]

(b) Cross-subsidies

The second distributional problem for transitions is cross-subsidies. When the main utilities were being nationalized by the Labour government in 1945–51, these industries were regarded as merit goods — part of the more general welfare state (see Dilnot and Helm, 1987). Each citizen was entitled to these basic social primary goods, regardless of income or location. Thus education and health were to be universally provided, and the provision of electricity and mains water and sewerage were to be extended to marginal areas without the recovery of the full costs. Water had never been metered at the domestic level, and electricity customers in remote areas have not paid for the full infrastructure costs or transmission costs. With the advent of telephone services and natural gas, a similar policy of cross-subsidy was employed.

Though this approach was strictly economically inefficient, its objective was distributional. It could be sustained indefinitely as long as the utility service providers were statutory monopolies. Revenue collection was, in effect, a form of taxation. Customers, faced with distorted prices, invested in capital goods to consume the utility services, and the choice of housing location was similarly distorted. House prices capitalized the actual rather than optimal utility prices (see chapter 2 by John Vickers in this volume for a discussion of the optimal structure of prices and access charges).

As noted in section 2(b), the effect of competition is to undermine cross-subsidies. Unless other policies are adjusted, there will be losers. Although there will also be gainers, it is likely that the former will be politically far more important than the latter. In practice, it may be possible to disguise these losses if exogenous costs drive down the real cost of services (such as in the case of gas). However, it is likely that the cross-subsidies across each of the industries are concentrated in the same geographical areas, and hence concentrated in their effects on household income, as many of the cross-subsidies are simultaneously unbundled.

The clearest example of this geographical distributional effect is perhaps the south-west, which is being affected by the unbundling of water, gas, and electricity tariffs. The biggest effect is in water, where the contributions from other areas and government to the higher regional

---

[12] Indeed, in the pilot for domestic gas competition in 1996, customers in the south-west were offered discounts of up to 22 per cent on British Gas's price by entrants (see chapter 5 by Waddams Price in this volume).

water and sewerage costs have ceased. Now around one and half million people in Cornwall and Devon have to meet the full costs of cleaning up around 30 per cent of Britain's bathing waters, improving water quality standards, and dealing with water shortages. Bills have risen sharply as a result and it has become a major local political issue (see the MMC report on SWW (MMC, 1995a)).

There are several possible policy responses. These fall into four broad categories:

- allowing a slow enough transition to permit adjustments in the capital stock and housing markets;
- adjusting the natural monopoly prices to deal with social costs;
- adjusting social security policy; and
- relying on the efficiency gains to offset the cross-subsidies.

The first has been pursued most notably in the electricity industry, where an initial 8-year period was established at privatization for a phased reduction in the franchise. In gas, the transition was only provided for less than 3 years, following the 1995 Gas Act. The second has been partially adopted for gas, where rebalancing of the transmission and distributional tariffs has been slowed. The third has not been adopted for any of the main utilities. Indeed, the unwinding of cross-subsidies has actually coincided with a number of reductions in social security provisions (and the introduction of VAT on domestic electricity and gas). Finally, the efficiency gains have only gradually been passed on to customers. For the period 1990–5, water prices were rising in real terms, as were some electricity distribution prices. Only after 1995 did real price cuts begin to provide a cushion in these industries. The exceptions were gas and telecoms.

(c) *Technology*

A third factor in implementing competition is technology. For many utility industries, competition requires complex information technology to facilitate customer switching. This may comprise data-handling, metering, billing, and system balancing. Unlike the monopoly situation, where errors in meter reading and estimations can be carried from one period to the next, switching requires accurate readings at the switch point. The development of remote reading and smart meters has, therefore, been important for the practical implementation of competition. In addition, billing systems need a substantial information technology resource. Finally, as customers switch, modelling the demands and supplies on systems which must be quickly balanced becomes more complex, and here again information technology is critical.

Until the 1980s such technology was largely confined to the telecommunications industry, and even here issues such as itemized billing and number portability were only beginning to be developed at the time of privatization, and in the latter case were only introduced in the late 1990s (see MMC, 1995b). In electricity and gas, metering has proved a significant impediment to meeting the 1998 timetable. In water, the absence of metering for many households makes competition at the domestic level practically impossible (see chapter 7 by Simon Cowan in this volume).

Thus, the necessary conditions for the implementation of competition vary over time and include not only the technical facilitation of competition, but also the political constraints. The latter reflect the distributional impacts on producers and consumers. In the UK, scant regard has been paid to these issues in the original proposals, and it is hardly surprising that the results in managing transitions have been at best mixed. Indeed, regulators have had to step in to fill in the details of the transitions. But, far from the expectation held out for the earliest utility privatization — telecoms — that after a transitionary period of just 7 years, regulation would wither away (Littlechild, 1983), regulation has in fact increased as competition has developed. Regulating for competition has proved much more difficult than regulation of monopoly.

4. Regulating for Competition

Partly in recognition of the difficulties in prescribing a complete transitionary plan — and, indeed, in having a full model of competition — the regulators were given general duties to promote, facilitate, or secure competition. This general competition duty is usually a primary one, along with the duty to ensure that the utility functions can be financed. (The exception is water.) In practice, the regulator has considerable scope to follow his or her own preferred course to achieve the competition objective. The discretion is great, and has resulted in some regulators pursuing market-share targets, while others have attacked structure and entry conditions.[13]

(a) Regulatory Control Over Transitions

The mechanisms available to regulators are both direct and indirect. A regulator can propose licence changes in pursuit of the competition duty. The regulatee can either accept such changes, or request a reference to the MMC. Usually the MMC reports back to the regulator, who then 'takes

[13] See Helm (1994b) and Hansard Society (1997) for a discussion of the discretion issue.

account of the MMC findings.[14] The Secretary of State sometimes has powers in this regard, for example to veto licence amendments.

But, in many circumstances, the regulator need not confine his or her actions to direct licence amendments. The *threat of regulation* can prove a powerful tool in gaining compliance. A good example was the 'voluntary undertakings' entered into by the two main electricity generators, National Power and PowerGen, to divest a total of 6,000 MW of plant (in the event, ironically, to Eastern Electricity which, as noted above, thereby integrated vertically) and to price in the Pool so as to meet an average price over a 2-year period. The divestment arose in the context of an investigation by the regulator into the separate matter of the costs and margins in contracts between the generators and the RECs for the period 1993–8. Since these were fixed, a change in their value had virtually nothing to do with competition. Yet the regulator, in effect, bargained for a divestment instead of a reference to the MMC over the contracts. The threat of action in one domain forced compliance in another.

In addition to the general duties, regulators also set price caps for utilities, both with respect to natural monopoly activities and those activities which are in transition to competition. Examples of the latter include caps on electricity and gas supply, and overall caps in telecommunications. In fixing the level, structure, and duration of these caps, regulators have considerable scope to influence the development of competition. If prices are set close to costs, and therefore with tight margins, customers benefit immediately, but the incentive to enter the market is blunted. Thus, the regulator trades off short-term price benefits against longer-term competition. In the case of electricity, a recent example is the supply price margin in Northern Ireland. As yet, few competitors have shown an interest in entering, and, therefore, the regulator intends to set a (low) margin of around 0.5 per cent (Offer NI, 1996).[15] The lack of entry might then become self-fulfilling.

In some cases, the regulator can influence entry directly by adjudicating on the cost pass-through of specific entrants' costs. Thus, the electricity regulator allowed RECs to pass through the costs of their contracts with new independent power producers' CCGTs in the price caps on supply, without competitive tender against existing incumbents (see Helm, 1994a). These new entrants have turned out to be expensive, not only against conventional coal stations, but also against subsequent gas stations.

[14] The extent of regulators' discretion in their interpretation of MMC findings is currently the subject of judicial review, after Northern Ireland Electricity objected to its regulator's (OFREG's) interpretation of findings by the MMC (MMC, 1997a).

[15] The Northern Ireland Electricity supply price control was subsequently subject to an MMC inquiry (MMC, 1997a).

Regulators also adjudicate on the input costs to be included in price caps. Comparative efficiency evidence is used to inform on best practice, but, in addition, regulators can specify rules for the use of competitive tendering. As noted above, these rules have been most significant in the water industry.

(b) *Anti-competitive Practices*

Some regulators have argued that even the powers mentioned above do not give sufficient control over the transition to competition. In particular, the Director General of Telecommunications has successfully proposed the granting of anti-competitive practices (ACP) powers which enable him to intervene and adjudicate over BT's conduct without BT being able to appeal to the MMC (see chapter 6 by Mark Armstrong). In effect, the Director General becomes the market referee, and the referee's decision is final, subject only to judicial appeal (see Oftel, 1996b).

It is possible that ACP powers will also be granted to the Directors General of Offer and Ofgas, and possibly even Ofrail as part of new competition legislation being introduced by the government into Parliament at the end of 1997. In each case, the interpretation of the requirement is likely to depend upon the incumbent regulator, and add to the discretion inherent in the British approach to regulation.[16]

(c) *Regulatory Reform*

Progress toward competition has been fraught with regulatory conflict in all the main utility industries. The introduction of number portability and the granting of ACP powers in telecommunications led to an MMC inquiry and a judicial review, respectively. The proposals for competition in water have been subject to major criticism by the industry. The pilot experiments in gas competition have witnessed major controversies over some entrants' conduct, and acrimonious exchanges between Ofgas and British Gas over the systems and support for the implementation of competition. (Indeed, dispute over the costs was a component of the appeal to the MMC triggered in late 1996 over TransCo's price formula.) In electricity, some of the companies have been accused of dragging their feet in preparing for 1998, and the earlier deregulation of the over 100 kW market in 1994 was described by some participants as a 'shambles', with customers left without proper billing and metering for some considerable period, and subsequent widespread disputes. The timetables for liberalization in 1998 for both gas and electricity are subject to considerable scepticism and, in the case of electricity, the costs

---

[16] There will, in consequence, be an effect on the general review of regulation which the government announced at the end of June 1997.

of the necessary information technology have increased greatly during the transition.

It is apparent that the regulatory aspects of the transitions in many of the utility industries have not been carried out as well as they might. There are two major faults: that the objectives and market design have not been properly specified; and that the exercise of regulatory powers has been subject to too much discretion and hence lack of predictability.

(i) Objectives and market design

The discussion in section 2 indicated that the design of the competitive market comprised several dimensions, and that this specification would determine in large part the type of competition which resulted. Too often, this design has been vague. Sometimes this has been deliberate, in order to facilitate privatization. In the case of rail, the model of competition (open access) was deliberately subverted to provide sufficient transitional monopoly to enable franchises to be let to train-operating companies. Sometimes the vagueness has been by omission, and sometimes the result of genuine ignorance as to how competition will evolve.

In general, the greater the extent of specification of market design, and hence the objective of the transition, the less the subsequent controversy on matters other than those of detail. Furthermore, to the extent that stranded assets are the inevitable consequence of a move towards competition, pre-specification of the method of recovery has greatly assisted the subsequent process.

Specification does not, however, mean a determined path. Rather, the specification should deal with how such matters as stranded assets and the cost-allocation rules will be handled as a result of the inevitable changes as the path unfolds. Where, for example, new information technology is required by the natural monopoly to facilitate competition, these costs may be subject to cost pass-through. The assignment of risk between the parties reduces the extent of *ex-post* conflict. When these risks are not properly assigned, then MMC appeals and public disputes are likely.

(ii) Limiting regulatory discretion

The main regulatory failures derive from the way in which the regulators were left to implement competition, together with the discretion granted to them through the general powers noted above. The exercise of these powers is not easy for investors or entrants to predict, with the result that the cost of capital may be increased, and competition may be weaker.

To improve upon the current unsatisfactory position requires reforms both to the system of regulation and the methods of implementation. The two are related: the design faults in the regime have encouraged the *ad-hoc* methods used by the regulators. Some necessary steps are:

- to limit the degree of regulatory discretion, by specifying the nature of the transition in greater detail;
- to require regulators to give reasons for their actions, together with the supporting analysis and evidence, thereby opening the exercise of discretion to public scrutiny and challenge;
- to specify responsibility for implementation, and encourage proper project management;
- to provide for pilots which properly test systems, and allow time for consultation and modification of the transition.

(d) *Dealing with the Current Transitionary Processes*

The specification of the transition path rules and the reduction of regulatory discretion are general lessons which emerge from the British experience. However, these reforms would be too late to deal with many of the transitions already in progress — particularly in electricity and gas. The 1998 programmes are now being implemented in detail.

This progress has, however, been highly controversial, for precisely the reasons given above. The regulator has not, in either case, put in place proper project management, there is no agreed mechanism for dealing with the costs of implementing competition as and when they arise, and the participants are very unclear as to the ways in which discretion will be exercised. In the case of electricity, as concern mounted over the timetable, the Director General eventually announced a phased programme of liberalization in 1998 which lacks credibility (Offer, 1996). In his plan there will be three steps to liberalization, beginning with a 6-week trial for 10 per cent of the market from April 1998, then the opening up of 25 per cent, followed by the rest in September 1998. The idea that a proper pilot can be conducted, evaluated, and acted upon in 6 weeks is not credible. In gas, the pilots have been more spaced out, beginning in 1996, but there is still doubt about the required systems, and little agreement about the treatment of TransCo's costs.

In such circumstances, what should be the policy response? Given the scale of the projects, and the permanent nature of the changes, there is a considerable premium on getting the transition completed in an orderly way. This refers not only to the liberalization timing, but also the secondary consequences. In particular, the type of competition remains ambiguous. Will it be short term, or will contracts be permitted which bind customers to upstream sunk costs over time? What will constitute anti-competitive practices? Will suppliers be able to integrate vertically? Can suppliers discriminate between customers?

Since none of these questions has yet been satisfactorily answered, there is a good case for a short pause to assess the evidence and redefine the transitional path. Such a reassessment would attempt to resolve the cost allocation rules, assign the risks between the parties for exogenous costs, and address at least some of the above questions. The result might be a delay of one or two years, but in the history of these industries, this is not particularly significant. Furthermore, for this period, customers are already protected by a price cap on supply in gas and electricity, so the prospects of monopoly exploitation are limited. Any resulting higher returns for the incumbent supply businesses from higher market shares for this period could be taken into account in the price caps.

The fact that the incoming Labour government has rejected this path, and that Ministers have taken personal responsibility for meeting the timetables, may turn out to have been costly mistakes. The problems will not go away and postponement of a thorough review now is likely to undermine or further delay the onset of longer-term sustainable competition.

5. Conclusions

The UK's experience in attempting to introduce competition into the utility industries provides important insights for other countries in considering liberalization policies and implications for the completion of the transition to competition in the UK.

At the policy design stage, it needs to be recognized that competition is a means not an end, and that each industry displays unique elements. In addition, there are different kinds of competition, and the type of competition which best meets the efficiency criterion depends upon the market failures and government failures which arise in each industry.

On structure, there is a general preference for the separation of natural monopoly from the potentially competitive activities. There is, however, no presumption in favour of spot over contract relationships, and the pros and cons of vertical integration between production and supply depend upon the industry characteristics. There should similarly, given technological changes, be no general presumption against integration along multi-utility lines.

The widespread prevalence of upstream sunk costs in the potentially competitive parts of the utilities gives rise to two related problems: stranded assets in relation to past investments, and contracting failures and risk assignment with respect to new investments. Stranded assets, in turn, create two related problems in designing the transition to competition. Without prior arrangements, those holding these assets are likely to block liberalization, as has happened in Europe in most utility industries. Where they are held by the state, they can be written off as part of the privatization package. Alternatively, the natural monopoly can carry a levy to finance these past costs. This is the model for nuclear stranded assets in the UK and the USA. In the former case these accrue to the state, in the latter to private shareholders.

An additional distributional problem in the transition to competition is the position of those who lose when cross-subsidies are unwound. The preferred solution here is adjustment to social security policy or a social levy on the natural monopoly.

The transition to competition in several British utility industries has been hindered by significant regulatory failure: in failing to assign the costs and risks of the transitional period, in failing to define the end-state type of competition, and in the exercise of regulatory discretion. In the cases of electricity and gas, these failures have called into question the timetable for completion of the transitions in 1998. It may be better to pause to review the current situation, set realistic pilots, and properly address the cost assignment, than to press on regardless of the mounting regulatory problems. The government may live to regret its hasty reaffirmation of the timetable.

2

Regulation, Competition, and the Structure of Prices

JOHN VICKERS*

1. Introduction

Competition policy in regulated industries has three broad aspects —
structure, liberalization, and conduct regulation. Structural policies
include break-up decisions such as those taken (or not taken) at the time
of privatization, merger controls, and scope-of-business restrictions.
Liberalization policy is about the removal of legal barriers to entry.
Conduct regulation, which may take the form of explicit monopoly
controls and/or competition policy measures, constrains the pricing and
other behaviour of dominant firms. Most obvious is the question of how
to regulate the *level* of prices charged by firms with monopoly power —
by RPI–X price caps or otherwise.

The purpose of this chapter, however, is to provide some theoretical
background for policy questions concerning the *structure* of prices
charged by multi-product firms in regulated industries.[1] Many competition policy issues in regulated industries come under this heading, for
example price discrimination, non-linear pricing (e.g. volume discounts),
cross-subsidies, predatory pricing, pricing of inputs (e.g. network access) used by rivals, universal service obligations, and geographical
averaging. Though the focus is on pricing behaviour, the economic

* All Souls College, University of Oxford. This paper was presented at the British
Association Annual Festival of Science at Birmingham University, and at the War-
wick Business School conference on Rebalancing Utility Prices in September 1996.
The paper was written during a period of sabbatical spent at London Business School.
I am grateful to the Economic and Social Research Council and the Office of Fair
Trading for research funding under the Contracts and Competition programme
(grant L114251038). Much of the paper reflects joint work with Mark Armstrong.
Thanks also go to Chris Doyle, John Kay, Robin Nuttall, and Jean Tirole for valuable
discussions and comments. The usual disclaimer applies.
  [1] For more detailed analysis, see Laffont and Tirole (1993, ch. 3) and Armstrong
et al. (1994, chs 3–5).

principles relating to non-price behaviour (e.g. refusal to supply) are often similar.

A major reason why pricing structure questions are difficult is the problem of conflicting objectives — or, perhaps more accurately, of too few instruments chasing a number of objectives. Thus *efficient resource allocation* calls for (marginal) cost-reflective pricing. But with economies of scale or scope, that leaves a problem of *cost recovery*. Where liberalization has occurred, pricing structure policies might distort *effective competition* by thwarting the entry of efficient firms or by inducing the entry and growth of inefficient ones. Further tensions might arise if *social objectives* (e.g. distributional concerns) or political constraints (e.g. uniform nationwide pricing requirements) are important. Section 2 below examines these issues, and resulting trade-offs, starting from the benchmark of Ramsey pricing.

Another fundamental source of difficulty has to do with information. Regulatory and competition authorities generally know less about cost and demand conditions, and about firm behaviour, than those in the industry. Decentralized information would ideally be used in setting prices, but it might be hard to elicit, and indeed firms might seek privately to exploit informational advantages to the detriment of the public interest. This suggests that firms should have some discretion over their pricing structure choices, but perhaps with constraints on the exercise of that discretion. For example, instead of many detailed price controls, the firm might be constrained by just one or two broad price caps, with supplementary rules on permissible ranges of price variation (sometimes called 'floors and ceilings') or cross-price restrictions (e.g. bans on kinds of price discrimination). Broad price caps and limits to discretion, the theoretical principles of which are only partly developed, are the subjects of section 3.

Section 4 brings wholesale prices, and their relation to retail prices, into the analysis. It discusses the problem of the terms on which an integrated dominant firm should be required to supply inputs — notably access to essential facilities such as natural monopoly networks — required by its rivals. This 'network access pricing problem' is perhaps the most controversial of all pricing structure questions in regulated industries.

The transition from more to less regulation, which, it is to be hoped, is in prospect in parts of the regulated industries, involves removal of some price controls. The resulting question of how remaining price controls should be structured so as to avoid distortions of competition and efficiency is taken up in section 5.

2. The Ramsey Pricing Bench-mark

(a) *Least-bad Departures from Marginal Cost Pricing*

Consider the pricing problem of a pure monopolist that supplies n different products (which might be differentiated by time, place, state of the world, or even type of buyer). Let c_i and p_i denote the marginal cost and price of product i, and assume for now that neither varies with quantity (but see below on non-linear pricing). Let $x_i(\mathbf{p})$ be the demand for product i, which generally will depend on the whole set of prices $\mathbf{p} = (p, \dots, p_n)$ and not just p_i. If $v(\mathbf{p})$ is 'aggregate' consumer surplus, then $x_i(\mathbf{p}) = -v_i(\mathbf{p})$, where $v_i(\mathbf{p})$ is the partial derivative of v with respect to p_i.

Assuming that there are no significant externalities or other distortions elsewhere — so that c_i measures social as well as private marginal cost — it is clearly optimal to set prices equal to marginal costs: $p_i = c_i$. Then, and only then, will prices reflect the resource costs caused by individual consumers' decisions, which is a requirement for efficient resource allocation.

The trouble is that marginal cost pricing will obviously not cover all costs if, as in major parts of the regulated industries, there are economies of scale or scope. Suppose that the monopolist has a fixed cost F in addition to its variable costs. Then its profit $p(\mathbf{p}) = S_i (p_i - c_i) x_i(\mathbf{p}) - F$. Marginal cost pricing would lead to $p = -F$. Unless this deficit can be covered by a lump-sum payment to the firm — which would have to be financed somehow, with resulting social costs caused by higher distorting taxes elsewhere in the economy — the firm will be unable to finance its activities. If the firm's revenues have to cover all its costs, the question is how best to do this. Ramsey pricing is the answer to this question.[2]

Formally, the problem is to choose prices $\mathbf{p}$ to maximize welfare $v(\mathbf{p})$ + $p(\mathbf{p})$ subject to $p(\mathbf{p}) \geq 0$. One might guess that the solution to the problem would be to have the same price/cost mark-up $(p_i - c_i)/p_i$ on each product. This is wrong: equal mark-ups are not generally optimal. Much closer to the truth is the proposition that optimal pricing causes the same proportional *quantity reduction* for each product, relative to quantities demanded at marginal cost pricing. More precisely, Ramsey prices are such that a small proportional change in 'tax' rates, where $(p_i - c_i)$ is the tax on product i, would cause the same proportionate reduction in the *compensated* demand — i.e. substitution effect — for each product.[3] Thus

---

[2] The classic paper is Ramsey (1927).

[3] See Mirrlees (1976). Note that the 'tax' is defined here as the difference between price and marginal cost, whereas the 'mark-up' is that difference in proportion to price. So taxes are measured in money units whereas mark-ups are dimensionless numbers (e.g. percentages).

the equi-proportionate quantity reduction principle is correct for small increases in taxes and provided that income effects are ignored.

This description of Ramsey pricing is much more general than the 'inverse elasticity rule', which says that price/cost mark-ups should be inversely proportional to elasticities of demand. That rule is, of course, implied by the more general principle in the commonly assumed case of independent demands and no income effects. In some special cases, the general principle implies equal mark-ups, but generally it does not. It follows that Ramsey pricing generally entails price discrimination: if $c_i = c_j$, the Ramsey prices p_i and p_j are likely to differ.

This discussion has so far assumed uniform pricing—i.e. that price per unit does not vary with quantity purchased. Non-linear pricing, in particular quantity discounts, can often do better. For example, consider two-part pricing, which involves a fixed charge as well as a price per unit. To be feasible, this requires consumption metering and no resale opportunities, conditions which are common in the utility industries, and, indeed, there are fixed quarterly charges for gas, electricity, and telephone services. The benefit of two-part pricing is that it enables the variable price to be closer to marginal cost, while the fixed charge contributes to the firm's fixed costs. Indeed, if no one got excluded from consumption altogether, two-part pricing with variable prices equal to marginal costs could achieve the first best (given the other current assumptions).

This accords with the Ramsey principles above. If demand for access to the service is perfectly inelastic, then all fixed-cost recovery should be done via the fixed part of the two-part tariff, and there is no demand distortion. If, however, the number subscribing to the service varies with the fixed charge, then there should be some mark-ups on the variable prices. Ramsey principles apply not just to uniform and two-part tariffs but also generally to the theory of optimal non-linear pricing—see Wilson (1993, especially ch. 5).

(b) *Distributional Concerns*

The principle that mark-ups should be higher on products for which demand is less price-sensitive, and especially its implications for the fixed element in charges, seems to conflict with concerns for income distribution.[4] High fixed charges on essential services, like poll taxes, are regressive. Ramsey principles can readily be adapted to accommodate distributional concerns and, moreover, the Ramsey tax problem is better

---

[4] Hancock and Waddams Price (1995) analyse distributional implications of pricing structure changes as liberalization happens in the British gas industry.

motivated when they matter, because otherwise a uniform poll tax would be rather efficient.

The 'many-person Ramsey rule' involves welfare weights. The welfare weight of consumer h is the increase in social welfare resulting from a small increase in h's income. Depending on one's attitude to income distribution, poor people might have higher welfare weights than rich people. Let the marginal social value of an income transfer (MSVT) to h be equal to h's welfare weight minus the costs of meeting the extra demands resulting from the transfer.

The Ramsey principle about equi-proportionate reductions in compensated demands still holds, but in relation to MSVT-weighted demands. With optimal pricing, a small proportional increase in 'taxes' would cause the total substitution effects—i.e. the (unweighted) compensated demand changes—to be proportional to MSVT-weighted demands. Depending on the welfare criterion, and on what has been achieved by other distributional policy instruments, the many-person Ramsey rule could even entail subsidies of some products. In any event, Ramsey principles are entirely capable of accommodating distributional concerns.

It certainly does not follow, however, that regulators have applied, or should be allowed to apply, anything like the principles of the many-person Ramsey rule. In practice, political economy considerations collide with normative welfare economics. Most of the taxes and subsidies implicit in utility prices historically are more plausibly the result of political incentives and pressures, coupled with inertia, than of rational normative calculation. Implicit taxes are subject less to legislative scrutiny and approval than explicit taxes.

Should regulators take distributional considerations into account in making their decisions? I think not—except perhaps where specific duties with distributional aspects, together with the financial and other means of carrying out those duties, have been given to them by government or parliament. The basic reason is that distributional policies are generally better pursued by other branches of government, which is not to say that the latter can achieve a distributional outcome that could not be improved by the use of regulatory instruments. Rather, the view is that the advantages of regulators having discretion to pursue distributional ends are outweighed by disadvantages of capture, influence activities, uncertainty, and unaccountability. Regulators, perhaps like central bankers, should have focused objectives.

(c) *Effects of Competition*

How does competition affect this analysis? If competition to the dominant firm takes the form of a price-taking fringe, it is straightforward formally to extend the Ramsey analysis to the competitive case. Let $s_i(\mathbf{p})$ be the supply of the competitor group function for product i. Then the residual demand curve facing the dominant firm is given by $x_i(\mathbf{p}) - s_i(\mathbf{p})$. If competitor profit and consumer surplus have the same welfare weight, then the principles in section 2(a) above, with residual demand in place of total demand, apply equally to the competitive case. If not, then welfare weightings modify the analysis along the lines of section 2(b).

Thus, in principle, it is quite easy to characterize the optimal pricing structure, given the need to cover fixed costs and given that the price vector $\mathbf{p}$ is the only instrument available. However, unless fixed costs are small and distributional concerns are modest, this constrained optimum may fall well short of productive efficiency.

If, for example, the optimum has a large 'tax' $(p_i - c_i)$ on product i, then the fringe will supply units of the product that could have been more efficiently supplied by the dominant firm—a kind of 'cream-skimming'. (The fringe supplying too much is analogous to consumers demanding too little of the product in question.) On the other hand, if product j is subsidized at the margin—for distributional or political reasons, perhaps—then there is productive inefficiency in the other direction as more efficient competitor supply is partially or wholly foreclosed. Moreover, a subsidy to product j that is not financed independently will generally increase the tax, and hence productive inefficiency, associated with product i.

There are three broad approaches to the possible conflict between liberalization and the tax/subsidy patterns that might exist in pricing structures. The first is not to pursue liberalization. Then monopoly profits can be used not only to cover fixed costs but also to pursue various distributional ends. But this fails to exploit the various benefits of competition, and tends to result in the persistence of some subsidies that are both inefficient and unwarranted.

The second approach is to liberalize but not worry too much about potential 'cream-skimming'. Indeed, some encouragement to entry via the 'tax wedges' $(p_i - c_i)$ might be thought legitimate, at least in the short term, in view of various barriers to entry that may exist, incumbent advantages, infant firm considerations, and so on. However, especially as liberalization extends, this is not a very satisfactory position either.

The third and most attractive approach is to address both the tax/subsidy issue and the entry barrier problem directly. Rebalancing of prices, which competition will sooner or later compel unless it is hindered, is the way to tackle subsidies that turn out not to be desired once their costs are exposed, and public subsidy or explicit taxes are needed to reconcile efficient competition with desired subsidies. (Indeed, liberalization might assist the provision of explicit subsidies by reducing and revealing their costs.) That is, an additional instrument is needed to remove conflict between objectives. This is entirely practicable, as the 'fossil fuel' levy in electricity and the proposed universal service fund for telecommunications illustrate.

The tension between competitive pressures and implicit taxes in pricing structures has been most acute in the context of network access pricing—see further section 4 below.

3. Pricing Discretion and the Problem of Information

Ramsey pricing requires a lot of information about cost and demand conditions. The regulated firm is likely to know much more about that than the regulator. Moreover, if price controls are committed for a period of years ahead, industry conditions may well change before they are reset. Rather than imposing a particular price vector upon the regulated firm, it therefore seems likely that in many circumstances it would be better to give some pricing structure discretion to the firm.

The general advantage of giving the firm some pricing discretion is that decentralized information can be exploited. Thus, provided that the regulated price index is reasonably well constructed, we might expect relative prices to reflect relative costs or elasticities better if the firm has some freedom over pricing structure. However, there are dangers that freedom will be abused, for example anti-competitively. Thus pricing structure freedom is often limited by more or less explicit restrictions on prices in relation to costs (as with rules against cross-subsidy) or in relation to each other (as with bans on price discrimination). The question of how best to influence and constrain the exercise of pricing discretion is a difficult one.[5]

(a) Global Price Caps

One proposal, which Laffont and Tirole (1996) have analysed, is to have a single *global price cap* on the firm's product range. This would cap an index $P(\mathbf{p})$ of the firm's prices but leave the firm free to choose its pricing structure subject to that cap. The general advantage of discretion can be

---

[5] The general theory of incentive design with multi-dimensional uncertainty is not well developed. Armstrong (1996a) examines the multi-product monopoly non-linear pricing problem, which is of this type.

Figure 1
Advantage of Pricing Discretion

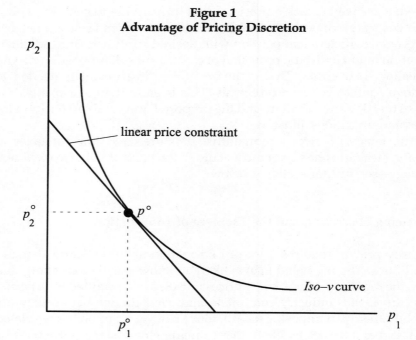

illustrated by Figure 1. Compared with the non-discretionary price vector $\mathbf{p}^\circ$, it would clearly be better to allow the firm freedom to choose any prices such that $v(\mathbf{p}) \geq v(\mathbf{p}^\circ)$ because the firm would generally do better and consumers (in aggregate) would be no worse off. (In this case the index $P(\mathbf{p})$ is simply $v(\mathbf{p})$.) This will induce a Ramsey pricing pattern, though probably with non-zero profits, but it does require a lot of knowledge about consumer preferences.

Less informationally demanding, and even simpler, is the linear price constraint given by $Sp_i^\circ x_i(\mathbf{p}^\circ) \geq Sp_i x_i(\mathbf{p}^\circ)$, which says that the firm can set any prices that do not increase the cost of buying the product bundle demanded at the non-discretionary prices — see Figure 1. Again, the firm will generally gain from having the discretion, and so too will consumers.

If the weights in a linear global cap are set correctly — in proportion to the quantities demanded at the resulting prices — then *Ramsey pricing is induced.* Thus a very simple form of price cap can bring about optimal pricing in a decentralized manner that appears not to be too informationally demanding for the regulator. It could be said that setting the weights exactly right would call for a great deal of information, but this does not upset the general point that pricing structure discretion is often desirable, and that it can be implemented in simple ways.

Armstrong and Vickers (1996a) analyse the desirability of pricing discretion, and the optimal form of discretion, for a series of examples involving cost or demand uncertainty. While some discretion is desirable when there is cost uncertainty, this is not necessarily so for demand uncertainty. Thus zero discretion might be best if the demand elasticity is higher in markets where the level of demand is higher. This is because the firm likes to charge higher prices in larger markets, but it is socially desirable (for Ramsey reasons) for prices to be inversely related to elasticities. When discretion is desirable, it is shown to imply Ramsey-like pricing in some simple symmetric examples, but departures from Ramsey pricing are optimal more generally for reasons having to do with asymmetric information.

(b) Floors and Ceilings to Combat Cross-subsidy and Predatory Pricing

Another, complementary, approach to the issue of discretion is to bound the freedom of the firm by prohibiting cross-subsidies or predatory pricing, perhaps by setting 'floors and ceilings' between which prices are allowed to vary. Thus Baumol and Willig, among others, have advocated the combined use of *incremental cost* floors and *stand-alone cost* ceilings on prices.[6]

The (average) incremental cost of product i is the addition to total cost caused by producing i rather than not producing it at all, divided by the number of units of product i, holding constant the production of other goods. The (average) stand-alone cost of product i is the cost per unit of producing i in isolation. Consider the example with constant marginal costs in section 2(a) above, and assume that the fixed cost F is completely joint—i.e. the entire fixed cost F is entailed by the supply of any product. Then the incremental cost of product i is c_i, and the stand-alone cost is $[c_i + F/x_i]$. These floors and ceilings must apply not only to individual products but also to sets of products. Thus, for example, the stand-alone cost of products i and j in combination is $[c_i + c_j + F/(x_i+x_j)]$. Otherwise a lot of profit could be made by charging the stand-alone cost for each product.

These incremental and stand-alone cost tests would be met in a contestable market thanks to the forces of potential competition, but why use them in a regulated monopoly? One point is that they do not require demand information. Another argument is that they give precisely the notion of 'subsidy-free' prices, because consumers of each product at least cover the extra cost that their consumption causes, so no financial burden is placed on others, and no consumers pay more than they would

---

[6] See, for example, Baumol and Sidak (1994, chs 5 and 6).

pay if they broke away and went to an alternative supplier with access to the same technology. Subsidy-free prices do not always exist, but under reasonable natural monopoly conditions Ramsey prices are in the non-empty set of prices that are subsidy-free, as are many other prices.

Baumol (1996), following the spirit of Areeda and Turner (1975),[7] has urged a similar approach to predatory pricing. Baumol argues that pricing above average *avoidable* cost does not threaten to drive out a more efficient rival firm and so cannot be predatory. Avoidable cost is the same as incremental cost, except that sunk costs are ignored. As with the subsidy tests described above, this test of predatory pricing applies to products in combination as well as individually. Which costs are avoidable depends on the time horizon. In the long run, for example, all costs are avoidable, and the approach boils down to average incremental cost (which is simply average cost in the single product case). Baumol (p. 62) argues that the relevant time horizon is that 'over which the price in question prevailed or could reasonably have been expected to prevail'. This might be hard to judge.

A number of the criticisms that have been made of the Areeda–Turner rule, for example its possible vulnerability to strategic behaviour, apply also to Baumol's proposal. We shall not rehearse those criticisms here since they do not concern regulation—see Ordover and Saloner (1989) for an analytical survey which also discusses alternative approaches. However, there is an important point about a possible effect that regulation might have on incentives for predatory behaviour. The discussion of pricing discretion in section 3(a) above, which was in a static setting, implicitly assumed that the firm always maximized profit, which rules out predatory pricing because a necessary condition for predatory pricing is (temporary) sacrifice of short-run profit. However, incentives for such behaviour might exist and, indeed, might be strengthened by broad price caps insofar as price cuts in one market allow price increases elsewhere, thereby reducing the profit sacrifice entailed by predatory pricing. This suggests that constraints to guard against predatory pricing—perhaps in the form of floors and ceilings—might be a sensible accompaniment to broad price caps (see further section 4 below).

(c) *Bans on Price Discrimination*

Unlike price floors and ceilings, which constrain pricing structure by reference to costs, bans on price discrimination do so by placing cross-restrictions on prices, so their enforcement does not require cost information. Price discrimination can be defined in general terms as the sale of

---

[7] Areeda and Turner advocated a marginal cost criterion in principle, proxied by average variable cost in practice.

different units of a product at prices not corresponding to differences in the cost of supplying them.[8] This definition covers non-linear pricing as well as cases where different terms are offered to consumers in different markets despite common cost conditions. It also covers cases of *uniform* pricing (e.g. geographically) where costs differ.

As explained above, optimal pricing generally entails price discrimination when there is a need to finance fixed costs (or subsidies that are not funded otherwise). So a benign social planner should be allowed to engage in price discrimination. However, it does not follow that the same is true for a profit-maximizing firm. Indeed, analysis for unregulated monopoly shows that the welfare consequences of profit-maximizing price discrimination are ambiguous (see Varian, 1989). Unless price discrimination causes output to rise, it is bad, but it might desirably open up new markets (e.g. markets for high-demand consumers in the case of non-linear pricing).

More relevant here are the welfare consequences of price discrimination by a *regulated* monopolist. Naturally, these depend on how the monopolist is regulated.[9] With linear price caps that have fixed weights proportional to demands, price discrimination is good for consumers as well as the firm — see section 3(a) above. But 'average revenue' regulation, which caps $[Sp_i x_i(\mathbf{p})/Sx_i(\mathbf{p})]$, though it causes output to rise, tends to be detrimental to consumers and can have very distorting incentives on pricing structure.

Another approach is to allow price discrimination subject to the constraint that no consumer is worse off than with uniform pricing — i.e. that all continue to have the option of buying at the uniform price. This may have attractions, especially in the case of non-linear pricing: discounts to large buyers could happen without harming smaller consumers (unless the latter are firms competing with the former).

A significant difference between this form of optional tariff and a global cap is that giving a discount to one consumer group does not relax the price constraint for others, and so any incentive to engage in predatory pricing may be diminished. Bans on price discrimination, by increasing the cost to the firm of predatory pricing — since price has to come down in all markets, and not just those where entry has occurred — might further reduce the risk of it occurring. At the same time, however, such bans might prevent the firm from legitimately and pro-competitively responding to rivalry.

---

[8] See Whish (1993, p. 503).
[9] See Armstrong *et al.* (1994, especially section 3.3.2).

4. The Pricing of Inputs Sold to Competitors

Rivals to BT and British Gas have had to obtain key inputs from them —
in particular, access to telecommunications or pipeline networks. The
pricing of access to essential facilities can be complex even when (as now
in rail and electricity) their ownership is separate from competitive
activities, but it is especially controversial when there is vertical integration. On the one hand, it seems that vertically integrated dominant firms
might have a strong interest in denying rivals access to key inputs on
reasonable terms. However, there are dangers of inefficient entry and
cream-skimming if access is required to be sold too cheaply.

The access pricing problem can properly be viewed as an instance of
the general pricing problem. Although the discussion in the previous
two sections implicitly supposed that **p** was a vector of retail prices, it
applies equally well if **p** includes wholesale prices. But the controversy
that surrounds the access pricing problem is such that it deserves a
section of its own. The two leading approaches to the problem are the
efficient component pricing rule (ECPR) advanced by Baumol, Willig,
and others,[10] and the Ramsey/global cap analysis of Laffont and Tirole
(1994, 1996).

(a) *The Efficient Component Pricing Rule*

Consider a vertically integrated firm M that supplies a retail output and
an 'upstream' input (say network access) necessary for producing the
output. Let p and a respectively denote M's retail and access prices. (In
more general analysis these would be vectors and non-linear pricing
might be allowed.) Let b and $b+c$ denote the marginal costs of access and
of final output, so c is the marginal cost of the downstream activity. Firm
M also has fixed cost F, which is assumed joint, so b and c are incremental
as well as marginal costs. Firm M faces price-taking competitor(s)
downstream whose product might be differentiated from M's. The
question is how a should be regulated.

In general terms, the ECPR says that a should be set equal to the direct
incremental cost of access plus the opportunity cost of (i.e. lost profit
from) supplying it. The ECPR is often expressed as the *margin rule*:

$$a = p - c, \tag{1}$$

which says that the margin $(p - a)$ between M's retail and access prices
should equal its incremental cost in the competitive activity. If M's
opportunity cost of supplying the input to competitors is $[p - (b+c)]$ per

[10] See, for example, Baumol and Sidak (1994, ch. 7).

unit, then (1) corresponds to the opportunity cost formulation since it can be expressed as

$$a = b + [p - (b+c)]. \tag{1a}$$

The reasoning behind the ECPR is that it is necessary for productive efficiency. A lower access price (in relation to the retail price) would lead to excessive entry by inefficient rivals, and a higher access price might deter more efficient rivals. On the face of it, the ECPR has the further advantage of being 'cost-based' and not requiring information about demand elasticities and so on.

The immediate natural objection that the ECPR is a recipe for the preservation of monopoly profits — and associated allocative inefficiency — is rebutted by its proponents when they say that its full validity is conditional upon the retail price p being regulated so that no supernormal returns accrue to the firm.

(b) Ramsey Pricing of Access

Laffont and Tirole (1994) analyse the problem of choosing p and a to maximize welfare when the fixed cost F has to be financed from revenues. Their base model has price-taking rivals who have constant returns to scale and whose product is differentiated from that of firm M. This being a Ramsey problem, it is not surprising that the (constrained) optimal access price has the form

$$a = b + [\text{Ramsey term involving super-elasticities of demand}],^{11} \tag{2}$$

which looks rather different from the seemingly 'cost-based' ECPR. Whether (2) gives a higher access price (in relation to p) than (1) is ambiguous. It is generally desirable that access revenues should contribute to the fixed-cost recovery problem, which the ECPR ignores. This is a reason for raising a above its ECPR level. On the other hand, Laffont and Tirole have product differentiation in their model, and this is a reason for lowering a (see further below).

The Laffont–Tirole model is more general than the simple ECPR model in two major respects — it takes account of the need to cover fixed costs and it allows for product differentiation. Its solution does not satisfy the necessary condition for productive efficiency because of the fixed-cost recovery constraint. As with Ramsey pricing more generally,

---

[11] Super-elasticities of demand take into account cross-price effects as well as own-price effects. Where products are (imperfect) substitutes, the super-elasticity of demand for each product is lower than its own-price elasticity.

the optimal prices are the best that can be done given the instruments available and constraints. If there were no fixed cost recovery problem, then marginal cost pricing would be optimal: $a = b$ and $p = b + c$. That satisfies (1), but the ECPR was hardly intended as a corollary of marginal cost pricing.

Laffont and Tirole (1996), responding to the common criticism that Ramsey pricing requires an unrealistic amount of demand information, have argued that an appropriate global price cap that embraces access and retail prices symmetrically can induce Ramsey pricing in a decentralized manner (and, moreover, avoid other competitive and regulatory distortions that asymmetric regulation might cause). The logic is essentially as described in section 3(a) above. The worry that such a global cap might encourage a predatory price squeeze against rivals — i.e. raising a while lowering p — could be met by supplementary constraints, possibly of the form $p - a \geq c$, which is similar to the ECPR margin rule (1).

(c) A Synthesis?

Notwithstanding this last point, the ECPR and Ramsey approaches appear rather different. Armstrong *et al.* (1996) attempt to provide a synthesis. They note, first, that optimality of the margin rule (1) depends on some key assumptions that have not always been made clear in expositions of the ECPR. These include:

- *homogeneous product* — the rivals and M supply the same retail product;
- *fixed coefficients technology* — one unit of output requires one unit of input; and
- *no bypass* — only M supplies that input.

When these assumptions are relaxed, and in the absence of a fixed cost recovery problem, the optimal access price a for a given (optimal or not) retail price p, is given by

$$a = b + s\,[p - (b + c)], \tag{3}$$

where s is the *displacement ratio* defined as [Change in M's sales of final output as a changes] divided by [Change in M's sales of input to rivals as a changes].

The second term on the right-hand side of (3) is the opportunity cost of access, and hence (3) can be regarded as a more general expression of the ECPR than the margin rule (1).

Only if the three assumptions above hold does the displacement ratio $s = 1$, in which case (3) and (1) are equivalent. Otherwise $s < 1$, so (3) implies a lower access price, for a given retail price, than the margin rule (1). Corresponding to the relaxation of the three assumptions, s can be decomposed into terms relating to product differentiation, variable coefficients, and bypass. Calculation of s necessarily involves a good deal of elasticity information (cross-price elasticities of demand, elasticities of substitution, the elasticity of alternative input supply). This is not apparent from (1), because (1) is correct only if assumptions hold which imply that the relevant elasticities are zero or infinite.

If the fixed-cost recovery constraint binds, then the optimal p and a satisfy an expression of the form:

$$a = b + s\,[p - (b + c)] + [\text{Ramsey term}$$
$$\text{involving standard own-price elasticity}]. \tag{4}$$

The last term in this expression is a standard own-price elasticity, not a super-elasticity as in (2). But since (4) addresses the same question as that answered by Laffont and Tirole, it should be equivalent to (2). Indeed, the super-elasticity in (2) can be expressed as the sum of the second and third terms on the right-hand side of (4). So if (4) does indeed give the precise meaning of the ECPR, it follows that the optimal access price derived by Laffont and Tirole can be viewed as the ECPR price plus a standard Ramsey term.

Thus the ECPR and Laffont–Tirole Ramsey approaches appear capable of some form of synthesis. The ECPR — in its general opportunity cost formulation, of which the margin rule is just a special case — gives the optimal access price for a given retail price when there is no fixed-cost recovery problem. Ramsey principles give optimal retail and access prices when there are fixed costs to be recovered. (Of course, they imply marginal cost pricing when there is no fixed-cost recovery problem.) One way of expressing the Ramsey access price is as the ECPR price plus a normal elasticity term.

(d) *Multi-product Implications*

Some of the main implications of the access pricing principles discussed above arise in multi-product settings. Suppose, for example, that there is just one basic kind of access, but that it can be used to provide a variety of different services.[12] Ramsey principles of efficient cost recovery gen-

[12] Section IV of Armstrong *et al.* (1996) contains analysis of the more general case with N final products offered by the incumbent, R final products offered by the competitive fringe, and M types of access.

erally imply that access put to different uses should be priced differently (according to elasticities, etc.). So if usage-dependent pricing of access is feasible, it is usually optimal.

If fixed-cost recovery is not a binding constraint, but M's retail price vector **p** is fixed by regulation (optimally or not), then (3) suggests that usage-dependent pricing of access is warranted because the opportunity cost to M — the product of the displacement ratio and M's retail margin — differs as between uses. Thus, access used by rivals to supply direct substitutes for profitable services supplied by M might be priced more highly than access used to supply services complementary to those offered by M. (In fact, matters are somewhat more complicated in the multi-product case because the overall opportunity cost to M is the sum of the opportunity costs on its various offerings.)

Further questions arise when the set of products is endogenous. There is a case for saying that access used to provide new services ought to be priced lower — e.g. temporarily exempted from Ramsey 'taxation' — in order to encourage innovation. There is a concern that adoption of the ECPR might encourage M to introduce products inefficiently in order to create and recoup opportunity costs that would not otherwise exist. These examples illustrate the general point that *ex-post* optimality (of pricing in our context) might distort *ex-ante* incentives — by failing to encourage desirable behaviour or by encouraging undesirable behaviour.

5. Price Control under Partial Deregulation

Firm M's retail pricing was assumed to be comprehensively regulated in the analysis of access price regulation discussed in the previous section. But what if some or all of M's retail prices are deregulated? This question is becoming increasingly important as liberalization policies in the regulated industries offer the prospect that the scope of monopoly price controls might be reduced.

In terms of the basic framework above, in the event of deregulation, the retail price p becomes endogenous and influenced by the regulated access price a. The way that $p(a)$ varies with a then enters the analysis of optimal a. If firm M still has some market power, there is reason to reduce a, relative to (3) above, in order to bring p closer to marginal cost $(b + c)$ and hence improve allocative efficiency. On the other hand, as a comes down, the margin $[p(a) - a]$ might widen, so that productive efficiency worsens as rivals inefficiently take more business from firm M. In any event, M's break-even constraint might limit the extent to which a can be reduced. It is not clear that the ECPR gives much useful guidance in these circumstances.

In multi-product settings, deregulation of a subset of prices requires amendment to global price cap proposals. Caps with partial coverage are not global—in effect the index weights of deregulated prices become zero. It certainly does not follow that the case for discretion over the structure of the prices that remain regulated is undermined, but care is needed to avoid distortions induced by regulation.

For example, suppose that firm M supplies an input ('access') and an output to each of two markets. At retail level market 1 is monopolized, but market 2 is reasonably competitive. Firm M has a monopoly on the supply of access to both markets. In natural notation its four prices can be denoted (a_1, a_2, p_1, p_2). If p_2 is removed from price control and if a single linear price cap is applied to the other prices with weights proportional to the quantities of them demanded, then an obvious distortion would arise. Firm M would have an excessive incentive to raise a_2 in order to induce a higher p_2. (Recall that M's rivals in market 2 require the access input from M. Their rivalry constrains the retail *margin* rather than the retail price level.) With appropriate index weightings this incentive could be curbed, but the design of a single price cap would appear to be significantly more complex when that cap ceases to have global coverage.

Pricing structure issues arising from partial deregulation are of considerable policy importance, but are imperfectly understood. They provide further open questions in the theory of pricing discretion.

3

Network Industries

MICHAEL KLEIN*

1. Introduction

A wave of infrastructure privatization activity is currently sweeping the globe, affecting about 100 countries and amounting annually to over US$60 billion of business on average over the past decade. It has become increasingly clear to policy-makers and firms alike that a major challenge is to ensure that such privatization activity will yield clear benefits. Existing empirical studies suggest that ownership change *per se* will often yield benefits, particularly where it leads to reduced non-commercial government interference. However, regulation that is required in areas with natural monopoly features may become overly intrusive and undermine the progress made. To generate lasting and sizeable welfare improvements the introduction of real competition is required. Effective competition requires that firms can fail. This in turn tends to require private ownership, as public firms may more easily count on being bailed out. It is in this sense that private ownership may be most clearly necessary for achieving lasting efficiency gains.

Many reforming governments want to employ competitive solutions. By way of example, consider recent policy issues faced by various reforming governments. Key questions were:

- Should we allow completely free entry into all telecommunications services or is there reason to fear uneconomic duplication of investment and services?

* Chief Economist at Shell International, formerly at the World Bank. I would like to thank Philip Gray for research support. I would also like to thank Sandy Berg of the University of Florida, Warrick Smith and other members of the World Bank's Private Participation in Infrastructure Group, and members of the World Bank's advisory group on private infrastructure for their helpful comments on the chapter. The views expressed here do not necessarily represent those of either Shell International or the World Bank.

- Should we introduce competition in power generation by unbundling generation and allow trade in transmission capacity rights, such that decentralized bargaining over such rights determines dispatch?
- Should we provide an exclusivity period for gas distribution systems or allow free entry?
- Should we separate rail track from rail service operations and let the latter be competitively supplied, or should we grant monopoly franchises combining track and service operations?
- Should we introduce auctions for landing slots at airports?
- Should we require that port concessionaires not be controlled by shipping lines, so as not to bias access opportunities for other shippers?
- Should we provide a measure of bankruptcy protection for private competing airlines to ensure essential services?

The answers often remain unclear and continue to be subject to—sometimes heated—debate. First, there is the debate about whether competition should be introduced and, if so, how. An example of the former question is whether free entry into telecommunications makes sense, given growing economies of scale in fibre-optic cables. An example of the latter is the great (and expensive) confusion regarding California's power sector reform debate about wheeling (decentralized trade in electricity contracts) versus poolco (system optimization via central dispatch based on price bids by generators). Second, there are the questions about the regulatory implications of sector deregulation. Will regulation remain necessary, and will it be easier or more complicated? Third, policy-makers are worried about whether private finance will come forth on reasonable terms to fund new investment in competitive segments of a network, where investors may face new and unclear risks, which they are not used to.

The presumption of this chapter is that the time is ripe to clarify and illuminate the debates about the competitive forces that may be brought to bear on network industries. The idea is not to provide perfect answers, but—in a reasonably dispassionate and intuitive fashion—to provide policy-makers with broad perspectives that may help them orient themselves. The goal is to identify the key considerations and arguments and how they hang together, to clarify what is known and what is not. Examples are drawn from various sectors to obtain richer insights by relying on what amounts to a larger set of (quasi)-counterfactuals. Such a broad view of competition in networks should, in particular, bring out questions about the nature of networks and the nature of competition, which may more easily be glossed over in 'technical' sector-specific debates.

The basic structure of this chapter is as follows. First and foremost ways of introducing competition in network industries[1] are discussed. Basic regulatory requirements are sketched along the way. Implications for financing industry expansion when competition is introduced are considered at the end.

The discussion on competition starts by sketching the concept of natural monopoly giving rise to the debates. The natural monopoly issue is then contrasted with a bench-mark view of 'ideal' competition in networks. This bench-mark serves as the key goal underpinning policy reform efforts, which aim at introducing effective competition in network industries. In particular, the role of market-driven prices and the need for spot markets is highlighted. This is then followed by a discussion of ways of introducing competitive forces, in the following order:

Competition for the market
  — bidding for monopoly franchises (e.g. solid-waste collection services);
Competition over existing networks
  — 'open access' — liberal policy towards access to monopoly segments and interconnection requirements (e.g. in natural gas, rail, or telecommunications systems);
  — 'pooling' — introducing competition in existing networks where central dispatch optimizes network-wide delivery of a fairly homogeneous service, while end-users and input suppliers contract competitively (e.g. in electricity or natural gas);
  — 'timetabling' — competitive determination of optimal service delivery in networks where non-homogeneous services need to be sent to specific end-points (e.g. auctions for airport landing slots or railway routes);
Competitive system expansion
  — decentralization of investment decisions for new capacity in networks (e.g. new transmission lines for electricity);
Remaining natural monopoly and the role of competition policy
  — options for reliance on competition policy instead of traditional utility regulation to deal with market power arising from remaining natural monopoly elements in a network industry; and

[1] The term network industry is used in a broad sense. For example, the whole road transport system including vehicles is considered a network, even though each vehicle is obviously physically separable from the road network. One may also think about all sort of activities that match suppliers and customers and incur some sunk costs in the process as network activities, e.g. marketing. However, the discussion here centres on network industries in transport, telecommunications, energy, and water/sanitation.

Competition among multiple networks
— conditions under which competition among several networks or bypass within a network may be desirable, including reliance on substitute or intermodal competition (e.g. for freight transport);
— the desirability of erecting policy barriers to entry, including arguments about cross-subsidies and financing of infrastructure projects.

2. Natural Monopoly and Ideal Competition in Networks Contrasted

Some types of networks, such as water pipeline systems, railroad track, gas pipelines, and power transmission lines, exhibit technical character-istics which appear to make them natural monopolies. In other words, it would be a waste for society to have several parallel networks of this type compete with each other. In fact, if they were competing, only one firm would eventually survive. Indeed, competing municipal gas and water systems have not survived the 19th century. Competing 19th century railroads in the United States ended up in monopoly areas carved up in private agreements among the companies. Competing gas transmission companies in Germany concluded demarcation agreements among themselves, delineating respective monopoly areas for each company.[2]

If entry into a market is easy and if it costs little (low sunk costs), then there will be potential competitors who will enter the industry when prices are 'too high' and compete prices down again. An example may be trucking markets. If a single firm in one area or line of business starts charging excessive profits, other firms may simply use trucks available elsewhere and compete the excessive profits away. The equivalent example of airplanes illustrates that the fixed costs (the cost of the airplane) may be high, but hit-and-run entry is still feasible because the investment (the airplane) can be moved to alternative use in other markets.

However, when specific investments with no economic alternative use are required to operate a network, then investments are sunk, as in the case of a water pipeline.[3] If the incumbent raises prices, a new firm

[2] The natural monopoly argument does not imply that complete systems of infrastructure need to be owned and managed by a single firm. Complete systems, e.g. a telephone or gas system, may be composed of several small interconnected systems, each being the sole provider in a particular geographical area. Examples are telephone franchises in Finland and Hungary (56 small systems), gas transmission in Germany, electricity distribution, water and sewerage systems, railways in the United States, road systems managed by differing regional government entities, etc.

[3] It is, of course, physically possible to remove the sunk investments in the network, i.e. water pipes, in this case. However, this would not generally be economic.

may enter, but it risks losing its investment if the incumbent lowers prices again, or the incumbent may be driven out of the market. In both cases some water pipelines may lie idle eventually — potentially wasteful duplication from the point of view of society, it seems. Once only a single supplier remains, it has the power to earn excessive profits. This gives rise to an issue of economic regulation so as to limit profits to normal levels and pass more benefits to consumers.[4]

In recent years, received notions about which network industry or segments thereof are truly natural monopolies have been challenged repeatedly. Deregulation efforts have successfully expanded the scope of competition in various sectors with network characteristics, such as airlines, trucking, natural gas, power, and telecommunications. By the same token, the extent of economic regulation in these sectors has shrunk, although in some cases it has become more complicated as a result.

In some sense the various policy experiments have tried to peel away competitive layers from regulated networks and lay bare the true remaining natural monopoly. How one can peel off competitive segments varies from sector to sector, depending on technical characteristics of the sector. Nevertheless, it helps to look at the problem from the perspective of several sectors, to sharpen the understanding of what is involved in expanding the scope for competitive forces and their nature in differing sectors. However, before exploring this agenda further, it may be useful to state the importance of establishing functioning spot markets.

The creation of a spot market yielding prices that reflect market conditions is essential for the introduction of effective competition. A competitive spot market yields a set of prices maximizing welfare — absent externalities. This requires *inter alia* that the market is large enough to sustain a sufficient number of competitors to avoid oligopolistic behaviour and that prices are free to vary by time, location, and customer. When there are such market prices, regulation in this market is no longer necessary, as competition will limit market power of market participants and yield efficient outcomes.

---

[4] Theoretically, one could forgo regulation if society were prepared to accept monopoly profits, which would always be limited to some degree by competition from substitute products. However, this is usually politically unsustainable. We, nevertheless, see that a number of sectors are not, or are only partially subject to economic regulation. Such is the case when substitute product markets exist and society for some reason accepts possible remaining monopoly rents, e.g. railways vs. trucks (United States, Argentina) and natural gas vs. petroleum products (Germany, Finland, Hong Kong).

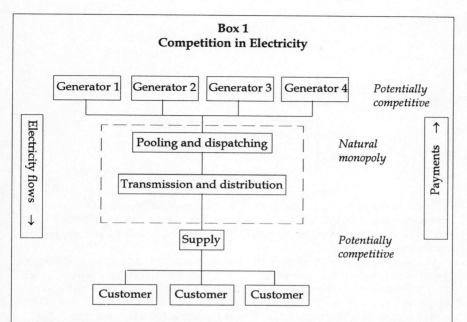

Box 1
Competition in Electricity

The diagram shows what elements of the system are potentially competitive or natural monopolies. In this diagram, supply, i.e. billing, customer service, and bulk purchase of electricity, is potentially competitive, as is the generation business. The 'wires' business, high voltage transmission and low voltage distribution, are natural monopolies. Pooling (operation of the market) and dispatch are also considered natural monopolies, although some believe that these two are potentially competitive through decentralized contract trading.

Box 1 shows an 'ideal' system in the case of electricity. Note, however, that even some parts termed 'natural monopoly' here could be potentially competitive. For instance, some experts believe pooling and dispatching are potentially competitive.

Furthermore spot markets allow buyers and sellers to buy and sell at short notice, to make up for shortfalls or excesses that may occur for whatever reason. This, in turn, allows buyers and sellers to conclude meaningful long-term contracts that even out price fluctuations in the spot markets and yield predictable payment and supply obligations (see Box 2). Long-term contracts also facilitate the financing of investments.[5]

Efficient spot prices are essential for decentralizing investment decisions in the network infrastructure itself. For this to be possible, spot prices in a network need to reflect the capacity constraints of the

[5] For long-term contracts to exist one needs to allow 'speculators', i.e. players who develop liquidity in a market and hence support the development of contracts with a long maturity period.

Box 2
Long-term Contracts

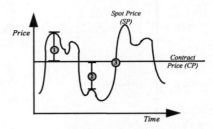

In many commodity and financial markets, buyers and sellers face a variable spot price. A wide variety of contracts exists to allow players to 'hedge' the risk of buying and selling at a variable price. This diagram explains the basic mechanism in the simplest case.

In a long-term contract, a buyer and a seller of a commodity agree to eliminate revenue risks caused by variation in the spot price through fixing a price at which they will contract. In the figure above, there is a variable spot price (SP) and the buyer and seller decide to fix the price at which they will trade (CP).

In a simple long-term contract a constant quantity (q) is traded.
(1) If SP> CP then the seller pays q x (SP – CP) to the buyer.
(2) If SP< CP then the buyer pays q x (CP – SP) to the seller.
(3) If SP = CP then no money changes hands.

If both parties are buying and selling the amount q in the spot market, then the financial flows in the financial contract will exactly offset the price variation in the spot market and essentially fix forward the price at which the trade is concluded.

network — given safety and other operating requirements. One way of thinking about this is that a bottleneck facility segments the market in several sub-markets, as long as there is congestion. Prices reflecting sub-market conditions will reign at all relevant nodes in a network (see Box 3). When capacity constraints are not binding at all, node prices will not differ and the whole system functions as one unsegmented market.[6]

Consider the example of a power system where electricity flow through the grid is optimized by a central dispatch system. Here, contracts for power supply need not be concluded by a single, central power company. Contracting can occur directly and competitively between generators and consumers, subject to the constraint that total power input into the system equals total output (including losses). Producers bid for dispatch, consumers bid for supply. The dispatch centre optimizes system operations subject to operating norms about

---

[6] See Schweppe *et al.* (1988) for a full discussion of the applied theory of congestion pricing for power systems.

Box 3
Congestion Prices

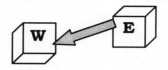

For simplicity, think of two markets, East and West, each comprising a series of buyers and sellers. Assume all transport costs are zero.

Example 1: No transport link: If no transport link exists between the two markets, then they operate completely separately, i.e. prices and quantities are determined by supply and demand conditions in each market.

Example 2: Limited transport: If there is a limited transportation capacity link, then there is partial integration of the two markets. If the price is such that E < W, then it will pay suppliers to divert units to W. The prices in the two markets will tend to converge. If after the capacity of the link is exhausted, there is still a price difference, then the difference is known as the 'congestion' price.

Example 3: Unlimited transport: If transportation capacity is infinity, suppliers and customers are effectively competing in the same market.

---

system stability, reserve margins, etc.[7] With complete pricing flexibility, the outcome is a system of spot prices, varying by time and location in the network (node prices), which reflect both the valuations of suppliers and consumers as well as the operating norms and capacity constraints of the system.[8] The spot prices will also provide appropriate signals for capacity expansion in generation. When spot prices are expected to rise and remain high enough to fund the cost of building and operating a new power plant, a new plant will be built. In times of over-capacity, on the other hand, spot prices will drop to low levels and investment will be discouraged (theoretically the price should follow system short-run marginal costs which could vary widely).[9]

To hedge price fluctuations in the spot market, generators and consumers can conclude long-term contracts for power delivery at

[7] Such markets for electricity have—with varying degrees of sophistication—been established for power in Chile (1978), the United Kingdom (1990), Argentina (1992), Norway (1992), Australia (Victoria) (1994), New Zealand (1996), and Sweden (1996). Other countries introducing electricity markets include Bolivia, Colombia, Peru, Poland, and the Ukraine, as well as efforts in such countries as Russia and India (state of Orissa).

[8] Such a market may be called a 'smart market', in this case embodied in the optimizing dispatch system. A 'smart market' is effectively any computer-aided market that uses a series of algorithms to facilitate the market-clearing process.

[9] A relevant analogy is the market for aluminium plants, i.e. plants with high fixed, sunk costs operating in a world market with flexible spot-market prices, reflecting market conditions.

agreed prices. To be able to fulfil such contracts producers must be able to purchase or sell power in a spot market. This is equivalent to trading arrangements in markets such as that for crude oil. For example, a producer of crude located in the Middle East may honour a sales contract to a customer in Brazil, by purchasing crude oil coming from Venezuela on the spot market, while selling crude from the Middle East in the spot market that may ultimately serve Europe. The contract for delivery is then separable from the actual flow of the product. This is always possible when there are multiple supply sources for the product traded and a spot market exists. The existence of the spot market makes it possible to honour long-term contracts efficiently and thus also to use them to secure debt financing.

An efficient node pricing system provides signals for new investment in 'transport' capacity expansion. The difference between node prices reflects the cost of congestion and system losses. As differences between node prices grow, investment in new capacity relieving congestion becomes economical. In theory, it should be possible to allow investors to come forth with investments in transmission infrastructure in response to expected node price differences.

If it is possible to create an efficient spot market that allows operating and investment decisions in all of the network industry to be decentralized i.e. left to market forces, then all that remains of regulation is 'normal' anti-trust or competition policy, which should help guard against excessive concentration in relevant markets and collusion.

As in the case of any other market, competition over networks will not be effective if the total system is so small that there is only a small number of competitors, e.g. in a power system with only two or three generating stations. Even when there is a large number of producing plants they must not all be owned by a small number of firms to minimize the incentives to collude and thus undermine the effectiveness of competition. Anti-trust rules may be needed to prevent collusion or mergers between the plants. But if unregulated investor responses are sufficient to take care of efficient network expansion, then there is no issue here that is different from those in any other market with workable competition.

Care needs to be taken in analysing the scope for competition properly. For example, the shape of the bottleneck part of the network, e.g. the transmission system, which may include 'treatment' facilities (e.g. gas or water treatment plants), may effectively create a series of small, segmented markets so that many suppliers are able to exercise monopoly power in 'their' part of the market.

As we will see, it may be that in some cases competing networks may sensibly be used to establish workable competition. In other cases it may ultimately be possible to create effective spot markets by means of 'smart' markets. The smart (computer-based) market is an auction system, where producers and customers of a good or service bid to produce or consume the good or service, subject to the constraints imposed by the bottleneck facility, including any rules governing system stability, safety, or the like. The smart auction system explicitly takes these constraints into account and optimizes the use of the bottleneck facility as it exists.

The smart market thus simultaneously optimizes utilization of the bottleneck elements of a network, and generates a system of spot prices based on bids for delivery and purchase of services by multiple producers and customers, who require the network for service delivery. It may thus be that the only 'real' natural monopoly element left is the establishment and operation of the smart market itself, whereas new investment in network expansion can be left to 'the market', based on the spot prices generated at all nodes in the bottleneck parts of the network.

Politically, it will be important that customers accept the bewildering and fluctuating array of prices that is required for effective spot markets in network industries. The world of such prices is almost diametrically opposed to often preponderant notions of uniform system-wide flat rates for services of network industries. A flavour of what consumers could expect is provided by airline pricing practices in a deregulated system such as that in the United States, where prices may differ by seat, by cancellation option, or by the time of booking, and are constantly adjusted by airlines on the basis of evolving demand for seats and competitors' behaviour. The liberalized long-distance telecommunications market in the United States provides another example of the kind of market that might confront consumers.

If the choices are extremely complex, it is possible that brokers will come into the market and provide a simplified 'menu' of choices for consumers. This is, in effect, what banks do for customers: provide an interface to the financial markets and provide marketable packages for customers. An example is the provision of fixed-rate mortgages: these are backed by derivatives or other hedging instruments in the financial markets, but customers do not need to know this. They simply face a choice about whether to fix their mortgage rate for a number of years and what the cost of this action will be.

3. Introducing Competition in Network Industries

(a) *Competition for the Market*

It has been argued that one way of bringing competitive forces to bear on natural monopoly segments of an industry is to delineate the monopoly franchise and auction it off to the bidder requiring the lowest price from consumers (see Demsetz, 1968). However, prices and related terms of the franchise (often known as a concession)[10] will have to be adjusted as time goes by in response to new events. There are two options to adjust prices, either by rebidding the franchise periodically or by instituting price regulation of the 'traditional' kind. Only rebidding promises an escape from a return to a standard natural monopoly case requiring regulation. Indeed, monopoly franchises for such activities as solid-waste collection have been auctioned off periodically with documented efficiency gains over regulated systems.

However, if there are significant sunk costs involved, assets need to be transferred at the end of the franchise period under a system of rebidding. These assets will have to be valued. One way is to let new bidders bid a value for the assets. For that they need to have information on future prices, which needs to be given exogenously. That could only be done by a 'regulator', as — by definition — there is no market setting the price(s). The other way is to value the assets and let the bidder offer the lowest price to consumers. The valuation, however, needs to compensate the incumbent such that incentives to invest and operate efficiently are maintained. Such a valuation exercise is almost identical to a rate review by a regulatory agency (Williamson, 1976). If the value for the assets is too low, the incumbent will have weak incentives to invest in and maintain the system. If the value is too high, it will lead to excessive prices for consumers under the new bids.[11]

De facto, there will always be challenges to incumbents in monopoly franchises. Such challenges may be infrequent and may not follow any

---

[10] There are a variety of other similar forms of contracts, for instance leases, build–operate–transfer schemes, etc. The differences between contracts depend on the degree of responsibility of the private operator (for instance, whether they are responsible for financing new investment) and whether the contract is to operate existing infrastructure or to build new assets.

[11] One alternative mechanism to avoid these problems was developed in Argentina and used for concessions in electricity distribution and transmission. In this scheme, the incumbent and the entrant bid. If the entrant outbids the incumbent, the value of the bid is paid to the incumbent. If the incumbent wins then no money changes hands. Theoretically, this system should overcome some of the problems described above. The difficulty with this scheme is that the customer derives no benefit from these periodic competitions. This scheme, therefore, either has to be accompanied by regulation, i.e. the customer receives the benefits of competition through periodic price reviews in which case the scheme does not eliminate the need for regulation, or a proportion of the proceeds of the auction have to be returned to the customer at the auction, e.g. 25 per cent of the value of the auction is returned to the customer. This then raises the traditional problems of franchising, i.e. the danger of less than full compensation for the transfer of assets and the potential advantage of the incumbent in bidding for the franchise.

prescribed set of rules, but no incumbent will forever be efficient and politically acceptable. The difficulties of setting appropriate franchise periods and of valuing assets — explicitly or implicitly — at the end of the franchise period will then be encountered by necessity. Historically, occasional, albeit infrequent, challenges to incumbents in monopoly franchises have often yielded at least temporary reductions in prices and efficiency gains (e.g. gas distribution in 19th century Canada, water concessions in France, or power generation plants in the United States after 1978).

By placing limits *ex ante* on franchises and requiring some form of competitive bidding for renewal of the franchise, governments will ensure that regular challenges are possible. If many different franchises exist there will be constant competition for renewal of some franchise, e.g. if there are 10,000 water franchises with an average length of 20 years, 500 will come up for bid annually. As long as firms are allowed to operate franchises in several jurisdictions they will then have an incentive to maintain some reputation to be able to be prequalified for bidding at renewal time. The incentive to maintain reputation will somewhat reduce the temptation to slacken efforts in franchises they currently hold.[12] However, during the life of long-term franchises economic regulation will continue to be required and the valuation problem at the end of the franchise period will remain.

(b) *Competition over Existing Networks*

(i) Open access

Open access to the bottleneck facility:[13] Sometimes, segments of a network industry have been identified as potentially competitive, e.g. long-distance services in telecommunications, power generation in electricity systems, gas production in natural gas systems, etc. However, for competition in one segment to be effective, access to remaining natural monopoly-type bottlenecks is required. As long as the network owner(s) are not engaging in predatory behaviour, competitive suppliers will have access to the bottleneck facility provided there is available capacity. An example might be rival gas suppliers using a single gas pipeline (the bottleneck facility). In the case where the pipeline owner has no interest in supply, it will always pay for them to allow additional access. The marginal cost, and hence the price of capacity, will be close to zero. For interruptible service, gas suppliers and their customers can thus count on available transport capacity and there will be an effective competitive

---

[12] Such reputational effects have been shown to exist in the only larger study of the issue that we know of, i.e. a review of experience with the results of the competitive award of cable TV franchises in the USA (Zupan, 1989).

[13] This is sometimes known as 'common carriage'.

spot market for interruptible service with the possibility of writing longer-term hedging contracts.[14]

When capacity constraints are binding, there will have to be rationing of access (interconnection) to the bottleneck. This can be achieved efficiently without regulation. An efficient outcome would be approximated if the owner of the gas pipeline could charge prices for the transport of gas that reflect the difference between consumers' willingness to pay and producers' marginal cost. The allocation of resources would then be optimal in the sense that the cheapest producers would sell gas to the consumers with the highest willingness to pay, i.e. the ones valuing gas the most.

In this case, the owner(s) of the bottleneck facility would receive monopoly profits. There is, therefore, again the need for regulation of prices charged by the owners of the bottleneck facility for access and of prices for any services they provide to final customers of the network industry. This could, for example, be achieved by way of a 'global' price cap on a basket of prices for all services rendered by the bottleneck facility, including the price of access (Laffont and Tirole, 1994).

Open access and interconnection rules: So far it has been argued that a market for capacity rights will not eschew the need for regulation. This was on the assumption that owners of the bottleneck facility do not engage in predatory behaviour. However, there may be incentives for them to do so, particularly when they themselves own part of the competing supply facilities, e.g. power plants, gas fields, or long-distance telephone transmission facilities. In those cases they may seek to raise access prices to the network to prevent competitors in the non-monopolistic segments of the network from gaining business and, eventually, to drive them into bankruptcy.

To prevent this from happening, regulators may impose certain access obligations and matching pricing principles to prevent owners of monopolistic segments from engaging in predatory behaviour. This rationale for regulation is thus different from the attempt simply to limit profits in the monopolistic segments. The former regulation is there to enable competition 'over the network' to take place and to prevent owners of the bottleneck facility from reaping excess profits, whereas the latter is there only to limit profits of the bottleneck owner. Of course, the limitation of profits on the bottleneck facility may well be the reason why

[14] 'Interruptibility' in gas refers to the ability of the pipeline owner to stop services to customers on interruptible contracts when demand is high. The conditions on which interruptibility can occur, e.g. number of times, length of interruption, etc., varies by contract. Unless the demand for gas is relatively constant, therefore, it is likely that some types of interruptible contracts will be possible in every gas system.

Box 4
The Efficient Component Pricing Rule

| Town A | Route AB | Town B | Route BC | Town C |

	Marginal cost (AB)	Marginal cost (BC)	Joint cost	Access price*	Price (average cost over AC**)
Incumbent	5	5	10		20
Efficient entrant		4		15	19
Inefficient entrant		6		15	21

This is a simple example of the efficient component pricing rule (ECPR), developed by Baumol as a principle for setting access prices. In Baumol's example, a vertically integrated incumbent offers a rail service between towns A, B, and C. An entrant wants to develop a rival rail service between towns A and C, but has to pay for access to the vertically integrated incumbent for its bottleneck service between towns A and B (route AB), and will provide the service itself between towns B and C (route BC).

The costs of the service are as follows. There is a marginal cost (assumed constant) of service for each leg of the route, AB and BC, of 5. In addition, there is a joint cost of service of 10 (an average fixed cost incurred by the incumbent for operation of the entire rail network), so that the average cost of the service, AC, is the sum of the marginal costs and the joint cost, i.e. 20. The incumbent charges the average cost of the service (20) and the entrant charges a price equal to its marginal cost over BC and the access price to AB.

As illustrated in the table above, the ECPR states that the correct access price to charge the entrant for the bottleneck service (route AB) is the sum of the marginal cost of access to the bottleneck, AB, which equals 5, and the joint costs of service 10 (the opportunity cost of entry to the incumbent). The efficient access price is, therefore, 15.

This example is illustrated by two entrants. The first, the efficient entrant, has marginal costs of 4 over the route BC. It can, therefore, profitably enter at the ECPR access price of 15 and undercut the incumbent with an average cost of 19, which is less than the incumbent's average cost of 20. If an efficient entrant has marginal costs for the route BC of 6, then it will have average costs of 21, i.e. more than the incumbent and hence will not enter. In other words, the correct access price induces efficient entry. An access price less that the ECPR (in this simple example) will induce inefficient entry.

Notes: * Access price (under ECPR) = MC(BC) + JC. ** Average cost (to incumbent) = MC(AB) + MC(BC) + JC; Average cost (to entrant) = MC(BC) + AP.

its owner might want to establish and exploit market power in the competitive segments. This then argues for imposing limits on vertical integration and separating ownership in the bottleneck facility from that in other parts of the system—a time-honoured way of ring-fencing the natural monopoly element since the time of canals in 18th and 19th century United States where, at times, canal operators were not allowed to operate barges on the canal.

As soon as access rights and prices are to be regulated, there may have to be non-price-based rules rationing access, such as first-come first-served (at the regulated access price). It is then no longer clear whether the outcome will be optimal. In particular, there may be excess demand for capacity, which may lead to excessive network expansion, if the network owner is obligated to provide access at given (low) rates.

A well-known bench-mark pricing rule for the regulator trying to preserve competition over networks is the efficient component pricing rule (Box 4). It essentially says that the access price charged by the bottleneck owner should compensate for the full cost of providing network access to a competitor in the competitive segment. That full cost consists of the marginal cost of access as well as any losses of profits that may be the result of new access. Clearly the bottleneck owner will then maintain its prior profitability, whether that included excessive profits or not. New entry will bring benefits to consumers under this rule if the new entrant is more efficient and can deliver a final service for a total price that is less than others charge, including, for example, a vertically integrated firm with control over the bottleneck. For the vertically integrated firm it will be economical to shut down its own capacity in the competitive segment, because it will be compensated for this through the access price.

The efficient component pricing rule defines, in effect, an upper limit for access prices, because it still allows the incumbent vertically integrated firm to make excessive profits — as in the past. A lower bound is set by the marginal cost of granting access to the network. The marginal cost may, however, fail to compensate the network owner for fixed costs of maintaining the network. Such costs should also be incorporated in the access price, possibly in the form of a two-part tariff — with a fixed charge covering network establishment costs (including the capital cost of the network owner) and a variable one covering the short-run cost of access. In effect, such an access price would be equivalent to the efficient component rule, without compensating the incumbent for loss of excessive profit.[15]

Pro-competitive regulation : Sometimes access rules and prices are used to provide an advantage to new entrants relative to the incumbent. The

---

[15] Kay (1995) argues that recent advances in accounting theory, in particular the activity-based costing rule, have to a large extent eliminated the distinction between costs that can easily be allocated to a specific activity and general overheads. Further progress could lead to a situation where access prices can 'simply' be based on the marginal cost of access provision without the need for further fixed-cost compensation.

rationale for such entry assistance is presumably similar to that for infant industry protection, i.e. ultimately based on arguments about learning externalities. It would also follow that such protection should be limited in time.

Resale of capacity:[16] Users of the bottleneck facility may buy rights to use capacity and may be allowed to resell them in various ways. The question is, what type of competition can such a resale market provide? Resale can yield more complex pricing of capacity than may be allowed under regulation for the primary sale of capacity by the bottleneck owner. Also, parties not having access to capacity because of some type of quantitative rationing may be able to obtain access through purchase in the retail market. If pricing in the retail market were unregulated, then the ultimate pricing structure would be the same as that of the bottleneck provider selling directly. Regulation would simply create a rent for 'primary dealers', i.e. companies buying capacity rights from the owner of the bottleneck. Therefore, for regulation to be effective it has to apply to resale of capacity in monopolistic segments as well. Consequently, prices for capacity cannot be set in a free market for capacity rights based on access regulation.

   While the creation of an open-access system is plagued by many detailed regulatory challenges, it can serve effectively to promote competition in competitive segments of the industry. An increasing number of examples across sectors illustrate the benefits of creating open-access systems in rail, telecommunications, and gas. Note that this issue is often combined with issues associated with the creation of new duplicate networks, for instance in telecommunications, i.e. the price at which a new long-distance fibre-optic network can gain access to the local network to provide a full service (see section 4(a)).

(ii) Pooling

The open-access rules outlined above attempt to enable competition over the network by selling rights to network capacity to competing firms on a non-discriminatory basis. However, it may be difficult to define, adjust, and enforce such rights in a manner that allows effective competition to take place. For example, in power systems a complete set of access or capacity rights may be indefinable. Power flows through a network according to Kirchhoff's law. What capacity is used or unused at any moment in any part of a power system is a function of all physical flows throughout the system and not a function of bargaining or individual transport decisions. It may not, therefore, be practical to define

[16] This is also known as 'contract carriage'.

capacity or access rights for power systems. What can be done, however, is to have a central dispatch system that optimizes system flows, instantaneously matching supply and demand. There is open access in such a system in the sense that the power of winning bidders will always — and by definition — be dispatched. The use of capacity is then flexibly determined by the dispatch system. There is no need for trade in capacity rights, e.g. in response to short-term shutdowns of power plants, and no need to compensate holders of capacity rights for the effect of power flows on available capacity.

This solution to competition over power transmission systems has by now been tried in several countries. Chile introduced a competitive power pool in 1978, when its system was still publicly owned. Least-cost dispatch continues to be on the basis of audited costs of power plants, not on continuous price bids by generators. Bidding thus takes place implicitly as costs are reset. The United Kingdom introduced a competitive bulk power market on the basis of half-hourly price bids in 1990 (see Box 5). However, both Chile and the United Kingdom continue to suffer from high market concentration in the generation segment and a lack of barriers against vertical integration. The Argentine system, introduced in 1992, places strict limits on horizontal and vertical integration thus effectively creating the conditions for workable competition. However, so far 'bids' are based on audited cost data rather than price bids by generators. All the foregoing systems set transmission prices in an essentially administrative way, i.e. they do not allow congestion prices to be established by the smart market. Norway introduced its competitive pool in 1992 and is trying to generate prices by the smart market including congestion prices. Most recently, the Province of Victoria in Australia is introducing a competitive bulk market for power. Results from the introduction of competition remain encouraging. In the United Kingdom, productivity of generators has roughly doubled within 4 years, including for the remaining public nuclear power operator. Productivity in the industry segments not subject to competition, i.e. distribution, has also increased, but only by about 10 per cent. In Argentina, the switch to a private competitive system quickly resolved all of the urgent problems of power shortages and created a situation of temporary excess capacity, essentially because the new generating firms efficiently rehabilitated and operated existing plants.

It might be argued that one could define and enforce capacity rights in systems with directed flow, such as natural gas transmission. However, trades may still be too complex to obtain efficient gas transmission on the basis of trade in capacity rights. In effect, the notion of trade in capacity rights entails that a complete path for the transport of gas from seller to buyer be obtained through purchase of a series of capacity rights,

Box 5
The UK Pool

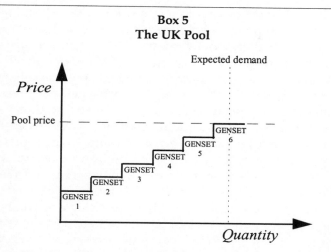

The price in the Pool in England and Wales is determined on the day ahead of operation. The price is determined by ranking the bids (the price at which it will generate and the quantity that it can generate at that price) of each generating turbine (genset) in the system. The price is determined by taking the highest price bid needed to meet expected demand in every half-hour period in the day ahead, as shown in the diagram above. The Pool price is therefore determined for every half-hour period on a given day. A sample of prices taken from the *Financial Times* is shown below.

Note that this is a very simplified explanation of the mechanism. In practice, there are other elements to the price and the bids are complex non-linear functions.

UK Pool Prices, 23 January 1996

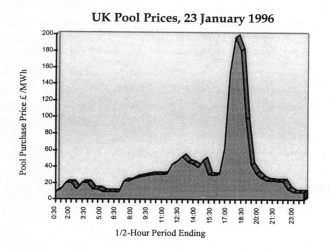

Source: Energy Settlements and Information Services Limited, 23 January 1996.

which are available at the time they are needed. Constructing such a system of 'straws' through a pipeline system that efficiently matches capacity rights with energy delivery may be so complex that efficient solutions may not obtain. The experience of the deregulated US gas industry is suggestive in that there are efficient spot markets for interruptible gas supply, i.e. supply flowing in times when pipeline capacity does not impose an aggregate constraint on the energy trades that are possible. Such markets are still rudimentary for trades when capacity constraints are binding, i.e. when capacity has value. A conceptual solution currently being investigated in the UK gas industry is to use a central optimizing dispatch system, as in the case of power mentioned above. It remains to be seen whether such a system can technically be put in place.

One might argue that, rather than relying on a single optimal dispatch system, one could conceive of a system where transport rights through a pipeline are originally allocated to several owners, who can than sell these rights. Private brokers could construct optimizing models that would match energy and capacity trades in the way a dispatch system would. The result of these trades would then yield the instructions to the actual dispatch centre. For electricity, such a system would simply have high transaction costs unless different brokers were to develop competing optimizing systems and unless such competition between optimizing systems were to yield sufficiently large benefits to offset the cost of the whole brokerage system.[17] That includes the issue of whether instructions generated by competing optimizing systems could generate a feasible and efficient set of instructions for the dispatch centre.

Under the solutions described above, the transmission systems remain natural monopolies and require regulation. There is no need to design an interconnection regime as discussed in the previous section. Rather, regulation of the cost of utilizing the transmission system appears to be equivalent to regulation of any bottleneck transport facility, e.g. regulation of a monopoly railway franchise. Regulation may thus be a little less complex than that required in the case of an interconnection regime, which does not rely on market structure regulation under which the bottleneck facility is vertically separated from the competitive segments.

(iii) Timetabling

In the case of power or natural gas it does not matter whether a customer receives electrons or molecules produced by the supplier with whom he has contracted for delivery, because the product shipped is sufficiently

---

[17] Logistics networks are a case where 'brokers' compete with competing optimizing methods. Markets for trucking and taxi services also see competing dispatchers.

homogeneous. A different issue arises in transport ventures, such as airlines, railways, or telecommunications, where a piece of freight, a passenger or a caller needs to reach a particular customer or point in the network. This imposes a more complex set of constraints on the network optimization problem than the 'simple' requirement that total inflows match total outflows (including storage). This problem is equivalent to the previously discussed issue of constructing an optimal set of 'straws' for natural gas systems—and adjusting it efficiently in the face of changing supply and demand conditions. However, for the sectors now considered the issue cannot be eschewed as in the case of the previously discussed industries.

For example, if one were to define rights to use the rail tracks and allocated them to multiple parties, secondary trading should yield the optimal set of paths (straws) through the network that maximizes welfare given the valuations by producers and consumers for the service in question, i.e. person or good x delivered to point y at time z. The optimal set of paths forms the optimal delivery schedule or timetable. The problem is whether an optimal timetable can be generated through decentralized bargaining or whether a smart market is needed that simultaneously generates the optimal set of paths through the network and the prices for all the paths contained therein. Because the value of each right to use a piece of track at a particular time is dependent on what happens with all adjacent pieces of track (all pieces are indirectly adjacent to all others) one may need a single optimizing smart market.[18] A further issue is whether short-run adjustments to the optimal schedule, e.g. owing to mechanical breakdowns or other emergencies, can be made in a timely manner by the smart market/dispatch centre, or whether the loss of vertical integration translates simply into higher transaction costs.

While the structure of the problem may be clear, it may also be too complex to solve for many systems.[19] Potential applications are conceivable in railways and airport slot auctions (to obtain an optimal timetable, pairs of slots need to be auctioned, i.e. a path through the 'network' of airports).[20] Sweden and the United Kingdom are currently investigating

[18] Once a set of paths is established, the right to use the paths in a specified way, e.g. by running a container train over a set of tracks, could be auctioned to—in this case—train service companies. The right to use capacity on the trains can, in turn, be allocated by price or queuing mechanisms or a mix thereof.

[19] We know now that, in the case of electricity, a smart market can be made to work, in which paths through the network need not be explicitly defined. Setting up smart markets that can derive optimal sets of paths would imply also that, in principle, capacity rights could be traded 'in' the smart market.

[20] In the future, remote intelligent traffic management systems could also bring the world of smart markets to road transport.

whether such smart markets can be established for railways. Experiments with such smart markets have been conducted in experimental laboratory settings.[21]

Implicit timetables: Timetables need not be preannounced. Optimal routing may be obtained through smart markets in other ways. Ideally, transport and congestion prices could be determined through competing segments of the transport network, each of which competed to provide the service. Through demand and supply conditions, prices on individual segments could be set independently and competitively. These systems have been the subject of experiments, particularly in the case of gas and electricity, where joint competing owners of transport infrastructure, i.e. specific gas pipelines, have been proposed.[22]

How might this work in practice? Two examples are provided here. The first is of a telephone network. Optimal use would be obtained if users of the system faced prices that led them to use the system optimally. For pricing in a phone system one might—as a thought experiment— imagine the following system. The caller would dial. The system optimizers (switching facilities in the case of telecommunications) would then determine the optimal path at the desired time and quote a price that would appear on the phone. The customer could then 'conclude' the contract by pressing a 'yes' button or abort the call attempt. This would yield a system of spot prices on the basis of which longer-term contracts could be established, enabling callers to have assured call rights at given prices at certain times. In a sense the price schedules of the phone companies mimic this 'long-term' market directly without explicitly letting callers make a spot market. Indeed, the information over the Internet is already conducted on a similarly decentralized basis, with individual 'packets' of information being sent across different routes of the network.

The second example is the road network. In theory, each road, or even lane of a road, could be under separate ownership, with each segment profit-maximizing given the constraints of competition from other routes and transport substitutes. Subject to the prices that arise from these routes, individual shippers, logistics firms, and other road users will decide on the traffic flows, hence establishing an 'implicit' timetable. Note that this is simply the price 'dual' of the quantity rationing which

---

[21] See McCabe *et al.* (1989)

[22] See Funk (1992). This system would essentially work by splitting up individual pipeline ownership into a series of individual owners competing to provide the transport service. Although there may be some difficulties monitoring the contracts and entitlements, this would not necessarily be impossible using advanced metering and computer systems.

exists today, certain routes are more congested than others and the time costs associated with heavily used routes determine traffic flows on a decentralized basis.

Why are some routes decided on a decentralized basis and others on a centralized basis? Clearly the answer is not necessarily to do with the cost of congestion, which is substantial in roads and still the subject of 'decentralized' timetabling. Part of the answer, at least historically, may be to do with the cost of short-term supply/demand imbalances, which are catastrophic in systems that have been traditionally centrally dispatched, i.e. railways with the danger of collisions, and gas and electricity with the danger of explosions or black-outs respectively. The other answer clearly is that timetabling and dispatching grows more complex as the number of players/routes etc. increases, making 'central dispatch' infeasible in the case of transport over the road network. New computer and monitoring systems, however, may reduce the need for centralized dispatch in future in the other infrastructure sectors, particularly telecommunications.[23]

(c) Competitive System Expansion

Under the various schemes for organizing competition over existing networks, users of the network will somehow have to pay for investment and operating costs of the network. It is notoriously difficult to allocate such costs in an economically meaningful way. The danger thus exists that sub-optimal charges for the bottleneck facility, e.g. power transmission, will result in bad location of facilities in competitive segments (power plants) or bad transmission expansion decisions (Newbery, 1995a).

The more information is reflected in prices, the better investment decisions can be and the more scope there is for decentralizing decisions. We have considered above arguments why price (and, simultaneously, scheduling) systems may require a — potentially unique — smart market, i.e. a natural monopoly of sorts. But once prices are established they can then guide decentralized decision-making. If one can obtain a price system that reflects opportunity costs by time as well as location, then it should, in principle, be possible to decentralize all trades and also investment decisions.

[23] The airline industry exhibits some features of this decentralization as well. In a deregulated system, airline seats are continuously repriced to reflect demand and supply conditions. Customers have a choice of buying in the spot market — sometimes literally bidding over seats in overbooked aircraft — or buying longer-term contracts that guarantee a seat at a price. However, as mentioned before, airline routes are not yet competitively allocated. Therefore seat-pricing currently optimizes given a route system, i.e. given a timetable.

Consider the above railway path/airport slot auction problem. Suppose a pure price system could operate that would yield different prices at different locations and times for the use of capacity train or airplane capacity. These prices would feed back into the valuation of complete paths. Prices would then reflect congestion costs. This is equivalent to node pricing referred to above for power systems.

At some point, the cost of congestion should lower the value of sales to producers so much that it would pay to invest in congestion-reducing infrastructure. Equivalently, the value of calls or travel might be so reduced. Will this lead to efficient decentralized investment decisions? Network customers, e.g. power plants, would need to form expectations about future node prices and the difference between them, i.e. congestion costs. That may not be more difficult than assessing future market conditions in any other competitive market.

Network customers, groups of customers, or developers on behalf of customers could then invest in extra capacity to relieve congestion. However, it may often be difficult to determine who benefits to what extent from the new capacity. For example, the owner of the existing 'path' or a part thereof may neglect maintenance and still not suffer much, because the new investor(s) have relieved congestions sufficiently. Or some firm could not be persuaded to join the consortium but still has access to the system, e.g. because access is rationed by price only. The question is whether sufficiently strong consortia can be formed that feel they can ignore the beneficial effects on others. In reality, some such attitude always prevails, e.g. when a firm constructs its own captive infrastructure thereby relieving constraints on others. The builder(s) of new infrastructure capacity benefit by collecting higher sales prices and by receiving future congestion rentals between the nodes that the new capacity connects.

Where free-rider problems are serious, whether in the 'maintenance example' or the 'consortium example', the key is to write contracts *ex ante* between the concerned parties that can be enforced *ex post*, e.g. maintenance obligations could be contractually specified or payment obligations under the consortia and other participants in the power system could sue when contracts are breached. What remains to be shown is that the solution to the free-rider problem is substantially different from 'regulation'. Also, if the solution of free-rider problems increases incentives and opportunities to collude, is anti-trust legislation sufficient to deal with this threat?[24]

---

[24] The answer to this question will also determine whether co-tenancy schemes, such as 'competitive joint ventures', are significantly different from 'straight' regulation.

One may ask: If new investment could be decided upon in the above decentralized way, why could trade in that capacity not occur in the first place? Maybe the answer is that a smart market—not decentralized bargaining—is first needed to establish prices that can then support a decentralized investment response.

(d) *Remaining Natural Monopoly and the Role of Competition Policy*

In a sense, the scheduling mechanism is the one that grants access to a system that is otherwise operated, maintained, and expanded in a decentralized and competitive fashion. To a degree, scheduling is equivalent to a permitting system, that allows firms to operate in an otherwise reasonably competitive market. Scheduling should, therefore, always be (vertically) separated from the rest of the system and probably be run as a non-profit organization, which represents all participants and, in particular, the users. That is in analogy to 'governmental authorities' or self-regulatory bodies, which govern and operate permitting or licensing systems in other parts of the economy.

By vertically separating the core natural monopoly element, namely scheduling, from the rest of the system, there can also be more latitude for allowing vertical integration in the rest of the system. If scheduling/ dispatch is carried out separately, the actual ownership of the transmission part of the network will not provide much in the way of monopoly power unless the owner can obstruct competitors by scheduling maintenance work in anti-competitive ways. While vertical unbundling may not be so important after all, a sufficient number of competitors (horizontal unbundling) may be required to achieve lasting benefits of competition. In many ways this is similar to basic principles of competition policy elsewhere, i.e. vertical integration is not much of a problem as long as the integrated company has no monopoly power in any part of the vertical supply chain.

In practice, rules and institutions of competition policy are, indeed, used more and more to deal with remaining issues of regulation in networks. As outlined in the following, a variety of approaches reducing traditional sector-specific price and quality regulation are being introduced in a number of countries.

(i) Reliance on economy-wide rules of competition policy

In the different infrastructure networks firms exercise varying degrees of market power. Some segments, for example, trucking, airlines, and natural gas production in the United States, have been completely deregulated and are no longer subject to traditional regulation. Market power may, however, be tackled by using anti-trust rules.

Some countries rely completely or to a large extent on competition from substitute services to keep prices in check, subject only to competition policy provisions. For example, gas supply to large users in Germany has for some time been unregulated, with market prices of competing petroleum products setting a cap for natural gas prices. Suppliers are free to negotiate any contract and practise price discrimination.[25] Competition policy authorities are meant to check market power abuse *ex post*, relying on outcomes in comparator markets, a form of yardstick competition, to assess industry performance. In fact, meaningful comparators are hard to come by and the competition policy authorities have largely allowed substitute competition, however imperfect, to determine outcomes (Mueller and Vogelsang, 1979).

Hong Kong has so far left natural gas prices completely unregulated, even for residential customers. Not having any competition policy rules or agency, Hong Kong thus relied entirely on substitute competition to discipline market power. However, currently there are moves to introduce some type of price regulation as the social and political legitimacy of the old unregulated system is eroding.

(ii) Special safeguards: market structure regulation

Segments of some industries, such as local telephony or power generation, are becoming more competitive and less subject to regulation. However, some doubts about whether workable competition may really be obtained persist. In such a case, a country may combine *ex ante* market-structure regulation (including *per se* prohibitions of vertical and horizontal cross-ownership) with *ex-post* reviews of abuse of market power in the system. This is the basic approach underlying the Argentine power generation market, where the government unbundled the sector horizontally and vertically to reduce the likelihood that generators might exercise undue market power (see Box 6 for arguments about unbundling).

(iii) Special safeguards: potential regulation.

Other governments have opted for forms of 'potential' regulation, i.e. they established mechanisms, which allow some regulatory authority to

---

[25] In fact, the law recognizes the natural monopoly characteristics of gas pipelines and allows private inter-firm agreements limiting competition, such as demarcation agreements, which define exclusive territories for gas transmission companies. The demarcation agreements are only binding for the participating companies. Other companies may build pipelines through the 'demarcated' territory, a strategy recently pursued by Wintershall, a subsidiary of the chemical giant, BASF.

Box 6
Restructuring Sectors to Facilitate Competition

In many cases, simple removal of regulatory barriers to entry may not be enough to ensure effective competition with minimal regulatory demands. Existing public enterprises may need to be restructured, horizontally or vertically. The key principles in this area are summarized below.

(i) *Horizontal restructuring*: Horizontal restructuring involves the creation of two or more entities in a single area of economic activity, such as power generation, water supply, or gas distribution. The rationale for this approach depends on whether the activity in question is potentially competitive or naturally monopolistic.

When the activity is potentially competitive, restructuring an enterprise into two or more separate firms allows the new firms to compete with one another. It also dilutes the market power of the incumbent enterprise, thus reducing barriers faced by new entrants to the market and reducing the burden on oversight by utility or competition regulators. When the activity is naturally monopolistic, restructuring into two or more firms creates opportunities for introducing yardstick competition between the new firms. It can also make competition for the market more effective, by increasing the number of local bidders for monopoly franchises. The optimal degree of horizontal restructuring — and hence the number of new firms created — depends in large part on economies of scale in the relevant activity and on market size.

(ii) *Vertical restructuring*: Vertical restructuring involves the separation of economic activities in different stages of the production chain. In utilities, the primary focus is separation of naturally monopolistic activities — such as power transmission lines and gas transmission pipelines — from potentially competitive activities, such as power generation and supply and gas production and supply. Vertical restructuring has two distinct but related objectives.

First, it facilitates regulation of monopolistic activities, by isolating relevant costs and revenues. This facilitates introduction of yardstick competition and reduces opportunities for manipulating regulation of different regulated businesses (e.g. power transmission and distribution) and anti-competitive cross-subsidies between regulated and unregulated activities (e.g. power transmission and power generation). In some cases, mere accounting separation into separate business units may suffice to meet these concerns, although there is a trend to require at least the creation of separate subsidy companies. Second, vertical restructuring reduces the potential for a vertically-integrated firm to misuse its market power to the detriment of competitors. When a single enterprise controls both a critical network facility (such as a transmission grid) and a competitive activity (such as power generation), it can use control over the network to stifle competition. To reduce competitive pressures in potentially competitive activities, it might charge new entrants prohibitive or discriminatory prices for access to the network, or discriminate in a range of other ways. When concerns of this kind exist, the creation of separate business units or subsidiary companies can facilitate regulatory supervision of such behaviour — and thus reduce the burden on heavy regulatory control. Full separation of ownership and control is usually required.

In evaluating the pros and cons of vertical restructuring, possible costs in terms of forgone economies of scale and scope need to be weighed against the benefits of facilitating effective competition without the need for heavy regulatory oversight. When a country has limited experience in economic regulation, the balance usually favours full separation of ownership and control, as illustrated by the approach to power sector reform in countries such as Argentina and Bolivia.

control prices and quality if and when unregulated outcomes are judged unsatisfactory (Sappington, 1994).

New Zealand's system of potential regulation of the telecommunications sector has attracted particular attention. The most widely known aspect is the treatment of access pricing to the telecoms network, which was left to the supervision of the Commerce Commission, New Zealand's competition policy authority, under its general rules.[26] However, there are also limits on price increases for residential customers and public call facilities contained in the 'golden share' retained by the government. Furthermore, under the Commerce Act of 1986, the Minister of Commerce can impose price controls, if he is satisfied that conditions of effective competition do not exist and control is necessary to protect network users or consumers.

When a new entrant, Clear Communications, attempted to reach agreement on interconnection policy with the incumbent, New Zealand Telecom, uncertainty about interconnection rules remained high, owing to the lack of sector-specific rules and guidelines. This led to protracted litigation in the courts, with the Commonwealth Privy Council in the United Kingdom as the final arbiter. The experience of New Zealand points to the continued usefulness of some regulatory rules that clarify price-setting principles in markets, where competition is still imperfect.

Another variant of *ex-post* review is found in the state of Nebraska in the United States. In the telecommunications sector of the state, entry and prices are unregulated. However, the regulatory commission may intervene if a certain level of complaints is reached. This form of potential regulation resembles reliance on competition policy by relying on a type of *ex-post* intervention, however, exercised by a regulatory agency, not the competition policy authority.

In the United Kingdom, pricing and entry in the power generation segment was initially unconstrained until the regulator, OFFER, introduced a price cap in this segment on the grounds that there was still reason to believe that existing generators exercised excessive market power.

In Mexico, the competition policy authority may determine whether conditions for effective competition in a market segment are absent and sector-specific price regulation is required. In the case of ports it has so far ruled that price regulation was not required.

Another variant of regulation may be characterized as implicit potential regulation. Requirements to publish prices, together with some

---

[26] Note that the licence for New Zealand Telecom requires accounting separation to generate information that may be used by the competition policy body to be able to apply its tests and rules.

surveillance or reporting mechanism, may be used to create publicity about the pricing behaviour of firms. Corporatized airports in Australia are subject to such a price surveillance regime. Another case in point is the requirement for Argentine freight rail concessions simply to publish prices. It may be argued that such publicity may lead to calls for reimposition of price controls if blatant abuse of market power were to persist. (On the other hand it is well known and supported also by experimental economics that requirements to publish prices may facilitate collusion.)

The examples show that the transition to reliance on economy-wide rules remains complicated in sectors where only a limited degree of competition can reasonably be introduced. Of course, there remain other sectors or market segments where traditional regulation remains inescapable for the time being, for example, water transmission.

(iv) Basic trade-offs in assigning responsibilities

The examples also illustrate that economy-wide rules (New Zealand) or sector-specific ones (Nebraska) may be used. Rules may be applied by economy-wide agencies (New Zealand) or by sector-specific ones (United Kingdom). Indeed, in Australia sector-specific agencies may apply some economy-wide rules and some sector-specific ones fall within the purview of economy-wide agencies. Furthermore, competition policy authorities may have concurrent rights to review cases subject to traditional regulation (e.g. Mexico), or they may be used as appeals bodies, as in the United Kingdom. Of course, final appeals will rest with the court system.

This raises the question about the basic trade-offs in the choice of rules and institutions empowered to apply them. Competition policy authorities may be less prone to capture as they are more distant from the players in a sector. On the other hand, they may lack the detailed technical competence required to deal with some sector-specific issues. The challenge is to strike a balance between these considerations while preserving coherent decision-making to reduce uncertainty for investors. This may, for example, argue for empowering the competition policy body to deal with fairly generic issues, such as collusion, while asking the regulatory agency to look after more sector-specific issues, such as interconnection rules, final pricing, or quality of service. In many systems, mergers in negotiated industries are subject to scrutiny by both industry-specific and economy-wide regulation.

(v) Change in rules and compensation

Whatever transition mechanism is chosen in the move towards increased reliance on competition in the market, such a transition implies an interference in the rights of industry participants. In particular, increased competition will tend to expose investment required by or prudently carried out under regulation—what are called 'stranded assets' in the United States.

Private firms ask for compensation when their assets are 'stranded' due to regulatory decisions, which, for example, allow new market entry. It may, therefore, be desirable to introduce competition before privatization where this is an option. This would tend to reduce protracted and inefficient negotiations for compensation,[27] a strategy chosen, for example, in Chile and the Ukraine. By the same token it may be desirable to introduce tough market-structure regulation initially, which may later be relaxed, rather than having to tighten regulation with possible consequent demands for compensation.

4. Competing Networks and Policy Barriers to Entry

(a) *Competition Among Networks*

The preceding discussion had suggested that the hard core of natural monopoly is the smart market, whether in its incarnation as dispatch or timetable optimizer. When will there be a single smart market or 'scheduling system'? In general, scheduling is necessary when temporary congestion is extremely costly, i.e. system-wide black-outs in the case of electricity and problems to a lesser extent in gas networks. It is in these networks that a 'hard core' natural monopoly in terms of centralized scheduling is likely to remain.

In a world of complete information 'traffic flows' should be centrally scheduled and dispatched accordingly worldwide and across different types of networks—what the just-in-time logistics network tries at the level of competing firms, should be done centrally for the world by a (benevolent and efficient) scheduler. The whole world would thus be a natural monopoly with regard to scheduling.

---

[27] One should, however, recognize that the potential greater ease of competitive restructuring in the public sector is due to the fact that the owners of the assets, the taxpayers, are not well organized to claim compensation. The taxpayers' displeasure may, nevertheless, find voice in complaints about give-aways and low sales prices for state assets. The situation is particularly visible for taxpayers—and therefore controversial—when assets cannot even attract a price equal to book value.

But, as we know, there may be a lack of benevolence and efficiency in monopolies and the problem is probably too complex anyway — just like the somewhat equivalent proposition of central planning that wanted to reduce the chaos of markets and its attendant costs.[28]

We also see a number of competing networks, e.g. petroleum product distribution systems competing with natural gas systems, or railways competing with trucks, cases where the theoretical benefits of complete and integrated scheduling are probably less important than the practical benefits from competition among networks. Competition is most useful where the central planning problem is hardest, i.e. where uncertainty and/or complexity is great. There are thus dynamic or informational benefits from incomplete scheduling, which allows competition on the basis of some level of 'redundancy' or duplication. Such redundancy can — by definition — only be suspected, but not unambiguously identified. Redundant capacity is necessary for new things to be tried out and for monopolistic behaviour to be checked.[29] For example, the introduction of competition for long-distance services in Chile's telecommunications industry in 1993 led to market entry by eight long-distance carriers and a fall in prices by 50 per cent by 1995.

But, as knowledge and practices evolve, the (ambiguous) boundaries of where the realm of redundancy starts and that of tight scheduling ends will shift. Practical questions that arise and have no set answer are: should port dockage slots be auctioned in pairs, like airport slots, to benefit from tighter scheduling? Or because, in most parts, oceans are still uncongested, might there not be significant benefits from tighter scheduling, which should normally arise from reduced investment requirements? The obverse may be true with roads, which are currently inefficiently priced and not naturally abundant. For example, if roads were to be priced electronically, a lot of long-distance freight traffic might shift to rail, where it can be more tightly scheduled (higher throughput) and causes fewer mainte-

---

[28] See, for example, Vickers (1994), who outlines the trade-offs in terms of a simple model where the incentive benefits of a number of competing firms are weighed against the duplicated fixed costs of entry.

[29] Once upon a time the socialist critique of market economies pointed to the allegedly wasteful duplication in chaotic markets, of which marketing appeared to be an obvious case. But while there might be some duplication in markets, the pressures generated by chaotic competition to work hard, to learn, and to innovate, apparently outweigh many costs of duplication. The theoretical benefits from coordination or planning, on the other hand, are difficult to achieve when matters get complex and markets tend to be better at generating useful information than planning bureaux. In other words, what some call dynamic benefits of competition appear much more important than static allocational benefits in many settings.

nance costs.[30] Scheduling economics also appear to be behind the debate of whether one should allow free entry into urban public transport, e.g. bus systems, or whether routes or set of routes should be (competitively) awarded as monopoly franchises. Likewise, the empirical finding that free entry into solid-waste collection services is less efficient than competitive award of monopoly franchises is likely to result from the advantages of tighter scheduling under the monopoly franchise.

As it is never quite clear *ex ante* what the extent of natural monopoly is, it might be useful to let markets determine whether monopoly is indeed natural. If a natural monopoly is truly such, then only one firm will survive under unregulated competition for a franchise.

Competition is often valuable for the very same reason that it is impossible to quantify *ex ante* that it will be valuable. A review of the deregulation experiments in the United States highlights the role of unexpected new ways of doing business which have followed deregulation and led to welfare gains (Winston, 1993). If one could predict innovation, whether organizational or technological, any old protected monopolist could match the competitive outcome. It is precisely because one cannot predict innovation that competition is beneficial and by the same token one cannot *ex ante* quantify its benefits.

The view is also supported by specific examples of the behaviour of protected monopolies. In many cases, administrative entry restrictions have clearly retarded investment and better service — witness the behaviour of monopolists such as India Telecom. At the same time, the monopoly holder has often *de facto* charged market-clearing prices to customers by asking for bribes or other special payments, for example, for the installation of a telephone service.

Many such monopolists were and are public enterprises, and the lack of profit motive for the firm as a whole may explain their lack of dynamism. But other examples show that the private profit motive alone may not be sufficient to instil dynamism in a monopolist. As long as Ghana had only one cellular company the company invested slowly and planned to expand only as retained earnings easily allowed financing of expansion. As soon as a second cellular operator was allowed, the incumbent started to invest aggressively ahead of the previously announced schedule.

[30] The Channel Tunnel provides a real world example of the fact that, when costs matter, it is cheaper to put trucks on wagons than to build a tunnel for trucks. This does not essentially depend on the higher cost for ventilation under a truck-on-road system, but on the possibilities to increase throughput with tighter truck-on-rail scheduling and smaller tunnel diameter, because safety margins are less — in other words, two benefits of tighter 'scheduling'.

Essentially all of the preceding arguments against erecting policy barriers to entry revolve around what some call dynamic benefits of competition, i.e. benefits originating in better incentives to expend effort, learn, and innovate.

(b) Costs of Competition and Policy Barriers to Entry

In some cases, policy-makers will be reluctant to allow free entry for seemingly sound reasons. For example, it may be difficult to see the benefits of allowing multiple water companies to tear up roads and sidewalks, or to allow multiple garbage collection trucks to fight for the trash of the same community. However, in the first case—if the costs of tearing up the 'street' are clearly imposed on the private firm, including a tax for externalities, such as disturbing traffic and general quiet—it is hard to see why anybody would enter the market, particularly if corporate takeovers were allowed, unless the new entrant had a superior solution for the problem of delivering water. In the second case, it is again questionable why anybody would enter the trash collection market if prices could be freely set. An area monopolist should be able to offer better terms to everybody than competing firms, unless competition yielded other benefits. Competitors would at all times be free to offer a new set of contracts to area residents and if they could sign up enough clients, they would oust the incumbent.[31]

But there may still be costs to letting markets pass the verdict on natural monopoly.

- The process of establishing the natural monopoly outcome may be wasteful and costly, e.g. when water companies competed in the 19th century by laying parallel lines. Today, studies suggest that competition among solid-waste collection companies for the same customer group is less efficient than competition for (temporary) monopoly franchises for solid-waste collection.
- There may be an unsustainable or suboptimal outcome from the competition for a natural monopoly under a policy of free entry. Suppose a single efficient firm is the cheapest solution to supply the whole market, e.g. a water company that is constrained to charge uniform single price tariffs in the service area. Suppose, further, that production technology is such that average costs are minimized when two-thirds of customers are supplied, but rise again when more customers are to be connected. A new entrant could then offer to supply two-thirds of the customers at a lower

---

[31] In cases such as trash collection, where sunk investments are minimal, a reasonably effective alternative to free entry is to auction off monopoly franchises in short intervals on the basis of the lowest price offered (Demsetz–Chadwick auction).

price than the incumbent and would drive him out of business. In this case one-third of the market would remain unsupplied.[32] Foreman-Peck and Millward (1994) use this argument to explain why service provision in 19th century water and gas systems was often limited.

- Regulation may provide incentives for excessive bypass (Laffont and Tirole, 1990). Vertically integrated incumbents would tend to try charging excessive access/interconnection fees, which will, by the same token, provide excessive incentives to bypass the system.
- Network externalities may create either excess inertia (too little investment while everybody waits for others to invest in the expansion of the network, which becomes more valuable the more it connects users to others) or excess momentum (too much investment as firms try to establish a first-mover advantage) (Tirole, 1988; Economides, 1994; Katz and Shapiro, 1994).

Altogether the arguments for erecting policy barriers for entry into natural monopolies point to excessive costs of service delivery under free-entry regimes or under-supply. To evaluate such arguments *ex ante* one would need to have a view on the magnitude of such costs and compare them to the likely losses of efficiency resulting from restraints on competition. Such a trade-off is by definition impossible to quantify *ex ante*, but the following general considerations may hold.

- *Costs of establishing networks.* Competition between networks may be desirable if the sunk costs of establishing those networks are 'small' relative to the cost of the ultimate service, e.g. lines in telecommunication networks.
- *Government capability.* In cases where government capacity benevolently and efficiently to recognize natural monopoly and establish barriers to entry is weak, it is more likely that entry should not be limited by policy (the award of monopoly franchises or exclusivity periods etc.). Likewise when monopoly firms are either owned or regulated by a 'weak' state, the case for allowing competition is strengthened.
- *Technical change.* When technical change is rapid it will be more difficult to circumscribe the domain of natural monopoly and the dynamic benefits of competition will be large.
- *Complexity of networks.* As argued above in the discussion of scheduling there is likely to be more value in competing networks the more complex the network is, e.g. logistics networks. This is

---

[32] This could be avoided where price discrimination is allowed, because the incumbent could charge two-thirds of the customers the minimum average costs and more to the rest so that the new entrant cannot offer better terms.

simply a case where the costs and benefits of maintaining a monopoly are little known and where competition is most needed to find innovative solutions.

(c) *The Political Economy of Natural Monopoly*

Most of these arguments are difficult to translate into practical measures that allow governments to assess the likelihood of wasteful duplication. It is harder still to assess the magnitude of dynamic benefits that need to be weighed against the costs of duplication. The easiest may still be cost function studies, as suggested by the contestability literature. But this says nothing about how to factor in dynamic benefits from competition. Arguments about network externalities and games among a small number of players can go both ways—in favour of or against entry barriers—depending how the games are specified. The foregoing arguments thus mainly characterize the logic of some arguments. Politically established biases will be the decisive factor in the end. Good policy should ideally take such biases into account, guarding against arguments to restrict entry that do little more than protect special interests.

The same governments that advocate entry restrictions, ostensibly to reduce wasteful duplication, tend to tolerate and subsidize duplicate networks of major proportions—witness transport networks, for example, rail and road. In the 19th century, competition from rail led to a decline of the private road industry in the United Kingdom. In France the government maintained the roads with subsidies in the face of competition from rail. Today the reverse holds and many governments heavily subsidize rail. Governments also tolerate highly inefficient price structures and usage of infrastructure. For example, inefficiencies in road and airport usage pricing have been estimated to amount to around US$15 billion each in 1995 prices (Morrison and Winston, 1989).

Entry restrictions, on the other hand, have often been set at the behest of incumbents and to keep out new technologies. A case in point is the fight of gas companies against power companies around the turn of the century. Entry restrictions are particularly hard to undo when the boundary of a protected company coincides with the political jurisdiction that grants the protection. There are obvious benefits from collusion between the political powers and the firm, which would be reduced if the firm operated across jurisdictions and several political entities had to collude to extract monopoly rents. Municipal monopoly franchises may be particularly difficult to undo, as history seems to suggest.

A variation on the theme can be found in arguments in favour of entry barriers that are based on the need to maintain cross-subsidies. Certainly cross-subsidies can only be sustained if competition is somehow limited and so-called 'cherry-picking' restricted. But the same subsidy can be provided explicitly and based on competition-neutral funding sources. Monopoly profits in one part of the network are not the only source of 'tax' revenues.

Another argument for entry barriers is based on attempts to lower the ostensible cost of capital for network service providers. The natural incentive for investors, investment bankers, and short-term revenue-maximizers in government is to argue for entry barriers when privatizing infrastructure firms or issuing concessions to build new facilities. Thus the call for exclusivity periods, long-lasting concession terms, etc. Indeed, monopoly rights will lower the ostensible cost of capital and render financing 'easier.' However, they do so by shifting risks to the customers, not by reducing risk overall, unless the entry barriers help avoid a social cost of the type outlined above, in which case the ease of finance and the cost of capital is not the critical argument.

Experience from the last century shows that investments not protected by entry barriers were, in fact, funded. Today, we also see that new investments in competitive segments of network industries will be financed, e.g. power plants in competitive markets in Argentina, Chile, and the United Kingdom. What is no longer possible, though, is project finance based on long-term power purchase agreements with the ability to attract long-term debt for highly leveraged projects. Rather, financing patterns resemble more normal corporate finance patterns, with low leverage, short maturities, and on-balance-sheet financing by the sponsor. A recent case which suggests that competition may effectively stimulate investment and lower prices compared to a monopoly franchise solution is found in Chile, where the government allowed two rather than one gas transmission line to be built to supply gas from abroad. The decision to allow a competitor brought contract gas prices to final users tumbling down by some 20 to 30 per cent.

(d) *Basic Policy Rule*

As there are so many questions about whether monopoly should prevail and whether government is capable of identifying such situations *ex ante*, perhaps the basic policy rule should be: in case of doubt do not restrict entry and, if you do, subject the entry restrictions to an automatic test after a set period of time and require a cost–benefit review to argue for prolonging entry barriers.

5. A Sketch of Sectoral Implications

Depending on the physical characteristics of each 'network' industry, ways to introduce competition will vary in nature and effectiveness and differ in ease of implementation. Broadly speaking, competition is, of course, easiest to introduce in industry segments where sunk costs are unimportant, e.g. in the case of many transport vehicles, such as ships, airplanes, trucks, taxis, etc. The basic policy solution here is free entry without economic regulation. Matters become more complex when economies of scale due to scheduling are important. In those cases it may be efficient to award monopoly franchises competitively, e.g. for urban bus transport or solid-waste collection services. As long as sunk costs are not important, as in the case of buses and garbage trucks, repeated franchise bidding can provide a good level of competition without the need for extensive regulation. To date, positive experience has been gained with competition in all of the above transport industry segments.

Where sunk costs are important, matters are more complex. For electricity and natural gas systems, which produce and carry fairly homogeneous products, the best conceivable solution would appear to lie in 'smart' competitive pools, wherever a sufficiently large market can be created to sustain workable competition. This argues, of course, very heavily for fostering international trade in energy services wherever possible. Competitive pools are still in an experimental stage, but with demonstrated effectiveness and clear promise. The greatest current challenge is whether fully flexible congestion price systems can be made to work and allow effective deregulation of investment decisions in the transmission and distribution networks. Water pipeline systems might also benefit from competitive pool solutions, if and when markets in tradable water rights in areas where the price of water is high are allowed to function. However, the politics of water may impede progress. Competition in water is also made difficult, because water sources can be quite heterogeneous and economies of scale in water treatment may render effective competition difficult in many cases.

Smart markets have yet to provide practical solutions to introduce competition in networks where goods and services are not homogeneous and where starting and end points of network flows matter. Attempts at solutions are being debated in the context of the Swedish and UK railway reforms. But, basically, the preferred option is some form of open access or common-carriage system with regulation of interconnection rules. This is particularly important in telecommunications, but also used in various other networks, such as railroads, airports, and natural gas.

To some extent ,the search for competitive, unregulated solutions can be facilitated if one simply relies on competition between 'networks', otherwise described as intermodal or substitute competition. Typically, that is an option for railways, which face competition from trucks in many cases. One can also rely on competition from the petroleum product market to discipline pricing behaviour, e.g. in the natural gas market. This is the case for natural gas in Finland, Germany, and Hong Kong (for large users). Large electricity contracts in Germany are also unregulated. Indeed, international comparison of regulatory regimes shows that the rail and natural gas sectors are most likely to remain unregulated and tend to rely most on substitute competition to provide pricing discipline.

Telecommunications services are more and more exposed to competing wireless services and, in many cases, competing line-based networks are being established as the cost of such infrastructure falls. Further technical progress may thus obviate the need for regulation. Countries with limited government capability to regulate can already rely on competition from wireless services to provide basic consumer protection.

The toughest regulatory challenges remain in electricity, water, airports, and roads. In electricity the solution may lie in the above-mentioned competitive power pools. In water, the effective introduction of competitive forces is a fair way off, although conceptually similar to power pools. Road management may be revolutionized as electronic traffic management in conjunction with road (congestion) pricing becomes more widespread as a result of current tests in countries such as Italy, Norway, Singapore, and the United States. Airport landing rights auctions are still awaiting the arrival of appropriate smart markets, which would also be required in order to manage road networks efficiently and decentralize investment decisions in these networks.

The key to the introduction of new solutions will remain technical progress in telecommunications and telemetry. In the telecommunications industry itself, technical change holds out the hope for workable competition among networks. In other industries, such as transport and energy, advances in telemetry and telecommunications, combined with computer-based smart markets, are crucial for new solutions.

The UK Experience

4

The Electricity Industry in England and Wales

RICHARD GREEN AND DAVID M. NEWBERY*

1. Introduction

By the time that the government started to plan the privatization of the electricity supply industry in 1987, it had become apparent that effective competition could only be introduced into formerly monopolized industries if structural changes were made. The White Paper, *Privatising Electricity* (Department of Energy, 1988), accordingly announced that the Central Electricity Generating Board (CEGB) was to be split into three parts: two generating companies and a transmission company. The transmission company, to be jointly owned by the twelve regional electricity companies (RECs) responsible for distribution, would act as a common carrier and facilitate competition. The generating companies would compete to sell to the distribution companies and large customers, and would face entry from new stations built by independent power producers.

The White Paper had a vision of a competitive electricity industry, although it was very short on the details of how it would operate. Most of these details were filled in over the next 2 years (although some were deferred until after Vesting Day, 31 March 1990, when the new structure came into being) and there were some consequential changes to the underlying structure. Most importantly, the government discovered that the costs of British nuclear power stations were higher than it had previously believed, and was forced to withdraw the nuclear stations from the privatization in July and November 1989. They had originally planned to create an unbalanced duopoly in generation. National Power would own 70 per cent of the capacity, including all the nuclear stations,

* Department of Applied Economics, University of Cambridge. Support from the British Economic and Social Research Council under the project R000 23 3766 is gratefully acknowledged. We are indebted to Dieter Helm and the participants at the *Oxford Review of Economic Policy* seminar for helpful comments. The views expressed are ours alone.

in the hope that this company would be large enough to absorb the risks of nuclear power. PowerGen would own the remaining 30 per cent, in the hope that it could act as a counter-weight to National Power. When the nuclear power stations were split off to form Nuclear Electric (with 20 per cent of the total capacity), the conventional generators looked unbalanced and the case for a dominant National Power was gone, but the timetable imposed upon the privatization was too far advanced to change it.

Another decision made in late 1989 concerned competition in supply to final consumers. The White Paper had suggested that large industrial consumers might be able to choose the identity of their generator, but it was decided to extend competition in supply to all consumers, in three stages. The 5,000 largest consumers, with maximum demands of more than 1 MW, would be allowed to choose their supplier from the start. These consumers take about 30 per cent of the electricity generated. Another 45,000 consumers, with maximum demands of more than 100 kW, taking 20 per cent of the total sales, would be allowed to choose their supplier from April 1994. Finally, in April 1998, all consumers would have the right to choose their supplier.

The decision to take a competitive supply cannot change the physics of the electricity industry. Electricity flows through the system from power stations to consumers according to physical laws, and it is impossible to say which station is actually supplying a particular consumer. System controllers employed by the National Grid Company (NGC) must ensure that generation is equal to demand at every moment in time, or risk a widespread failure. Since demand is uncertain, and power stations sometimes break down, this means that some capacity must always be held as spinning reserve, ready to operate at a moment's notice. Demand at the peak on a cold winter's day (around 48 gigawatts, GW)[1] can be nearly 50 per cent greater than the trough reached that night, and more than twice the minimum level of a summer night (perhaps 18 GW). Some stations are taken out of service for maintenance during the summer, but less than half of the capacity on the system can hope to run on 'baseload', generating whenever it is available. Most stations only generate for part of the year, and a 'merit order' system should be used to ensure that the cheapest stations are run most intensively. The most expensive stations spend most of the year in reserve, and may only be operated during winter weekdays.

To take a competitive supply, known as second-tier supply (first-tier customers are those who still buy from their local REC), a customer must

---

[1] The normal unit of consumer demand is the kilowatt (kW). One gigawatt equals 1,000 megawatts (MW) or 1 million kW.

make special commercial arrangements. They must install a meter which records half-hourly electricity consumption, and sends the information daily to the Electricity Pool. Practically all generators have to sell to the Pool, rather than to individual suppliers, which reflects the way in which they send electricity out to the system, and not to specific end-users. Bilateral generation contracts do exist, however, in the form of contracts for differences (CfDs) between generators and suppliers, which are used to hedge around 80 per cent of the sales through the Pool. The metered information from second-tier customers is used to calculate how much their suppliers must buy from the Pool, and what they should pay the local REC for the use of its distribution system, and NGC for high-voltage transmission. The prices for transmission and distribution, and for supply to franchise consumers who cannot choose their supplier, are regulated by the Director General of Electricity Supply (DGES). The DGES, at present Professor Stephen Littlechild, is based at the Office of Electricity Regulation (Offer). His legal duties, set out in the Electricity Act 1989, can be summarized as protecting consumers and promoting competition. He has fewer powers over generators than over the RECs and NGC, because generation was intended to be a competitive market not needing regulation.

(a) *How Does Competition in Generation Work?*

The electricity market is actually a number of interacting and interdependent markets. The spot market, or Pool, is a physical auction market which sets a half-hourly price, called the System Marginal Price or SMP, that equates supply to demand at the price of the most expensive bid accepted. Capacity payments reward generators for the capacity declared available to be despatched, whether or not it is called upon. These payments are based upon the calculated Loss of Load Probability (LOLP), multiplied by the net value of capacity (the Value of Lost Load, or VOLL, set administratively, less SMP, the marginal cost of energy). LOLP is calculated by the scheduling programme, as the risk that the available capacity will be less than the actual level of demand. It uses the capacity of each generating set which has been declared available, and the risk that the set would become unavailable during the forecast period (based on historic data), together with the forecast level of demand, and the variance of this forecast. The VOLL was set at £2/kWh in 1990, and is increased each year in line with the retail price index (RPI). LOLP is frequently zero, but when the level of spare capacity falls, LOLP rises, and capacity payments have sometimes exceeded 50p/kWh, more than ten times the level of SMP at those times. On average, over the first 6 years of the Pool, capacity payments account for about one-tenth of the money

Table 1
Annual Average Pool Prices
(pence/kWh or £/kW/yr)

	1990/91	1991/92	1992/93	1993/94	1994/95	1995/96	1996/97
Time-weighted p/kWh							
SMP	1.74	1.95	2.26	2.40	2.08	1.94	2.06
Capacity	0.00	0.13	0.02	0.02	0.32	0.45	0.35
PPP	1.74	2.08	2.28	2.42	2.40	2.39	2.41
Uplift	0.09	0.16	0.14	0.23	0.24	0.20	0.19
PSP	1.84	2.24	2.42	2.65	2.64	2.59	2.60
Demand-weighted p/kWh							
SMP	1.81	1.99	2.31	2.44	2.19	2.07	—
Capacity	0.01	0.17	0.02	0.04	0.45	0.61	—
PPP	1.82	2.16	2.33	2.48	2.64	2.68	2.58
Uplift	0.10	0.18	0.15	0.22	0.27	0.24	0.20
PSP	1.92	2.34	2.48	2.70	2.91	2.92	2.78
Demand-weighted at 1995/96 prices, p/kWh							
SMP	2.11	2.21	2.49	2.59	2.26	2.07	—
PPP	2.12	2.40	2.51	2.63	2.73	2.68	2.52
National Power + PowerGen total revenue from generation at 1995/96 prices, p/kWh		3.90	3.87	3.52	3.56	3.42	
Capacity payments at 1995/96 prices, £/kW/yr	0.47	19.91	2.80	2.55	29.13	39.30	

Sources: Offer (1994a); *Pool Statistical Digest*; company accounts.

passing through the Pool, though in recent years the share has increased sharply, as Table 1 shows.

SMP and capacity payments together make up the Pool Purchase Price, PPP, to which is added Uplift, covering services needed to keep the system in electrical equilibrium, to give the Pool Selling Price, PSP. The evolution of these prices since Vesting is shown in Table 1 and Figure 1.

The contract market allows generators and suppliers to hedge the volatile Pool price, typically with a CfD, under which a generator receives, in addition to the normal Pool price for any sales, a sum equal to the specified strike price *less* the Pool price, multiplied by the specified number of units contracted. In addition to CfDs, there is a market for electricity forward agreements (EFAs) which trades moderately standardized contracts for 4-hour slices of time every weekday or weekend for some period. This is a form of embryonic futures market, which would have a completely standardized contract traded through a clearing house — and such a market may emerge as competitive trading increases.

The generators have to make three strategic choices — how to bid in their available plant each day, what level of contract cover to arrange,

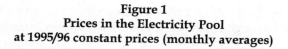

Figure 1
Prices in the Electricity Pool
at 1995/96 constant prices (monthly averages)

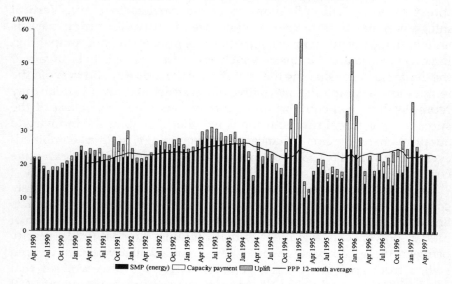

and how much plant to make available (normally each year when connection charges are incurred, but plant must also be withdrawn for maintenance). Together these choices determine the daily range of the PPP and the long-run average around which they fluctuate. The spot and contract markets are closely inter-related, and the contract price must be close to the expected spot price, otherwise buyers or sellers will prefer one to the other. Both are influenced by the amount of capacity, which will depend on the decisions of incumbents and entrants.

Anticipating the argument below, there are two routes to effective competition in generation. The first and obvious route is to ensure that capacity is divided between enough competing generators that no single generator has much influence over the price—an option available but not taken at privatization. The second, indirect route is to induce generators to sell a sufficiently large fraction of their output under contract, and expose them to a credible threat of entry if the contract price (and average Pool price) rises above the competitive level. Contracts and entry threats are complementary—entry threats encourage generators to sign contracts, and contracts facilitate entry.

The advantage of the first approach is that it does not need to rely on the continued contestability of entry, and it works well even when the competitive price is well below the entry price, in periods of excess capacity. In either case, one would expect generators to seek ways of reducing the intensity of competition in order to enhance their profits. Firms selling homogeneous products in fiercely competitive markets will be attracted to merge to create market power, while firms facing the threat of entry will endeavour to create barriers to entry. Vertical integration may be attractive in either case as a way of securing markets and reducing the intensity of competition. A proper study of competition in newly restructured industries such as electricity needs to be aware of the dynamic forces shaping the evolution of the industry and to avoid the temptation of comparing alternative initial structures, few of which may represent long-run equilibrium configurations. The proper test of the success of the initial restructuring is whether it enables the industry to adapt to changing circumstances (new technology, such as combined-cycle gas turbines (CCGT), or changes in fuel prices) without excessive cost, prices, or profits.

We argue that the initial structure of generation was not adequately competitive to achieve this objective, though we recognize that contracts and entry threats had a considerable restraining effect on the exercise of market power. Our argument is that dividing the coal-fired capacity between more companies would have avoided the excessively rapid switch from coal to gas-fired generation. We are also worried that competition in supply after 1998 may weaken the disciplining effect of entry before the development of adequate competition in generation. To demonstrate this line of argument, we shall first look at the relationship between the number of generators and competition in the Pool without contracts, and then examine the effect of contracts and the threat of entry to see how far they can encourage competitive behaviour with few price-setting generators.

The key market to examine is the Pool, which differs from normal auction markets in that it determines 48 half-hourly prices from one set of bids (submitted the day ahead by each generator). Instead of a single price, each bidder submits a whole schedule of prices and quantities, which can usefully be thought of as a supply function (giving the price required to elicit the next unit of generation as a function of total supply offered up to this price). Indeed, National Power explicitly refers to its bidding strategy as one of submitting a supply function. Suppose initially that there are no contracts. A generator with a small fraction of capacity at each price is unlikely to set the price in any period, and thus acts as a competitive price-taker. Such a generator's best strategy is to bid at short-run avoidable cost. A generator with a significant share of capacity in some active (i.e. price-setting) part of the aggregate supply function sets price for some fraction of the time, and can, by raising the price over this range, increase the SMP and its revenue from all despatched plant. If the bid price of the set is too high, then another generator would undercut, set the SMP, and the plant would not be despatched. The spot market is in equilibrium when each generator is content with its own supply function, given the chosen supply function of all other competitors.

(b) *Competition without Contracts*

Green and Newbery (1992) showed how to find equilibrium supply functions using the theoretical model of Klemperer and Meyer (1989), calibrated to the cost and demand conditions of the electricity industry in England and Wales of 1990. They showed that in the absence of contracts, and with no threat of entry or collusion, there was a wide range of possible equilibrium supply functions, lying between a high-price function that would maximize collective short-run profit, and a low-price function. Any one of the possible equilibrium supply functions would be self-enforcing, in that any generator deviating while the others continue to supply as before would reduce its profits. The range of possible equilibria would, however, be dramatically reduced by increasing the number of competing generators from two to five.

Figure 2 illustrates this finding. The line labelled 'marginal cost' represents a smoothed approximation to the marginal avoidable generation costs of the two main generators in 1990 in £/MWh at each level of total output. Since 1 MWh (megawatt hour) is 1000 kWh, £20/MWh is equal to 2p/kWh in units familiar to domestic consumers. Output is measured in gigawatts and demand is shown varying over a winter day. AD represents the highest-price feasible equilibrium aggregate supply function of a symmetric duopoly (each firm would submit half of the total amount shown at each price). It meets maximum demand vertically at D, and is equal to marginal cost at zero output at A. The lowest feasible equilibrium duopoly supply function, AB, meets the marginal cost schedule at B horizontally, and defines a range of feasible uncontracted duopoly supply functions shown as the backward-sloping shaded area, ABD.

If the available capacity were to be divided equally among five companies (and, conveniently, such an allocation of the conventional power stations is feasible), then the highest feasible equilibrium supply function would be AC, and the lowest one AB, defining the forward-sloping shaded area ABC of feasible equilibria. (Again, each company would bid a supply function one-fifth of the total). AC also meets maximum demand vertically and AB hits marginal cost horizontally, and these two features define the bounding equilibrium supply func-

Figure 2
Feasible Supply Functions, Duopoly and Quintopoly
(calibrated for England, 1990)

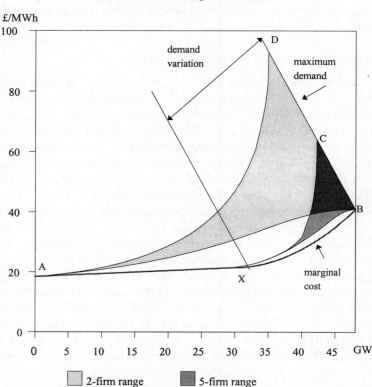

tions — any outside this range would be infeasible, either turning back or down, neither of which would be accepted by the scheduling program.

Note that the range of equilibria is dramatically reduced by increasing the number of competitors from two to five, and that for much of the range of output the two ranges do not overlap. Green and Newbery (1992) calculated that if the duopolists coordinated on the high price equilibrium, average prices would be well above costs, causing large dead-weight losses.[2] Had the generating plant been divided among five equal-sized companies, then each generator's market power would dramatically decrease. The five-firm supply function converges rapidly

---

[2] The deadweight losses vary with demand — at peak demand they are equal to the roughly triangular area DBX formed by dropping a vertical from D to meet the marginal cost line at a point X. As demand varies, it intersects the supply function and marginal cost function at different points to define smaller triangles, whose average is total deadweight loss.

towards marginal cost at lower levels of demand, and losses would have been reduced to only 6 per cent of their duopoly value.[3]

(c) *Competition with Contracts*

Contracts and the threat of entry dramatically alter this picture. Consider the effect that contracts have on the incentives that generators have to bid high. If a generator has sold CfDs exactly equal to the amount despatched in some period, then its income is entirely determined by the strike price of the CfD. It would have no incentive to manipulate the Pool price to either raise or lower the SMP, as this would not affect its revenue. Indeed, if it bid a set above its avoidable cost, it would run the risk that it would not be despatched and would lose the difference between the SMP and the avoidable cost, while if it bid below avoidable cost it might have to run the set at a loss. It would therefore do best by behaving as a competitive price-taker and bidding at short-run avoidable cost. More generally, the incentive to raise Pool prices depends on the amount of un-contracted Pool sales, since only this benefits from the higher prices. The larger the contract cover, the smaller the incentive to manipulate Pool prices, and the more competitive the resulting Pool prices will be.[4]

The second reason for keeping prices low is the threat of entry. In many markets, incumbents are forced to keep prices down to the level of entrants' costs, knowing that if they do not, entry will occur and they will lose market share. Unless they can deter entry, it is best to move quickly to the entry price (if it will soon prevail in any case), forestalling entry and retaining a high market share. Electricity generation might seem like a market in which entry could be deterred, for power stations are long-lived, specific assets, involving high sunk costs. Only an incumbent, or an entrant backed by a very large company, would want to take the risk of building a station which depended upon the fluctuating spot price. The contract market makes entry into generation contestable, however. An entrant can arrange back-to-back contracts for electricity sales and for fuel supply, making its project safe enough for debt finance, so that relatively small companies can enter the market. As long as there are electricity suppliers (or others) willing to buy the entrants' contracts, the incumbents will have to offer comparable terms, or lose market share. That is why the ending of the franchise market is potentially worrying,

---

[3] This result is reminiscent of, but more powerful than, the effect of varying the number of competing Nash–Cournot oligopolists, n, supplying a market with linear demand and constant marginal cost. In that case total deadweight loss falls as $1/(n+1)^2$.

[4] We should add that a generator with market power might attempt to raise the spot price, despite being fully contracted, if it thought that this would increase the price of next year's contracts.

Figure 3
Entry-deterring Supply Functions: The Effect of Contracts
(England, 1990)

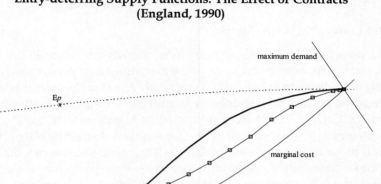

······ 2 firms, no contracts ──□── 5 firms, no contracts ───── 2 firms, 30 GW contracts

as the franchise market provides the guaranteed market that allows the RECs to sign long-term contracts with potential entrants.

Contracts are thus doubly critical for competition—contract cover reduces the incentive to exercise market power in the Pool, while contracts make entry contestable. This gives the incumbents an incentive to keep Pool prices down, which they can do by selling contracts.[5] Figure 3 illustrates the effect of contracts, enlarging the right-hand part of Figure 2. The entry price is shown at £28/MWh—the estimated average contract price that would cover the total operating and capital costs of a new CCGT generating station at the gas prices in 1990. The lowest duopoly supply function without contracts, AB of Figure 2, is shown as the continuous dotted line in Figure 3, and the point Ep is the expected or average price as demand varies, considerably above the entry price. With five firms and no contracts, the lowest supply function (shown dashed) has an average price just below the entry price, and would deter entry. But if the duopolists were to sign baseload contracts for 30 GW, their residual equilibrium supply function (i.e. the uncontracted excess supplied at Pool prices) can be brought down as shown (the heavy S-shaped line), and the average price could be held down to the entry price

---

[5] Green and Newbery found that, in the absence of contracts, the duopolists could not coordinate on an equilibrium price low enough to forestall all entry.

(if desired) by increasing the level of contract cover. Indeed, the best strategy for entry-deterring duopolists to coordinate on is to choose a level of contracts and a residual supply function that maintains the average price just below the entry price, while making the residual supply as steep as possible. This will maximize the spread in prices between peak demand and the trough, and give the highest revenue to the duopolists, who increase their output at times of peak demand, compared to the entrants who run on baseload. Over time, the volatility of Pool prices (i.e. the range from peak to trough) has increased as the incumbent generators have adjusted to this contracting and bidding strategy.

(d) *The Choice of Capacity*

The generators can further influence both the average price and its volatility by removing capacity from the system. Capacity payments are extremely non-linear in the margin between capacity declared available and peak demand—if this margin falls from 20 per cent of capacity to 10 per cent, then the capacity payments increase from negligible levels (a few pence per MWh) to more than £20/MWh. In deciding whether to pay the connection costs and the work-force needed to keep the least efficient power station available (as compared to disconnecting and keeping it on a care and maintenance basis), the company can estimate the annual capacity payments and the Pool revenue from the small number of hours it will run, to see if it covers these costs. If not, it is withdrawn, until system capacity falls enough to increase capacity payments. One of the curious features of the industry since privatization is that in the first 5 years, despite substantial new capacity coming on stream, the total declared capacity actually fell as the incumbents adjusted capacity to produce satisfactory returns to marginal or peaking plant, further adding to Pool volatility. The last line of Table 1 above gives the annual capacity payments in £/kW of capacity, showing this increasing from less than £1 to £39 in 1995/96, considerably above the amount required to keep a station available.

2. Progress in Introducing Competition

As noted above, the industry was restructured and privatized in 1990 to introduce competition into generation and supply, initially just to the 5,000 or so customers taking more than 1 MW, to be extended to increasing numbers later.

Figure 4
Generation in England and Wales

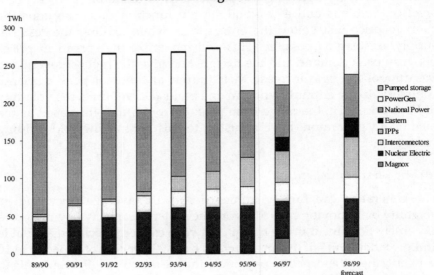

(a) *Competition in Generation*

Granted the imperatives of the parliamentary timetable which led to a flawed structure, the flotation was skilfully managed to ensure a smooth transition to private ownership. The two fossil-fuel generators were sold almost fully contracted, both for the sale of electricity and the purchase of coal. This gave predictability to revenue streams and dividend forecasts, delayed the impending politically divisive collapse of British Coal, while providing incentives to the companies to cut costs and equip themselves with the commercial expertise needed to trade in the Pool and contract markets. Full contract cover created incentives for competitive bidding in the Pool, and Pool prices were considerably below contract prices, though naturally they increased to the entry price over the next few years as contracts came up for renewal, as shown in Table 1.

The effect of restructuring and competition on generation has been dramatic. Figure 4 shows the generators' output since 1989/90, together with a prediction for 1998/99, based on Monopolies and Mergers Commission (MMC) (1996*a*). The increase in Nuclear Electric's output is due largely to the improved operating performance of the company's stations, encouraged by, but not solely due to, the competitive environment that the company faces. Imports from France and Scotland also rose when the trading rules were changed with the restructuring: the importers now sell at the market price in England and Wales, rather than at the (lower) average of the two system's costs, as before.[6] There has been a dramatic increase in independent generation, while PowerGen's and (particularly) National Power's output has fallen.

There has also been a dramatic switch from coal-fired to gas-fired generation. There was no gas-fired capacity in 1990, but 13 GW had been commissioned by the end of 1996, with another 2.5 GW under construction. Just over half of this was built by independents. By 1995/96, gas was the fuel for 19 per cent of the electricity sold in the Pool (*Pool Statistical Digest*, 1996; NGC, 1996). The main source of these changes was the rapid development of CCGT technology in the late 1980s, which offered potential entrants a technology that could be introduced at modest scale (300–600 MW), short construction times (24–36 months), and with low capital and operating costs. At the same time, the European Commission (EC) rescinded its prohibition on gas-fired electricity generation, and tightened emission limits for sulphur dioxide. To meet the limits, National Power and PowerGen would have to retrofit some of their coal stations with expensive flue-gas-desulphurization equipment, or to replace some of their coal burn with gas, which emits no sulphur dioxide. Given the relative prices of gas and coal, National Power and PowerGen decided to replace small old coal plant with CCGT technology rather than retrofit.

Eleven of the 12 RECs also invested in CCGT stations, generally in partnership with independent power producers (IPPs). The stations sold long-term contracts (typically 15 years) for their expected output, on terms which allowed them to be largely debt-financed. The RECs were able to argue that these contracts were competitive with the prices then being indicated by the major generators, although the generators might claim that there were no serious negotiations about those prices. Indeed, the RECs may have been somewhat ambivalent about the prices charged by the IPPs, since they were equity participants in the stations, and expected to pass their contract costs through to the franchise market until 1998. Thereafter, they might still hope for continued market power over domestic consumers, which would allow them to pass on their electricity purchase costs.

The RECs could also argue that the IPPs were desirable on wider grounds than price alone. The regulator had made it clear that he would welcome more competition in generation, and the new stations would provide this. Furthermore, a switch towards gas generation would

---

[6] In fact, Electricité de France also benefits by an exemption from the Fossil Fuel Levy which effectively allows it to sell at the market price for generation *plus* the levy of a tenth of the *final* price of electricity — this was worth £95m in 1991/92.

reduce the risks associated with coal's environmental impact. In the early 1990s, the EC was discussing a carbon-energy tax which would have fallen more heavily on coal-fired than gas-fired generation, while the UN Second Sulphur Protocol (not finally agreed until June 1994) similarly threatened to increase costs for coal-fired generation (House of Commons, 1993).

The resulting collapse of the British coal market and the closure of more than half the remaining deep pits prompted a parliamentary inquiry, which asked whether the new investment was justified on economic grounds. The eventual conclusion was that the ever-tightening sulphur limits would indeed require a shift of this magnitude to gas generation by the end of the century, but that about half of the new capacity could usefully have been delayed several years, since the relevant economic comparison was between the total cost of new CCGT generation against the avoidable cost of coal-fired generation valuing the coal at import parity prices (Newbery, 1994). The option existed for the incumbent generators to import coal, and although the vesting contracts for coal specified a substantially higher than import-parity price, these contracts were take-or-pay which, if anything, depressed the opportunity cost below import parity. The incumbent generators undoubtedly increased their bargaining power with British Coal by reducing their domestic coal dependence (they also invested in coal import capacity to the same end), making their choice of gas commercially sensible, if not necessarily socially least-cost.

The initial contracts, followed by rapid entry, and the recognition that contracts could be used to manage Pool prices and deter excessive entry, meant that the outcome was more competitive than might have been expected, given the duopolistic nature of the original structure. Even so, the generators were unsuccessful in avoiding the intervention of the regulator. He had criticized them on a number of occasions, and two Parliamentary Select Committees had recommended that he consider referring them to the MMC. When he announced his decision, he noted the growing discrepancy between rising Pool prices (Table 1) and falling fuel costs since vesting, and specifically the sharp increase in Pool prices in April 1993, as the previous year's contracts were replaced on 1 April (Offer, 1994*a*). He also noted that the two generators set the Pool price 90 per cent of the time, and concluded that their market power had enabled them to raise Pool prices above competitive levels. Faced with the alternative of a reference to the MMC, the generators agreed to a price-cap on Pool prices for the two financial years 1994/95 and 1995/96. They also agreed to divest 6 GW of plant (4 GW from National Power compared to its capacity of 26 GW, 2 GW from PowerGen compared to

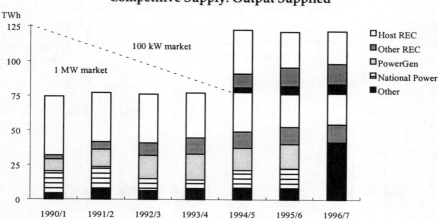

Figure 5
Competitive Supply: Output Supplied

Note: 'Other' includes PowerGen and National Power in the 100 kW market and in 1996/97.

its capacity of 20 GW) which they duly did, selling it all to Eastern Group, the largest REC.

The price-cap was presumably intended to restrain the exercise of market power until the divested plant was in the hands of competitors who would increase competition in the price-setting part of the market. The price-cap specified both a time-weighted level of 2.4 p/kWh and a demand-weighted price of 2.55p/kWh (both in October 1993 prices, which in 1996/97 prices would equate to 2.6 and 2.77p/kWh). As a measure of the ability of the two generators to control Pool prices, demand-weighted prices were within 1 per cent of their capped level each year.

(b) *Competition in Supply*

Figure 5 shows sales volumes in the part of the market opened to competitive supply. In the first year that the 1 MW market was opened to competition, the RECs lost two-fifths of their sales volumes, and their market shares have continued to decline. In 1996/97, Offer estimates that first-tier suppliers will meet less than 30 per cent of the demand in this market. Figure 6 shows that the RECs have retained a greater proportion of the sites in their home areas, however, and even in 1995/96, nearly half the sites in the 1 MW market bought from their local REC. (This average figure hides wide variations, for Yorkshire supplied three-fifths of the sites in its area, while South Western Electricity (SWEB) kept fewer than one-fifth of its own).

Figure 6
Competitive Supply: Share of Sites

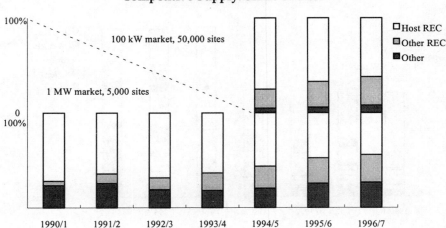

At first, most of the customers who switched supplier bought from National Power or PowerGen. The generators' sales were initially restricted to 15 per cent of the market in each REC's area, but these restrictions were relaxed, and then lifted altogether, following pressure from customers who wanted the better deals which the generators were offering. The RECs were generally slow to enter the second-tier market, but since 1993/94, they have (collectively) supplied more than half the sites taking a competitive supply. The RECs' supply businesses have a much lower share of sales than of sites, however, for the largest sites tend to buy from the generators, or other 'independent' second-tier suppliers.[7] In 1995/96, the 1 MW sites buying from a REC supply business (whether first- or second-tier) had an average demand of just under 10 GWh, while those buying from a generator or an independent supplier had an average demand of just over 30 GWh.

The size of the competitive market increased in April 1994, when the 50,000 sites with demands of between 100 kW and 1 MW were allowed to change their supplier. One-quarter of them did so in the first year, and second-tier suppliers are expected to supply almost half of the electricity sold in this market in 1996/97. The RECs' second-tier businesses have been more active in the 100 kW market than other second-tier suppliers and (collectively) have a greater market share, measured by either sites or sales. Offer's survey of suppliers indicates that competition has been effective even among the smallest sites in this market, those with

---

[7] A few of the largest customers act as their own supplier, and buy from the Pool on their own account.

demands of under 300 kW, for one-quarter of them bought from a second-tier supplier in 1995/96. Price controls in this market were lifted in 1994, when competition was introduced, and the ability to change supplier seems to have been sufficient protection for most consumers.

The expansion of supply competition in 1994 was a public-relations disaster for the industry. Teething troubles were expected and tolerated when the new system was introduced in 1990, but the expansion of the market in 1994 caused chaos which might have been avoidable. A number of changes to systems and procedures were needed to cope with the larger number of customers, many but not all of which fell within the Pool's remit. This meant that there was no single forum where all the changes could be debated and resolved, and no person or organization with overall responsibility for implementing the changes. Many important decisions were not made early enough to allow systems to be developed and tested. Customers who wished to change supplier would need a new meter and a communications link to transfer data to the Pool, but many of these were not installed, or installed but not properly registered. It was decided that these consumers should be allowed to change supplier anyway. In the event, some customers received two bills, some received none, and many of those bills were based on estimated data, sometimes wildly inaccurate. It took more than a year to sort out some of the problems, amid acrimonious debates over who had caused the chaos.[8]

(c) Competition in the Capital Market

If private companies have market power, the product market may not be able to provide adequate incentives for cost-cutting and the search for increased efficiency, as the survival of the firm will not be imperilled if it fails to make such improvements. The worry is that managers will seek to enjoy a quiet life rather than relentlessly minimizing costs. But publicly quoted companies can be bought on the stock exchange by those who believe that costs can be cut and profits increased, and the threat of takeover, and particularly the threat that lazy managers will be fired, is argued to be an important spur for efficiency. The RECs had been privatized with the government holding a golden share in each that could be used to block any takeover, but these shares lapsed in 1995, soon after the regulator had reviewed distribution prices, cutting the compa-

---

[8] Candidates included the electricity companies, for delaying decisions; the regulator, for insisting on several simultaneous changes; and the meter operators, for failing to install meters when promised. None of the parties faced financial penalties for failure to meet their obligations, and the industry recovered the additional cost of sorting out the chaos from a levy on consumers!

nies' revenues by £2½ billion over the next 5 years. The subsequent takeover wave culminated in the attempted restructuring of the electricity supply industry by vertical integration between generation and distribution.

The first bid, Trafalgar House's attempt to buy Northern, was made in December 1994, but was beaten off by a counter-offer from the target. This was a Pyrrhic victory, since it revealed the size of the cash mountain on offer to raiders, and persuaded the DGES to reopen the Distribution Price Control Review. In July 1995, he announced that he would cut the RECs' prices by a further £1 billion over the next 4 years. In the following few months, eight of the 12 RECs were targeted and six were successfully acquired. Two were bought by their local water and sewerage companies (also regulated utilities), one by the vertically integrated Scottish Power, one by Hanson plc, and two by US utilities. The remaining bids, by National Power and PowerGen, were referred to the MMC. The Commission proposed conditions under which the mergers were acceptable, but the bids were subsequently blocked by the Department of Trade and Industry (DTI). One of the target RECs, Midlands, was bought by another US utility group soon afterwards. Three more US utilities made successful bids in late 1996, and one in early 1997, so that by July 1997, only Southern Electric remained independent.

The generators' bids are discussed below, but why were the RECs so attractive to the bidders, and what lessons can be drawn for the regulatory process? First, the RECs were sold with little debt, and generous price caps, while their investment has generally been covered by their (current cost) depreciation charges. This allowed them to run down their debt from their large cash flow, but they soon had surplus cash, and effectively faced three options. Some sought profitable investments outside the regulated business, although they had little expertise, and some made large losses. Another choice was to hand back large dividends to shareholders while choosing a higher and more appropriate gearing (as Northern successfully did in its defence against Trafalgar House). The third choice was to carry on as before, enjoying large profits and handsome managerial rewards, with little pressure to cut costs. Those that chose the last route were vulnerable to takeovers which effectively returned their surplus cash to the original shareholders. The effect of privatizing the RECs with lax price controls and inadequate debt has been to capitalize a strong cash flow into transfers to shareholders, rather than reductions in the national debt.

Could this have been avoided in the distribution price control? Although the initial controls were widely agreed to be too lax, Professor Littlechild resisted attempts to bring forward his scheduled review, or to claw back past profits, because this would reduce the companies' future incentives to cut costs. The review cut prices by £2½ billion over the next 5 years, but even this reduction was based on a relatively generous treatment of the RECs' asset base. The assets inherited at flotation were included not at their initial market valuation, but at a 50 per cent premium to it (Offer, 1994b). The second review reduced this premium (to 15 per cent) which, with some other adjustments, produced a further £1 billion for customers (Offer, 1995). But a tighter price control might have been justified, and would have reduced the RECs' cash flow, transferring rents to consumers rather than shareholders. When more investment is required, the regulator should try to ensure that it is financed by issuing debt to create a more balanced and appropriate capital structure. Although much of the damage was done by the initial controls, part of the problem lies in the lack of information available to the regulator, and more especially to outside observers. The UK urgently needs to move to complete disclosure of all information on the accounts and operations of regulated monopolies such as the RECs, on the US model.

3. The Future Development of Competition

The main planned development is the abolition of the franchise market in 1998, bringing full competition in supply. This will also affect competition in generation, however, and has already done so; the coal contracts agreed in 1993 had to expire in 1998. Until then, the RECs could pass on the cost of expensive British coal to their franchise customers, but there will be no way of forcing small consumers to pay above-market prices after that date. The gas franchise will also end then, by which time the restructuring of British Gas should be complete. A gas spot market is rapidly developing, making interactions between the two markets stronger, as CCGT operators can choose whether to bid into the Pool or sell their gas into the spot market on a daily basis. This might result in the independent CCGTs setting the Pool price more often, increasing competition in the Pool. We also consider the moves towards vertical integration, partially blocked (for the time being) by the government's decision not to allow the two major generators to take over RECs.

(a) *The Abolition of the Franchise Market*

The RECs' remaining franchise is scheduled to disappear in April 1998, and the industry has been preparing for this change since 1994. It is clear that the arrangements thought suitable for customers in the 100 kW market would be completely inappropriate for domestic consumers. Half-hourly metering and settlement can cost around £800 per year, which is tolerable when compared to an average bill of £40,000 per year in the 100 kW market, but is twice the average domestic bill. At present, companies read their customers' meters at intervals of several months, and learn how much electricity each customer has used in total since the previous reading. This is adequate for billing the consumer, but the Pool needs to assign part of this consumption to each half-hour so that their supplier can be charged for it. A set of eight load profiles will be used for this task. Each profile shows the typical consumption shape for a group of consumers, and each consumer's total consumption will be spread over the half-hours since their last meter reading, in the proportions given by their profile.

This is the only realistic way to allow competition for small consumers when the Pool price changes every half-hour. It is effectively the system used to calculate tariffs at present: domestic tariffs are based on the average cost of buying electricity to meet the average consumption patterns of domestic consumers. There have been complaints that profiles will not give people any incentives to shift their consumption away from peak times, but those incentives are weak at present,[9] and the transactions cost of strengthening them would be greater than the benefits of doing so. In time, more sophisticated meters may become cheap enough to allow more differentiated tariffs, and these can be brought in alongside the profiles, but this does not seem cost-effective at the moment.

The industry is now working on the computer systems needed to introduce competition, but most companies have admitted that they will not be ready by April 1998. The regulator, who has gradually taken on much of the direction of the process, has ruled that competition will be delayed in each area until the local REC's systems are ready and have been tested. Even then, competition will be 'rolled out' across distinct sub-regions over a period of 6 months, with the possibility of suspending the process if problems occur. This is a much more pragmatic approach than that taken in 1994, which was to open the market on schedule 'at any cost'. To give the companies an incentive to make progress, however, the regulator has ruled that no REC may compete outside its area until its own customers are open to competition, and has also suggested that consumers should be compensated for any delays to the start of the market.

---

[9] A referee pointed out that some existing tariffs (e.g. Economy 7) have lower off-peak rates, and that profiles will support these. The cost messages in these tariffs are still averaged over long periods.

The cost of introducing full competition could run into hundreds of millions of pounds, but it remains uncertain how many customers will take advantage of the opportunity to change their supplier. One-third of a typical domestic bill (before VAT and the fossil fuel levy) is made up of regulated transmission and distribution charges which are common to all suppliers. Generation costs account for nearly 90 per cent of the remainder, and although these depend upon the supplier's individual portfolio of contracts, those contracts exist to hedge Pool prices which are also common to all suppliers. The supplier's own costs and profit combined, together with the tax on this part of the bill, average little more than £20 per household per year. This appears to leave very little room for entrants to undercut the established suppliers, although there may be profitable niches, such as larger customers (who have a bigger margin) who pay by direct debit (which costs less to administer). Even assuming that the margin on supply can be halved, and that some suppliers can 'beat the market' on the cost of generation, few customers are likely to be offered an annual saving of more than £15. It seems unlikely that more than a small proportion will switch in response to such a small saving (at best 5 per cent of the bill).[10] Switching costs and inertia mean that most customers will remain with their REC, and will need to be protected against the significant price rises that unregulated incumbency would make profitable. There is a risk that tariffs will change in ways which harm customers with low demands, and vulnerable groups, as discussed (in the case of gas) by Waddams Price in chapter 5. Offer will now have to worry about the temptation to cross-subsidize the competitive part of the supply business from the captive regulated part, while allowing RECs both to act competitively and to respond to competitive threats to segments of the market.

(b) *Competition in Generation*

National Power and PowerGen have now sold 6 GW of mid-merit plant to Eastern Group, the largest REC. The duopolists' share of generation has fallen from 54 per cent in 1995/96 to 46 per cent in 1996/97 as a result. The price cap in the Pool has been lifted, in the hope that the industry would not now be vulnerable to the exercise of market power. Average prices in 1996 remained below the level of the price cap, although it is too

[10] Chapter 5 in this volume by Waddams Price reveals that only 20 per cent of gas customers in the south-west have switched supplier in the first 6 months of competition, despite being offered savings of up to 25 per cent. British Gas had to pass on the high cost of its historic gas purchases, while its competitors bought at the much lower current prices. The RECs' competitors are very unlikely to have a similar advantage with their energy costs, and will only be able to offer small savings.

soon to tell what long-term effect the removal of the price cap and the divestitures have had on bidding behaviour.

One of the competitive issues that the regulator had to address was the way in which the divested plant was to be sold. The generators wished to make the transfer on long leases with an 'earn-out clause' under which the buyer would pay the selling generators £6 per mega-watt-hour generated (The Energy Group plc, *Introduction to the Official List*, p. 27). This, it was argued, would raise the buyers' bid price to ensure that the buyer bid into the mid-merit or price-setting part of the market, where extra competition was required. It would also enable the two duopolists to run their higher-cost, clean-coal stations, Drax and Ratcliffe, which remove 90 per cent of sulphur from their emissions, ahead of the transferred coal stations, which lacked such emissions controls. If the fuel cost of the leased stations is £14/MWh, then their minimum bid would need to be £20/MWh, which would indeed lead to mid-merit bidding, as half-hourly prices are less than this for 40 per cent of the year.[11] Critics claimed that by ensuring that their rivals based their bids not on true costs, but costs inflated by these earn-out fees, the duopolists would mute competition in the price-setting part of the market. The regulator accepted the proposals but indicated that any such 'earn-out' would have to expire within 8 years.

One reason for the divestitures was that, so far, almost all entrants have run their stations on baseload, and rarely, if ever, set SMP. This may change in future. More CCGTs are being planned, tempted by improve-ments in efficiency and a fall in gas prices (from over 20p/therm for a long-term contract in 1992 to 15p/therm in 1996, with much lower prices for spot purchases). Nuclear stations, imports, and existing CCGTs already meet practically all of the baseload demand, and so any signifi-cant increase in CCGT capacity will push some stations into mid-merit running. Which stations move down the merit order may depend as much on their contracts as on their underlying costs. Many CCGTs bought gas on take-or-pay contracts, which would once have implied that the marginal cost of their fuel was close to zero, but the UK now has a gas spot market. As long as the station is allowed to resell its gas in this market, the spot price will represent the marginal cost of burning gas for electricity generation. The marginal benefit of doing so should be the

---

[11] Two of the three stations sold by National Power, Rugeley B and West Burton, bid less than £15/MWh and had load factors of over 70 per cent, while the third, Ironbridge, bid £15–23 (October–December 1995) and had a load factor of less than 50 per cent (1994/95). The two PowerGen stations, Drakelow C and High Marnham, bid £29–36 and had load factors of less than 40 per cent. (*Pool Statistical Digest* March 1996; MMC, 1996a, p. 72; 1996b, p. 73).

electricity spot price determined by the Pool.[12] This means that many stations will be able to arbitrage the two markets, and that stations with a high thermal efficiency (and a lower opportunity cost) should be used more intensively. Stations which are not allowed to resell their gas, or are forced to generate by their power purchase agreement, may end up displacing more efficient stations, however. There are also concerns that if the prices of gas and electricity do not reflect their true values, then this arbitrage might cause power cuts when electricity was actually more valuable than the gas needed to generate it.

Abolishing the supply franchise may have mixed effects on the efficiency of competition in generation. It may make it less attractive for RECs to sign long-term contracts with new entrants, making entry harder and increasing the market power of the incumbents. It may also make the RECs less willing to contract as fully as at present, reducing the contract cover of generators and giving them more incentive to bid higher in the Pool. Increased volatility and customer switching may increase demand for short-term contracts, however, and the greater liquidity in this part of the market might reduce the premium between contract and Pool prices. It is almost certain to make investments in more durable, capital-intensive generation (such as nuclear and coal-fired stations) harder if fuel prices were to move against gas. These stations have a higher ratio of fixed to variable costs than CCGT stations and hence require longer-term contracts to offset the higher risk. A trend against long-term contracts could reduce options for future fuel diversity.

(c) *Vertical Integration and the MMC References*

The RECs were protected from takeover until April 1995, but three bids were launched in July 1995, and cleared by the competition authorities. PowerGen announced a bid for Midlands in September 1995, and National Power responded with a proposed merger with Southern shortly after. These bids were referred to the MMC, which reported to Ian Lang, the Secretary of State for Trade and Industry, on 29 March 1996. The MMC found that the bids could be expected to act against the public interest, but recommended that they be allowed to proceed under certain conditions, with one dissenting member. On 24 April, Mr Lang announced that he was rejecting the bids by National Power and PowerGen and therefore not accepting the recommendations of the MMC. Most

[12] This is not the case for some stations with power purchase agreements, which fix a price for each unit actually generated, but does apply to a station with a standard CfD, in which case the contract payments do not depend upon actual generation and the marginal payment for generating is SMP.

commentators noted that the government's rejection of the advice left the electricity industry unsure of the government's intentions for its desired evolution and its policy more generally on competition. In response to speculation about a bid for National Power, on 2 May, the government announced that it would block any bid for National Power or PowerGen, at least until 'there is adequate competition in the generation and supply markets' (DTI Press Release, P/96/329, 2 May 1996).

Horizontal mergers between water companies have been strongly resisted, and similar mergers between RECs would certainly be referred to the MMC, if only because they reduce the number of comparators and hence the quality of information needed to set the distribution price controls, but there have been no such attempts to date. Mergers between RECs and companies in other sectors or countries have been accepted subject to safeguards on the ability of the REC to finance its investment even if the parent company runs into financial difficulties. The previous Conservative government took a very relaxed view on foreign (US) ownership of English RECs, confident in the ability of the regulators to protect English customers, but the incoming Labour government re-ferred the first bid by a US company (Pacificorp) for the Energy Group, of which the REC, Eastern, is a subsidiary, to the MMC after it had been cleared by Offer and the Office of Fair Trading. The Secretary of State stated that she considered that the merger raised important regulatory issues that needed thorough investigation — the first time a utility had been referred for reasons other than competition.

The government had already privatized the Scottish electricity indus-try as two vertically integrated companies. Regulated vertically inte-grated utilities might be preferable to an unbundled structure for small and isolated systems. Because the Scottish interconnector to England was fully committed to exporting power, the Scottish generators have been protected from competition from England. ScottishPower had also been allowed to merge with Manweb without a merger reference, perhaps because ScottishPower's maximum share of the Pool in England and Wales was so small, at less than 5 per cent. The RECs had been allowed limited vertical integration into generation,[13] and most (except Manweb) had taken advantage of this possibility. Eastern, purchased by

[13] The limits, set in megawatts of capacity, were based on 15 per cent of the maximum demand in each REC's area. The limits were based on the REC's share of the equity in a station, rather than its purchases, and most RECs had equity partners who did not buy electricity, so that a REC might buy 250 MW from a 'stake' of 150 MW. If a REC has a maximum demand of 1,000 MW, its average sales will be at most 700 MW, and sales to the franchise market will almost certainly be less than 500 MW. This implies that the 15 per cent capacity limit could allow a REC to buy more than half the energy it needs for the franchise market.

Hanson, was allowed by the DGES to buy all of the 6 GW of divested plant from National Power and PowerGen, thereby creating a significant vertically integrated utility entirely in the English market. The limit on own generation had to be lifted to allow the purchase to go ahead. Why, then, were the two vertical mergers involving the two main generators deemed to be undesirable?

The normal argument is that if vertical integration does not affect market power either upstream or downstream, it will only be privately profitable if it lowers costs, and this will be socially beneficial. If integration reduces competition either upstream or downstream, then there must be sufficient cost savings to offset any reduction in competition. The RECs' ventures into generation probably increased total generation costs in the short run, but were allowed partly because they increased competition in generation. Most competition policy decisions involve balancing damage against gain, and this one is no exception.

The MMC reports recognized that market power is primarily exercised by setting prices in the Pool and deterring entry (MMC, 1996a,b), but thought that, with safeguards, competition could be made adequate to remedy the damage. A dissenting report raised the dynamic issue of whether approving the mergers would create pressure for further mergers and vertical integration, possibly ending with an industry of four or five integrated companies. The author of the dissenting report believed that the electricity market would not become sufficiently contestable for the mergers to have no adverse effect on competition.

The key questions are how much power over price-setting these generators would have, whether they could use this power to deter entry, and whether vertical integration would affect the extent of this power. It is clearly difficult to predict the bidding strategies of the players in the future, particularly as Eastern has only recently acquired 6 GW of plant, but there is reasonable agreement that the two generators will maintain a dominant position in non-baseload generation, which will set the price most of the time. The MMC estimated that the two generators' share of the non-baseload market would fall from 85 per cent in 1995/96 to 58–65 per cent in 2001, confirming their dominant position in terms of combined share—see Figure 4.

The mergers will have no effect on these figures, and are argued, therefore, not to affect the degree of competition in the market, which is described as 'a broadly satisfactory competitive environment in generation from 1997 onwards in the absence of the merger' (MMC, 1996a, para 1.6). The main argument that the duopolists will not be able to exercise market power in the price-setting part of the market is that competition to supply baseload will be intense, as 38 GW of nuclear, CCGT, and large coal-fired plant could be competing for 21 GW of baseload by the turn of the century (MMC, 1996a, para 5.93). Any attempt by one company to raise Pool prices by bidding high, runs the risk that some of this potential baseload plant (particularly CCGT, the divested plant, and electricity supplied through the interconnectors) would underbid and be preferentially dispatched, thereby setting the price at a lower level.

The second main plank of the MMC's argument on competition is that entry will continue to be relatively easy, as it argues that the market for the contracts needed to assist entry will remain both broad and liquid. But past entry was predicated upon two important features that will no longer continue. First, IPPs signed contracts for 15 years for baseload power with the RECs, because the RECs had a franchise market on which to write such contracts. Second, older coal-fired baseload stations were vulnerable to entry by cheaper CCGTs. In 1998 the franchise market ends, and RECs are likely to be more cautious in signing long-term contracts with IPPs. By 1998, nuclear and gas generation together should account for nearly 28 GW, considerably above the summer minimum load of 21 GW. Entry will now be in direct competition with existing similar-fuelled generation which is both young and of comparable performance. The fact that the 1-year CfD market may be liquid is little consolation in the absence of longer-term contracts, because an acceptable entry-supporting baseload CfD for 1 year offers no guarantee of likely future prices.

The dissenting report argued that the proposed remedies to counter the adverse effects of the mergers did not address the problem of market power, and that it was too soon to tell whether the ending of the franchise market would encourage competition or discourage entry. In addition, vertical integration would greatly increase the difficulty of regulating against discriminatory contracts. To conclude, the worry is that the two generators would be able to keep Pool prices high while keeping contract prices (and direct sales prices from their downstream businesses) low enough to deter suppliers arbitraging the Pool price, and targeting the customers of entrants with rather more favourable deals, undermining those customers' willingness to sign long-term contracts with entrants.

It may be that the supply market becomes sufficiently competitive, and that futures markets in baseload power develop to increase liquidity and transparency, making such price discrimination ineffective, in which case the market power of vertically integrated companies would be adequately curtailed. If so, there is little lost by waiting, for if the vertical mergers create genuine cost-savings, future mergers will still be attractive (and feasible, if the new owners sell out to the generators, or buy up the generators). If entry threats cease to exercise adequate discipline (perhaps because gas prices rise), then the option remains to allow the generators to divide their generating assets between a larger number of RECs to create an adequate number of vertically integrated companies to increase competition. In short, the option of waiting to see how competition develops after the ending of the franchise is valuable, and would be foreclosed by premature restructuring.

4. Was the Restructuring Worth It?

Since privatization, costs have fallen dramatically in generation, but the margin between fuel costs and prices has increased, and the efficiency gains elsewhere in transmission and distribution are only being passed on to consumers in the period after 1995. Competition in supply has eliminated cross-subsidies from the competitive part of the market, and suppliers have an incentive to give customers a higher standard of service.[14] Supply itself only accounts for a small proportion of the industry's costs, however, and the main savings, if any, must come from changes in generation.

Newbery and Pollitt (1997) have looked at these changes, reconstructing the accounts of the four successor companies to the CEGB and comparing the out-turn with various counterfactuals about what might have happened without such restructuring. In the 5 years since 1990, labour productivity in the successor companies has more than doubled. Delivered coal prices fell by 20 per cent in real terms and purchases of British coal fell from 74m tonnes to 30m tonnes a year. Fossil fuel costs per kilowatt-hour fell by 45 per cent in real terms. The switch from coal and the 'dash for gas' has reduced the number of British coal miners from nearly a quarter of a million at the time of the 1984–5 coal miners' strike to about 7,000 in the now privatized coal industry, and has contributed to the substantial drop in acid rain and carbon-monoxide emissions. The collapse of the British coal market was the subject of a Parliamentary inquiry and resulted in a clear statement of the government's commitment to market forces as its energy policy. The events of the past 5 years have therefore transformed British energy policy as well as the electricity and coal industries.

The fall in unit costs was not translated into corresponding falls in prices, but into increased profits, and since privatisation, electricity share prices have outperformed the stock market by over 100 per cent.

[14] In practice, this may not have extended to simplifying the design of their contracts. Many customers have had to employ consultants to compare the bewildering variety of terms they are offered!

Although real consumer prices have fallen, fuel costs have fallen faster, and the margin for the electricity industry's own costs and profits has risen by almost 0.5 p/kWh, or by nearly 25 per cent of the industrial average mark-up. In current cost accounting terms the successor companies have tripled their return on assets from 3 per cent to 11 per cent, now 1 per cent higher than non-North Sea British companies.[15]

Discounting at the public-sector discount rate of 6 per cent real, the net cost saving of switching from coal to gas was £3 billion. The £3.3 billion saved by abandoning the British nuclear construction programme was largely transferred to Electricité de France by allowing it to sell its nuclear power into the English Pool at the specially favourable nuclear price. Valuing the reductions in sulphur emissions at £250/tonne and carbon monoxide at £12/tonne carbon gives environmental benefits worth £2.3 billion, more than the fuel benefits alone. Restructuring cost £2.8 billion, but the efficiency gains from cutting non-fuel costs were estimated to be worth £8.8 billion. The final balance sheet shows a present value of net gains of £9.6 billion ignoring the environmental benefits, equivalent to a permanent reduction in generation costs of 7 per cent. If the environmental benefits are added, the present value rises to £11.9 billion, or 48 per cent of the capital value of the CEGB of £25 billion. At a discount rate of 10 per cent, the permanent cost saving (ignoring environmental gains) falls to £5.2 billion or 5 per cent of generation costs. These effects are large enough to be robust to moderate changes in the counterfactual assumed, although the study does not ask whether privatization with a more competitive structure might have yielded still greater benefits.

Newbery and Pollitt (1997) also attempted to find out how these efficiency gains were distributed between consumers, shareholders, and the government, according to various views about how future electricity prices will evolve and would otherwise have evolved under public ownership. Prices increased relative to plausible views of what might have happened under continuing public ownership, but costs are falling and at some stage competition should transfer some of these cost reductions to consumers. If prices converge to the public ownership counterfactual by the year 2000, then at a 6 per cent discount rate, consumers lose £1.3 billion in present value terms, the government loses £8.5 billion in revenue streams, but sold the industry for £9.7 billion, and thus gains £1.2 billion including sales receipts, while shareholders received after-tax profits with a present value (at 6 per cent) of £19.4

---

[15] The conventional historic cost accounts show a rise from 14 per cent pre-privatization to 24 per cent, but historic asset values for such a long-lived industry are highly misleading.

billion for their outlay of £9.7 billion, or a net gain of £9.7 billion. If, however, prices are not expected to converge until 2010, then consumers lose £6.1 billion, the government loses £3.7 billion (including sales proceeds), while shareholders gain £24.2 billion gross, or £14.5 billion net of the purchase cost. The distributional impacts are thus very sensitive to future price movements, which are unknown, and also to the effective marginal rate of taxes on profits—the sums reported here are based on an assumed marginal rate of 25 per cent, but if the rate were equal to the average 1991–6 rate of 14.5 per cent, a further £6 billion in present value terms would be shifted from the government back to shareholders. These calculations also exclude the windfall profits tax of £2 billion on the post-CEGB companies announced in the 1997 July budget.

5. An Assessment of the Regulatory Framework

Any assessment of the regulatory framework must note that there have been both successes and failures. There is no doubt that the second-tier supply market is competitive, and that competition in generation has greatly increased since 1990, but the path has not been a smooth one. The regulator was forced to fight a running battle with National Power and PowerGen, until the threat of a reference to the MMC finally forced them to agree to sell some of their mid-merit stations. Even after that agreement, it took more than 2 years to negotiate the sales, whose long-term effect remains uncertain. The industry's own solution, the CCGTs built by the RECs, contributed to the reduction in the major generators' market power, but hastened the decline of the British coal industry. The credible threat of entry has restrained average prices in the Pool, but increased their volatility, and it remains to be seen whether the market for entry remains contestable once the franchise market ends in 1998.

The regulatory regime for generation seems to have been set up on the assumption that the sector would be competitive from the start, and that little oversight would be needed. This placed the regulator in a difficult position, for he had few powers to intervene when it became apparent that the market was not competitive. If the problems had been anticipated, could the regulator have been given more powers over the companies' conduct? This might have restrained prices, but would have conflicted with the hope of moving towards a competitive market in which regulation was unnecessary. That required a structural remedy, not one based on rules about conduct. Professor Littlechild was able to use the threat of the MMC to bring about voluntary structural changes, but only as long as the companies expected the cost of an MMC reference to be greater than the cost of obeying him. If the regulator pushed too hard, one or both of the companies could decide that they would be better off with the MMC, especially as they would have a chance to lobby the government (which would decide on the MMC's recommendations) if they lost at the Commission.

The regulator's powers are also limited when dealing with changes to the Pool and its rules. Significant changes have to pass through a network of committees and a series of votes, which has the advantage of protecting the commercial interests of minorities, but can allow them to block sensible reforms. Offer is required to act as the 'court of appeal', a role which is incompatible with championing particular changes. Many of the arrangements for supply competition after 1998 have to be agreed by the Pool, although most of the RECs appear to feel that they have little to gain from competition, and much to lose. Perhaps for this reason, progress on agreeing the necessary arrangements has been slow, and the timetable for designing and running trials with the new computer systems is now frighteningly tight. The regulator is the only plausible central coordinator for the changes, but does not have the powers to ensure that others fulfil their own roles in the process.

6. Conclusions

The generation market exhibits the same divergence of view about industrial and competition policy that is familiar elsewhere in Britain and Europe. Do mergers lead to strong export-oriented national champions to be encouraged, or lazy local monopolies to be opposed? The national champion defence is that although only two (and from 1996, three) generators own almost all of the price-setting power stations, the fact that entry is contestable keeps the average price at competitive levels. As old coal-fired stations are retired and replaced by CCGT stations, so the older CCGT stations will move down the merit order and start to set the price, extending competition from entry with its effect on the average price to bidding in the Pool and hence to setting the spot price. Creating two large generators allowed them to exploit the expertise they obtained in the English market by a vigorous programme of overseas investment which five smaller generators might never have managed. Vertical integration would allow them further competitive advantages abroad.

We resist this view, and share the MMC's scepticism about the benefits of the integrated companies' increased ability to compete in international markets. Five conventional generating companies would have kept prices low and made it difficult for RECs to justify their generation investments and contracts to a regulator happy with the state of competition. This would have reduced the amount of excess entry of new gas-fired generation, and created a more liquid and competitive contract market that would have transferred more of the gains of fuel price falls to consumers. More competition in generation would have allayed fears about cost-saving vertical integration, and reduced worries about the effect of the loss of the franchise market on the contestability of entry. Instead, competition will be created by the more costly route of excess entry, and market dominance will continue to require the heavy hand of regulatory oversight that competition was supposed to replace.

What policy recommendations, if any, arise from this diagnosis? Should the government encourage further restructuring, either by forced divestment or by encouraging the development of four or five vertically integrated companies with a balanced portfolio of plant? The simplest solution is to await or encourage the development of liquid contract and futures markets and then see how the industry develops, while taking a fairly hostile position on any mergers that do not offer reduced concentration in generation. Forced divestment would require strong evidence of market abuse that seems unlikely while a regulator oversees the competition.

5

The UK Gas Industry

CATHERINE WADDAMS PRICE*

1. Introduction and History

The UK gas industry epitomizes a general shift in policy towards the regulated utilities over the last 10 years. It was one of the first three to be privatized (in late 1986) and alone has required major new primary legislation to redefine its competitive role. This new Gas Act in 1995 paved the way for competition in the residential market which was certainly not envisaged in the original privatization Act. Gas has also been subject to perhaps the most intensive discussion on the appropriate form of its structure and liberalization, and has been assessed by regulatory authorities not merely on its conduct, but on the effect of that conduct in the market. In this section we record the main events in the gas industry since privatization, and in the next section identify some of the key issues. Section 3 discusses access pricing and section 4 the development of competition to date. In section 5 we assess the regulator's role, and in section 6 discuss price discrimination and some distributional aspects of competition. Section 7 concludes and considers future regulatory strategy.

British Gas (BG) was privatized in 1986 as an integrated monopoly, despite contemporary criticism of this policy (Energy Committee, 1986). It would have been a comparatively easy task to separate BG into a national transmission network and 12 regional boards, recreating its structure prior to 1972, but the vehement objection of the chairman, Denis Rooke, would have delayed the sale. The gas industry had traditionally divided its markets according to volume consumed: users of very large quantities (over 25,000 therms a year) were supplied under individually negotiated and confidential contracts; others were charged

* University of Warwick. I am pleased to acknowledge the help of British Gas Trading in supplying information which forms the basis for Figures 2 and 3 and would like to thank Tim Jenkinson, Ruth Hancock, Morten Hviid, and a referee for helpful comments and suggestions on various aspects of this chapter.

through a published tariff consisting of a standing charge and a single running rate. These were known as the contract and tariff markets respectively. At privatization the industry argued that although there was no competition in piped gas, there was sufficient potential competition from new entrants and actual competition from other fuels to regulate only the tariff market. This argument was accepted and the tariff market was subject to a cap on average revenue, while the contract market was left unconstrained.

The 1986 Gas Act established a regulator, the Director General of Gas Supply, and Office (known as Ofgas) from August, and the industry's shares were sold in November 1986. The Gas Act placed upon the regulator the duty to 'enable persons to compete effectively' in the contract market, and this involved publication by BG of indicative prices for the access to pipelines which would be required by any competitor. Despite the (reluctant) publication of these and considerable informal government pressure to institute some competition in gas, which had been legally possible since the 1982 Oil and Gas (Enterprise) Act, BG's *de facto* monopoly continued.

However, a significant chain of events was initiated by the referral of the contract market to the Monopolies and Mergers Commission (MMC) in 1987. The particular issue which gave rise to the referral was the discrimination in prices charged to different contract consumers. The MMC (1988) found that this discrimination was an abuse of monopoly power, and recommended that prices both for supply of gas to the contract market and for carriage of gas by potential competitors be published and non-discriminatory. It also suggested that a proportion of new gas finds in the North Sea be made available to competitors, and, most significantly, that the effect of these measures be assessed by the Office of Fair Trading (OFT) after 3 years.

The government accepted and implemented the MMC report and BG introduced price schedules for supply and carriage of gas in 1989 (British Gas, 1989*a*, *b*). Despite this increased transparency (in competitive pricing and costs) for potential competitors, entry for piped gas supplies was slow. When the OFT reviewed the market in 1991, it found that although BG had complied fully with the MMC's requirements, this had not resulted in effective competition. To remedy this, BG agreed to sacrifice market share in a phased programme, culminating in a target loss of 60 per cent of its contract market by 1995, and to separate its transportation and storage unit from its supply function, to account for it separately, and not to discriminate between BG and other competitors in charging for these services. Ofgas and BG sought to reach agreement on an appropriate pricing regime for transportation and storage services, but by mid-1992 these discussions were deadlocked, and BG was referred to the MMC for the second time since privatization.

Meanwhile, events elsewhere in the energy sector and the gas industry were having a significant effect. The European Community removed the prohibition on the use of gas for power generation, and the form in which the electricity industry had been privatized (see chapter 4 by Green and Newbery, in this volume) encouraged the installation of combined-cycle gas-turbine generators, the so-called 'dash for gas'. In 1991 the price constraint on the tariff market was reviewed, and a tighter cap agreed just before the OFT reported on competition in the contract market. A few months later the government announced the lowering of the tariff threshold, which defined BG's monopoly, to 2,500 therms a year, transferring 216,000 commercial and industrial consumers and about 7.5 per cent of the total demand from the monopoly tariff to the potentially competitive contract market.

The 1992 reference to the MMC was broad and encompassed all BG's markets. In the summer of 1993 the Commission recommended that the company be separated, so that the transportation and storage functions were undertaken by a different company from the supply function. 'In our view this dual role [as both a seller of gas and owner of the transportation system] gives rise to an inherent conflict of interest which makes it impossible to provide the necessary conditions for self sustaining competition' (MMC, 1993b, Cm 2315). The Commission remained cautious about extending competition to all consumers, including the residential market: 'the removal of the monopoly should follow measures to ensure the neutrality of the transportation and storage system, which we regard as the principal condition for effective competition'. It recommended that a further tranche be opened to competition by 1997, with the remainder of the market, which included most residential consumers, able to choose suppliers by 2002.

After some months delay and further informal enquiries, the government rejected the MMC's recommendations that BG's transportation and storage be separated into a different company before competition, and announced that the market would be fully liberalized by 1998, the year when the monopoly franchises of the regional electricity companies (RECs) were to expire. Liberalizing the gas market in this way required primary legislation, since this possibility had not been anticipated at privatization, and legislative time was scarce; it was not until the Queen's Speech in November 1994 that the government's intentions were confirmed. The 1995 Gas Act prepared the way for competition to be phased in between 1996 and 1998, as well as tidying up some aspects of Ofgas's responsibilities. Competition for half a million residential consumers in the south-west of England was introduced in April 1996, and extended to a further one and a half million customers in the south of England in February and March 1997; the whole market will be opened in 1998.

In the meantime, other developments facilitated competition: a transportation charging system was agreed (and modified), a network code developed to facilitate the mechanics of competition, and a spot market in gas introduced. Meanwhile, BG underwent significant reorganization, and in 1997 implemented just the separation between transportation and supply which the 1993 MMC report had recommended, and which it had previously so strongly resisted. Liberalization had left BG with long-term contracts to purchase gas from the North Sea, but without the markets in which to sell. These were take-or-pay contracts, and falling gas prices left BG committed to purchase gas (for which it had lost much of its market) at a price higher than it could realize from other sellers of gas. The demerger of the company separated these liabilities, held by the supply operation, Centrica (supplying gas as BG Trading), from the main assets which went to the transportation section, BG Transco.

Relations between the first Director General of Gas Supply, Sir James McKinnon, and BG had always been strained, and the appointment of a new Director, Clare Spottiswoode, from November 1993 brought at least temporary relief from this tension. But relations with the new regulator soon became confrontational. Ms Spottiswoode spent much of 1996 consulting on the regulatory regimes to come into force in 1997. A price cap was agreed with BG Trading, but BG Transco refused her proposal for their prices, so a third referral was made to the MMC in the summer of 1996 to arbitrate on these concerns. The report (MMC, 1997b) broadly supported the Director General's proposals, although there have been continuing disagreements about some of its implications.

The main events in the development of competition in the gas industry are listed in Table 1.

2. Issues

As the account above shows, the decade since privatization has seen gas change from an integrated monopoly with no competition and without the structure necessary to encourage it, to an industry moving rapidly towards full competition. Like the other 'early' flotations (British Telecom and British Airports Authority) it was privatized as an integrated monopoly; it had no regulation in the bulk market, and light regulation in the tariff market. Within 10 years it faces liberalization in all markets, and has decided to separate its transportation and supply activities. Of

Table 1
Main Events in the Gas Industry since Privatization

1986	Gas Act: privatization of integrated monopoly with statutory monopoly for supplies below 25,000 therms p.a. Appointment of James McKinnon as first Director General of Gas Supply
1987	Referral to MMC on price discrimination in the contract market
1988	First MMC report
1989	Introduction of price schedules for contract market and gas carriage
1991	New price cap agreed for tariff market. OFT report on competition in contract market
1992	'Monopoly threshold' reduced to 2,500 therms p.a. Second referral to MMC
1993	MMC recommends breaking up BG before liberalizing entire market Clare Spottiswoode succeeds Sir James McKinnon as DG of Gas Supply Government rejects MMC recommendations and announces rapid introduction of competition
1994	Full liberalization confirmed in Queen's Speech
1995	Gas Act allowing competition in the residential market
1996	First phase of competition in the south-west of England
1997	Competition extended to 2m consumers in the south of England Transco and Centrica 'demerge' MMC broadly supports DG's price restraint proposals for BG Transco, which accepts them
1998	Full competition throughout Great Britain
2004	Competition in the residential market may be extended to Northern Ireland

the four utilities, it was arguably the most leniently treated at privatization, but faces the greatest threat of competition a decade later. The transformation has been remarkably rapid, particularly for a company which has resisted change at almost every step.

One reason that competition for domestic consumers was not envisaged at privatization in 1986, but was built into the Electricity Act in 1989, was the development of information technology which widened the technical possibilities for dealing with the necessary data. This not only enabled creation of the detailed consumer records necessary for recording supply by different shippers, but also the development of a balancing regime, enacted through the network code, and a spot market for gas. It was partly to test the feasibility of these systems that choice of supplier has been introduced on a gradual basis. Both the gas and electricity markets experienced considerable technical difficulties in opening markets to smaller industrial and commercial users, and it was considered advisable to 'pilot' the liberalization of the domestic market initially in a relatively small group of residential consumers. The choice of the south-west of England reflected both fears that, in the long run, the area might be disadvantaged through higher transportation charges because of its distance from the beachhead and where gas is landed, and political pressures.

The timetable for introducing competition was ambitious, and inevitably slipped by a few weeks. The process of transferring suppliers itself revealed considerable problems, with confusion and misidentification of consumers who were changing supplier. These technical difficulties have been acknowledged in dividing the second phase into two stages, and the real test will be in the extent to which the technical problems of the first phase have been overcome for the 1997 trials.

The introduction of competition for residential gas consumers is seen as a prototype for the gas and electricity markets throughout Britain, but it is important to recognize how it differs from the rest of the energy market. Geographic phasing is possible for gas, because the incumbent supplies the whole country, but would be inequitable for electricity where there are local monopolies (the RECs). Moreover, the gas incumbent labours under a unique handicap from the gas contracts which were commitments made when BG expected to retain a monopoly over most of the market.

Accustomed to supplying the whole market, BG had signed up extensive supplies of gas from the North Sea during the 1980s and early 1990s. As BG surrendered an increasing proportion of its market, it was stranded with inappropriately large supplies under take-or-pay contracts. These were contracts to buy a minimum quantity of gas from North Sea suppliers at specified (indexed) prices and to pay for it even if it were not used within the specified year. BG found itself overcommitted and was unable to sell on the supplies it had purchased except at a loss, because the spot market price of gas had fallen below the long-term contract price. It was in response to this pressure that BG chose to separate its major liabilities (the contracts for gas supply) from its main assets, the pipelines. To increase the viability of Centrica, responsible for the contracts and gas supply, it will also inherit BG's own substantial Morecambe gas fields.

BG has asked to be released from its long-term take-or-pay contracts on the grounds that they were negotiated in good faith when it had reasonable expectations of a near monopoly in the gas market. Both the government and Ofgas have declined to intervene but some companies seem to be willing to renegotiate, perhaps because they believe that the courts would not enforce the contracts if BG were to renege. Since take-or-pay contracts were originally introduced in the USA in response to frequent violations of gas supply contracts, this would be an interesting test case (Masten and Crocker, 1985).

Because the spot price for gas in 1996 was much lower than the price for gas included in these contracts, new entrants could obtain supplies much more cheaply than the incumbent. This has accounted for most of the substantial savings which were offered by new entrants (over 20 per cent for some users). Such savings are not necessarily a direct result of greater efficiency, and in part at least represent a transfer from BG to consumers, via the new entrants. The discrepancy in the cost of gas to different suppliers makes it difficult to identify how much the lower prices do reflect greater efficiency.

However, the changing *structure* of tariffs clearly is due to liberalization. Before competition in the residential market was confirmed, BG charged only two tariffs in this market: one for those using prepayment meters, and one with standing charge and commodity charge for everyone else. BG introduced a discount for consumers paying by direct debit as a direct response to the confirmation of competition, and all but one of the entrants have followed suit and offered discounts for direct debit payment, reflecting the lower costs of administration and risk of default for consumers paying in this way. These changes deliver most benefits to consumers of large quantities on credit or direct debit tariffs, while there are fewer discounts from new entrants for prepayment consumers to gain. We show in section 6 that this has important distributional implications, which may be serious if the tax and benefit system cannot be adjusted to take account of these changes.

3. Charges for Access to the Pipelines

The monopoly element of the gas system lies in its pipes, particularly those used for local distribution. For long-distance gas transportation, the quantity of gas to be carried may be four or five times the capacity of the optimal sized pipelines (there are several main feeders bringing gas south from the Scottish landing points). But, at the local level, demand is unlikely to justify the duplication of distribution pipes, which therefore constitute an 'essential facility' to which all suppliers need access. Bypass is prohibitively expensive, particularly at local level, and technology requires fixed proportions of input (carriage) for each unit of gas delivered. The pipelines constitute a natural monopoly, owned until 1997 by the incumbent monopolist and, after the separation of the two parts of British Gas, by BG Transco.

Unlike in the electricity industry, there is no division between bulk high-pressure transmission and the more local distribution system, though access to different levels is separately priced. Development of competition depends crucially on both the level and the structure of prices for access to the pipes, which have been the subject of lively debate between the industry and its regulators. In particular, the form of price cap and its dependence on rate of return have provided significant incentives to the company which seem to have influenced its charges.

The issue of separation between access and product prices has been pre-empted by the incumbent's own initiative to split pipeline and supply activities into separately owned companies. This provides stronger guarantees of independence and reduces the company's potential to cross-subsidize, but restricts the regulator's options. In particular, she must allow the pipeline company to recover its average costs (indeed, the Gas Act can be interpreted as imposing on her a statutory duty to do so), sacrificing the potentially more efficient instrument of pricing access at marginal cost. The incumbent's regulated prices to the final market include a 'pass-through' factor which incorporates the cost paid to Transco for transportation. The level of the cap on Centrica is based on Ofgas's estimate of efficient *average* costs, and the charges between consumer groups are expected to reflect their allocable costs, with a proportional mark-up to cover the unallocated element (Ofgas, 1996a). This satisfies one aspect of the efficient component pricing rule (ECPR), in that both incumbent and entrants pay the same charge; entrants should only be attracted if they are more efficient than the incumbent supplier. But it ignores both the dynamic element of 'loss-leading' to gain a foot-hold in a newly opened market, and the possibility of entry by a company whose marginal costs lie above Centrica's marginal costs (so it is less efficient), but below its average costs.

While BG was integrated, the regulator had imposed some elements of ECPR in determining the structure of the access price for the residential market, i.e. the balance between the fixed ('standing') charge per consumer and the price per unit of gas used (Ofgas, 1994a). The cost per consumer paid by suppliers to the pipeline company was capped at a level which reflected the balance of final prices then charged by the incumbent. This was probably largely for political and distributional reasons, which will be assessed further in section 6.

Table 2
Balance of Capital and Commodity Charges in Access Prices

November 1986	(1.82) indicative charges[a]
June 1989	1.52
May 1990	1.50
September 1990	1.545
September 1991	1.700
September 1992	1.773
September 1993	1.739
September 1994	1.296
September 1995	1.297

Note: Ratio of charges for 30 per cent load factor to 90 per cent load factor, showing changing ratio of capacity to commodity charge. The higher the ratio, the higher the proportion of capacity charge. [a] For derivation, see Price (1989).
Source: BG's indicative charges, November 1986, and BG Gas Transportation Services publications.

There was also a lengthy debate about the structure of transport charges, and in particular the division of charges between using the system at peak, and a commodity-related carriage charge (British Gas and Ofgas, 1993). Virtually all the costs of the system (overwhelmingly the capital cost of the pipelines) are determined by the size of peak demand, but BG wanted to recover only half the costs through peak charges. Table 2 shows its rebalancing between these elements. In the long debate about the capital/commodity split in access charges, it was generally acknowledged that the marginal cost of expanding the system was about half the total average costs. Ofgas (1995) recognized the efficiency arguments of Ramsey pricing, in which mark-ups above marginal costs are inversely related to the responsiveness of demand to price increases, but rejected it because of its informational requirements about elasticities and possible distributional consequences. Eventually the regulator agreed, somewhat reluctantly, that the remaining 50 per cent of access costs could be recovered entirely from the commodity charge, even though the marginal cost of extra non-peak supplies is close to zero. This 50:50 split would be efficient only if demand for off-peak gas were completely unaffected by price, which seems unlikely. This is also the condition which would make this strategy the profit-maximizing path for BG.

A more likely motivation for BG's insistence on minimizing the charge for peak is the encouragement of peak demand, so expanding the capital base which would in future determine allowed return, consistent with behaviour under rate-of-return regulation (Sherman, 1989). The new access prices also increased the proportional charge made for use of the medium- and low-pressure systems, reducing the distance-related element, and making entry to the market of 'small users' more costly for competitors. In early 1997, Transco is moving away from the 50:50 split, perhaps reflecting that lower peak charges also benefited its own supply arm, with its more 'peaky' demand—a consideration no longer relevant once the two parts are separated.

BG encouraged entry into the industrial market chiefly by lowering its transportation costs. These fell dramatically, by nearly 50 per cent in real terms in the years when there was most pressure on BG to lose market share. The disagreement between Ofgas and BG Transco on the price control from 1997 centred on the level of prices to be allowed; in particular, there was disagreement about the appropriate capital base. But the two parties also took a different view on the timing of depreciation allowances (Ofgas, 1996d). The gas transportation system had been rebuilt and renovated in the 1970s to distribute gas from the North Sea, and most of the assets added then had a lifetime of 50 or so years and were adequate to meet expected demand. Transco thought it should be allowed to recover depreciation throughout the lifetime of the assets, while Ofgas believed that it was more appropriate to allow higher revenues at the time when more investment would be needed. This raised questions of regulatory commitment to allowing such revenues over several future price reviews, and the incumbency of regulators as yet unappointed. It also underlines the traditional problems in industries where price needs simultaneously to give two messages: to those determining present consumption about current costs; and to those choosing fuel-burning equipment and appliances about likely costs over the lifetime of their investment. Where present and future costs diverge, this is a problem with no obvious solution, particularly if forecasts of future prices are difficult to make credible.

4. Development of Competition to Date

(a) The 'Industrial' Market

Pressure to make competition in the bulk (contract) market effective *de facto* as well as *de jure* followed the 1988 Monopolies and Mergers Commission report. Transparency was increased by publication of price schedules for the bulk market and for access to the transportation system; progress in development of competition was to be reviewed 3 years later. This monitoring provided a novel form of regulation. The incumbent knew it had to lose an (unspecified) market share: if not, it would be subject to further constraints; if it was successful it might be

Figure 1
Real Gas Prices in Final and Access Markets
(1995 prices)

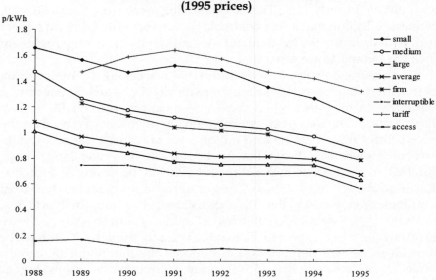

Source: Digest of UK Energy Statistics, 1990, 1993, and 1996.

able to revert to individual and confidential contracts. The application of this stick and carrot were to be determined not just by the company's actions, but by its effectiveness in encouraging entry.

The OFT (1991) review was not encouraging: although it concluded that BG had fully complied with the requirements of the 1988 MMC report, the loss of market was judged insufficient, and further negotiations to improve market penetration by new entrants ensued. In March 1992, BG agreed to 'lose' 60 per cent of its bulk market[1] by 1995. The monopoly market was narrowed to supplies under 2,500 therms a year in 1992 as recommended by the OFT report. The proportion of this wider market which BG was to lose was amended to 45 per cent, the equivalent of the previous target.

Entry to the 'contract' market was likely to depend on the gap between BG's final prices and the access charge it made for carriage. Prices for 'contract' consumers fell more than in the regulated tariff market (Figure 1), despite BG's target to lose market share. Access charges were based on distance over which the gas was carried, while final prices were geographically uniform (British Gas, 1989a, b); the most profitable markets for competitors were therefore those close to a beachhead and with an evenly distributed demand through the year. The MMC (1993b) found

[1] Over 25,000 therms per year but excluding power station supplies.

Table 3
Loss of BG's Market Share, 1990–6

Market	Oct90	Oct91	Oct92	Oct93	Mar91	Dec94	Apr95	Jun96
Small firm supply (<2,500 therms p.a.)	100	100	100	77	67	52	45	43
Large firm supply (>2,500 therms p.a.)	93	80	57	32	20	9	10	19
Interruptible (exc. power)	100	100	100	100	99	93	57	34
Power stations	no market	9	26	12	12	17	32	24
Total (exc. power)	97	91	81	77	65	47	35	29

Source: Ofgas (1994b,1996b).

little significant difference in market penetration by region, but did find the price discounts by competitors were higher near beachheads, and that competitors were supplying less 'peaky' demands than was BG.

BG's loss of market share after 1991 was dramatic (see Table 3). Ofgas removed permanently the need to publish tariffs for the above 25,000 therm market in 1996, although it retained the requirement (in suspension) for supplies between 2,500 and 25,000 therms a year. Return to price discrimination is forbidden by a clause in BG's licence (see section 5 for more discussion). The market for bulk supplies for electricity generation developed somewhat differently. It was accelerated by both the removal of the European Union ban on gas for such purposes, and the privatization of the electricity industry. BG was caught out by the rapid development of this market in the early days, and at one stage imposed a large price increase to restrict demand.

(b) Competition in the Residential Market

The timetable for residential competition announced by the President of the Board of Trade at the end of 1993 was rapid, and there were concerns about its practicality. To test this, the regulator decided to introduce competition in phases. Nine new suppliers offered gas supplies. In the second phase 12 companies have entered, all but one already involved in energy. Eight are RECs.

The programme was rushed and there were a number of technical difficulties. It was remarkable that the regulator managed to constrain delays in the introduction of competition itself to only 4 weeks, so that the first 'competitive gas' flowed at the end rather than the beginning of April 1996. On the first day, about 30,000 customers of the potential half million or so changed suppliers, representing the outcome of 6 months

Figure 2
Proportion of Consumers Using Each Payment Method who Switched in Wave 1 and Wave 2
(residential gas consumers in the south-west of England)

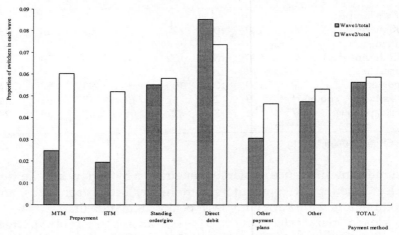

Notes: MTM is mechanical token meter; ETM is electronic token meter.
Source: BG Trading.

Figure 3
Proportion of Consumers who Stayed and Went in Each Wave, by Consumption Level

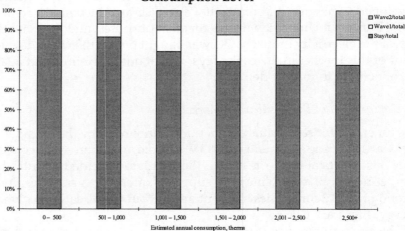

Source: BG Trading.

of fairly intensive marketing.[2] The numbers and gas consumption characteristics of the customers who changed in the first 6 months are shown

[2] Some of this was judged to be overzealous by the Gas Consumers Council and the local Trading Standards Board.

in Figures 2 and 3. These divide consumers into two groups: those who changed on the first day according to BG's records, and those who changed in the following 5 months: about equal numbers, identified respectively as 'wave 1' and 'wave 2'. The figures show that consumers of large quantities of gas, and those paying by direct debit, were more likely to switch in both waves; but that prepayment consumers, who were very unlikely to change in the first wave, were more likely to do so in wave 2. These results are a cautionary message to view these early results as indicative rather than definitive.

The difficulties of transition were exacerbated by the very regulatory safeguards put in place to prevent BG from exploiting its ownership of the distribution system. 'Chinese walls' were erected between Transco, the pipeline company, and British Gas Trading (BGT, later Centrica), the supply company, to protect the identity of the successful competitor from BGT. But this also imposed a very complex process for changing supplier, and a number of consumers were misidentified, causing problems which were beyond the capacity of either BGT or the local Gas Consumers Council to deal with in the short run. Inevitably, such transitional costs fall disproportionately on the incumbent, whose name and telephone number are familiar to households, and the regulator has recognized this in her price control for British Gas Trading from 1997 (Ofgas, 1996c).

It seems likely that the present programme of extending competition to the residential consumers of most of southern England in early 1997 and to the whole of Great Britain in 1998 will continue broadly on schedule, despite some of the early problems encountered in the southwest. New entrants are offering lower prices than BG (see Table 4 for savings in 'phase 2'), but it is difficult to tell at this stage whether they represent real efficiency gains, or merely marketing strategies and the benefits of lower gas purchase price. Many of those involved, including the regulators, are keen to demonstrate the success of competition. This will be likely to influence developments and encourage extension of the market as widely as possible.

5. Assessment: The Regulator's Role in Competition

The regulator's initial responsibility for competition was confined to the over 25,000 therm market; consumers taking less than this were protected by a price cap on average final prices. As liberalization proceeded, the regulator took on responsibility for the level of the access price (which was non-existent at privatization) and for the extension of competition to the entire market. Price caps on the access charge and on the

Table 4
Percentage Discounts on BG's Price Offered by New Entrants in Phase 2 of Competition in the Residential Market for Different Levels of Consumption[a]

Supplier	Standard tariff			Direct debit[b]
	Large	Small	Medium	Medium
Amerada Hess	18	15	15	9
Beacon	14	22	17	12
British Fuels	21	18	18	15
Calortex	18	18	18	14
Eastern	20	20	20	20
London	14	13	14	11
MEB	20	19	20	16
Northern	22	19	21	21
Norweb	17	20	17	14
Scottish Power	17	14	16	21
Southern	20	17	19	15
SWEB gas	20	17	19	17

Notes: [a] Large consumption: 40,000 kWh/year; medium (average) consumption: 20,500 kWh/year; small consumption: 10,000 kWh/year. [b] Note that for a medium BG consumer there is 7 per cent discount on the standard credit tariff for paying by direct debit.
Source: Consumers Association.

final prices have become important instruments in encouraging competition. The industry's structure as an integrated monopolist was not conducive to competition. Even regional monopolies would have provided the regulator with more information for comparative purposes (yardstick competition), as in electricity supply.

The regulator was also initially handicapped by the lack of accounting separation, unlike in electricity. In gas, separate regulation of the access charges and, indeed, the charges themselves, had to be developed from the beginning. Liberalization on its own proved insufficient to attract competitors into the bulk supply market and had to be reinforced by quantity constraints, partly because of the structural integrity of BG. In the residential market, competition is becoming established more quickly, partly because some of the mechanisms had already been established in the industrial market. This market, helped enormously by BG's take-or-pay contract liabilities, is strategic in developing competition throughout the residential energy markets in 1998. The gas regulators have faced the inevitable contradiction between constraining the incumbent where there is monopoly power and encouraging the development of competition. In the industrial market there was no price cap so the conflict did not arise directly, and the MMC recognized the potential difficulties in rejecting its possible introduction (MMC, 1988).

The pipelines will continue to need regulation into the indefinite future, and this has been the focus of the controversy in the 1996 price review discussions. Most of the public debate between industry and regulator has lain with the level of price cap being imposed (e.g. arguments over the capital base and the rate of return to be allowed) rather than with detailed price structures. To minimize the barriers to extending competition, the regulator has been anxious to remove remaining monopoly throughout the industry. For example, in the rapid development of competition in the industrial market in the early 1990s there was virtually no competition for interruptible supplies,[3] more than half BG's original contract market in volume. This was almost certainly because of the peak balancing which BG could undertake with respect to its still monopolized residential market, where demand is highly variable over the year.

The regulator has been active in developing a network code under which gas could be traded directly, thus 'unbundling' the commodity from various 'value-added' services. Such unbundling should help in distinguishing the commodity itself from the particular services which it renders to customers. But it is a complex process: both for the company which has traditionally provided vertically integrated services not only in the commodity, but in ancillary services such as connections; and for consumers who have very little understanding about how competition can work if similar gas continues to arrive through the same pipes. There is particular confusion about responsibility for safety: Transco is responsible for the safety and integrity of the system, while suppliers are concerned with ensuring supply. This division of responsibility may lead to confusion and additional costs, at least in the short run.

6. Structure of Tariffs

(a) Price Discrimination

Discussions of tariff *structures* have emerged both between and within all three markets: Figure 1 shows real average charges in residential and industrial markets, all showing considerable falls beyond the reduction in the cost of gas from the North Sea.[4] Within the contract market, the

[3] This is gas to industrial premises which can be interrupted for up to a specified number of days each year at the supplier's discretion, to help in balancing demand and supply at times of low temperatures and high demand.

[4] These are mark-ups over the average beachhead price, and do not include VAT on residential supplies (introduced in 1994).

initial referral to the MMC in 1987, less than a year after privatization, was to examine the issue of discrimination in the charging to different consumers under confidential tariffs. It was clear that BG was, indeed, using first-degree price discrimination in setting these prices:

> BG told us that its current contract pricing policy was to sell gas as profitably as possible at prices competitive with the alternative fuels which the customer could substitute for gas, subject only to the 'top stop' of the maximum prices published in accordance with BG's authorization[5] and the 'bottom stop' of not selling gas below marginal cost. (MMC, 1988)

This was a very efficient policy, but clearly did not encourage competition (at this time BG was concerned only about competition from other fuels); and was viewed as inequitable, particularly by those who paid higher prices. The MMC recommended increased transparency and pricing schedules to remedy the situation; these schedules were to be related to characteristics of supply which affected costs rather than consumers' willingness to pay.[6] It proposed that BG's licence be amended so that the requirement not to price-discriminate was extended from the price-regulated to the contract market. The possibility of price discrimination as evidence of monopoly power continued to be monitored in the competitive market by the regulator, who could find no evidence of such behaviour (Ofgas, 1996b).

The next debate on price structure arose in charging for pipelines discussed in section 3 above. The third investigation of undue discrimination arose explicitly after BG rebalanced its prices in the residential market, in anticipation of competition. Until then, BG had charged only two rates: a credit tariff for consumers who received bills for consumption in the previous quarter; and a more expensive prepayment tariff for consumers who paid using coins, tokens, or electronic cards to 'activate' their gas supply. From January 1995, however, BG offered a considerable discount for consumers who paid by direct debit, and later (partly under Ofgas pressure) introduced a (smaller) discount for those who paid promptly by other means.

BG was thus able to maintain its average prices within the cap, but rebalance considerably between prepayment consumers and the two new categories of prompt payers. This rebalancing partially redressed the cross-subsidy which had previously existed from prompt to late payers. The regulator conducted two investigations, which emphasized

---

[5] This top stop related to the price of gas in the tariff market, and was rarely binding.

[6] Though the inclusion by the MMC of size of demand is more likely to reflect a consumer's willingness to pay than any cost differences to BG.

the importance of the asymmetry of information since she was dependent on the company for providing the appropriate cost information in a timely manner. The regulator made clear her principle that prices should be broadly related to the attributable costs of each category of consumer, and that non-attributable costs should be recovered *pro rata* to these, independent of demand conditions. This amounted to a fully distributed cost allocation, rather than any form of Ramsey pricing. It is not clear that this is necessarily efficient; a monopolist will want to raise non-allocable costs from consumers whose demand is least price elastic. In general, these are high-income direct-debit consumers whose costs of supply are lower (Waddams Price, 1996), so the profit-maximizing price structure, which is close to Ramsey pricing, will be a fairly flat tariff, with highest mark-ups on lower-cost direct-debit customers. This is just the price structure which monopoly RECs and BG have maintained until liberalization of residential markets became imminent. But competitors will target these high mark-up markets, so incumbents must rebalance to protect their most profitable consumers. Suppliers will never want to charge any group of consumers less than the avoidable costs of supplying them. It is recovery of the *non-allocable* costs which will differ with liberalization. The equal mark-ups which will presumably characterize equilibrium are likely to be less efficient for the market as a whole.

(b) *Distributional Implications of Competition*

We have seen that competition induces rebalancing of prices, both between and within sectors. Its early effect was to alter the balance of prices between sectors, as Figure 1 (above) shows. Competition drove down the price in the industrial sector more than regulation managed to constrain it in the tariff market. Within the residential sector the threat of competition has also had a distributional effect. This has arisen from BG's rebalancing of prices, lowering prices for those paying by direct debit. At the same time, an increasing number of consumers with debt problems have been moved on to prepayment meters which also carry a higher charge. Ofgas found that these prices were broadly justified by the higher costs which BG incurred (Ofgas, 1996a)

Even if these changes represent improved efficiency there are two grounds for concern. One is that high-cost consumers will become a monopolized 'ghetto' because they are unattractive to competitors. Their costs may escalate further for a number of reasons. Companies will increasingly tempt the best of the group away with other offers, lowering the number remaining in the group, and worsening their average 'credit worthiness'. This will mean that both their marginal and average costs will rise, as the overheads of supplying a particular group are spread

Table 5
**Characteristics of Households According to Method of Payment and
Access to Bank Account**
**(percentage of households with each characteristic within each
payment method)**

	Gas-consuming households, paying by			Non-gas-consuming households
	C/SM –BA	C/SM +BA	Monthly payments	All
Poorest quintile	59	16	15	18	23
Richest quintile	1	23	22	21	16
Pensioner household	42	26	17	24	32
Single parent	13	2	5	4	4
On income support	53	8	11	12	16
Disabled	16	8	10	9	11
Sample size	360[a]	3,103[a]	1,838	5,301	1,440

Note: C/SM–BA = credit/slot meter, no bank account; C/SM+BA = credit/slot meter, has bank account; [a] Of those with no bank account, 67 used slot meters (column 1); of those with a bank account, 111 used slot meters (column 2).
Source: Hancock and Waddams Price (1995).

increasingly thinly. At the same time, the lack of competition means that the incentives to lower costs which appear elsewhere in the market are lost, and inefficient costs, both within the group and from elsewhere in the organization, will have to be recovered from them. It is interesting that of the nine new entrants in the south-west, only three initially offered a prepayment tariff. Early indications are that a higher proportion of consumers paying by direct debit have been recruited to other competitors than those paying by other means (Figure 2).

Consumers not paying by direct debit are among the more vulnerable households. In particular, those without access to a bank account, and those who are paying by standard tariff contain a disproportionate number of pensioners and consumers in the lowest income quintile. This is even more marked for prepayment consumers, where discounts are generally much lower (Table 5). Similarly, those who switched supplier in the south-west are more likely to be high-income owner-occupiers with large consumption and paying by direct debit (Hancock and Waddams Price, 1997). Three factors exacerbate the situation. This is a trend across all the utilities (except water, where competition is not a realistic possibility), so, for these households, tariffs for all services will be rising relative to those of the average consumer. Second, most price caps constrain average prices and so provide no protection for those whose prices rise within the average (though the new Ofgas caps on each element of each tariff described in the next section will provide some protection). Third, benefits and pensions are uprated by the retail price index, based on average expenditure, so that benefits may go down more than the prices paid by households who are dependent on them. The majority of gas consumers seem likely to benefit from competition (depending on potential increases in efficiency and economies of scope), but for a small and particularly vulnerable group competition may cause significant difficulties. Even outside competitive areas the regulator's emphasis on increasing cost reflectivity has distributional effects by raising the charges for customers using small amounts of gas, who often have low incomes.

7. Future regulatory strategy

The regulator's chief strategy in encouraging competition is to prevent discrimination—either in the operation of the system or in the prices which are charged in various markets. The 1995 Gas Act imposes restrictions on undue discrimination by any dominant company in the industry, for which BG Trading alone qualifies at present. This will be increasingly important in final markets as competition becomes established, but Centrica remains dominant in some sense. The regulator defines a competitive market as one with no barriers to entry, regardless of the amount of entry actually made, either by numbers of suppliers or proportion of market supplied. Though such a 'contestable' definition is intuitively appealing, it is very difficult for an observer to be sure that there are no 'invisible' barriers to entry, such as reputation. Achieved entry in substantial amounts is a reassuring confirmation that effective barriers to entry are absent.

These factors undoubtedly influenced the regulator in the form of the final price control to be imposed in the residential market from 1997. Until then, the basic constraint had been on the average revenue which BG could raise in any one year, but this is difficult to impose at a time of changing market share. While BG attempts to reduce the prices to those consumers who cost least to supply to minimize 'cherry-picking', it is unlikely to be able to adjust fully to costs, and so would lose fastest those consumers whose prices were cheapest, effectively tightening the revenue constraint under a current weighted price cap. In the residential market an average price cap poses problems for competition because it can so easily be combined with an anti-competitive price structure, lowering prices most where threat of competition is greatest. In response to these two problems Ofgas has implemented a cap on each tariff in place in April 1997 and each element of the tariff (standing charge and commodity charge), with the onus on Centrica to justify any new tariffs which it introduces. However, the proposal discourages Centrica from rebalancing and lowering its prices before that date, complicating its short-term reaction to competitive entry.

An important part of the regulatory armoury on which Ofgas relies is transparency — in the early days of competition for industrial and commercial consumers the MMC and Ofgas insisted that BG publish price schedules, though competitors did not have to do so. There is clearly a danger that such a practice could be used as a collusive device, and in early competition in both the industrial and residential market the prices have been expressed as discounts from those which BG was offering. In the industrial market competition has become established, but this has been driven much more by the requirement for BG to shed market share than by the transparency of its prices.

In terms of operating the system, this entails unbundling services such as storage, connection, and metering wherever possible, to ensure non-discriminatory access to the transportation and storage system. Equal access to such ancillary services, as well as to the pipelines themselves, is crucial if the aim is to ensure the legendary level playing-field. The eventual shape of the industry is likely to depend crucially on the way in which it develops. Such development will also be heavily influenced by the progress of competition in the electricity industry, and it is clear that one consequence of liberalization will be a growth in cross-ownership and multi-utility providers. For example, there are concerns that plans to liberalize meter provision are more advanced in the gas than the electricity industry, allowing the entry of RECs into the gas metering market while their own markets retain monopoly protection.

Some of these cross-industry issues will become an issue for general competition authorities, but they also call into question the shape of the regulatory structure over the next few years. Closer cooperation between the two energy regulators seems inevitable if they are not to introduce distortions to the market rather than remove them; a combined regulatory office may seem sensible, though some competition is likely to be as beneficial between regulators as in the markets which they regulate. If competitive metering becomes a reality in both gas and electricity it may reduce consumer costs through shared services. But utility provision is likely to remain a highly specialized area. Dealing with a large number of residential consumers, requiring access to their homes, and the complex social implications may well restrict entry to the market. We already see a proliferation of pricing offers which leaves many consumers confused, and an inertia among consumers unwilling to change suppliers even for quite large gains. This is a familiar pattern from the personal financial sector, and the energy markets are likely to develop with a similar small number of suppliers, some of whom may target 'niche' and specialist markets. This may leave incumbent suppliers with a disproportionate number of inert and high-cost consumers.

In the first 10 years of privatization the development of competition in gas can be seen as a triumph of regulatory determination against what appeared overwhelming odds in 1986. These far-reaching changes, legally possible under nationalization, could not be effectively enforced until the industry was transferred to the private sector. The price discrimination in the contract market, referred to the MMC within a year of flotation, had been known and monitored for years by the Department of Energy, but action was not seen as feasible. Similarly, gas-to-gas competition, using BG as a common carrier, had been legal since the 1982 Oil and Gas (Enterprise) Act, but did not become effective until the pressure of the 1991 OFT enquiry. There are a number of reasons why effective competition may be easier for the government to impose on an unwilling private than a similarly resistant nationalized industry. Problems of commitment (for example, through making budget constraints really binding) may be greater for nationalized industries, and the government may find it easier to distance itself from unpopular effects of its policies if they are implemented by a private company. The personalities may be too strong and too close to impose effective punishment on a public company (quite a credible explanation in Denis Rooke's case). The changes in the gas industry suggest that arm's-length regulation has been more effective than public ownership in reforming the industry.

Alternatively, supporters of the privatization programme might argue that the change of ownership released efficiency savings through the powerful incentive scheme provided by the regulatory structure, which could then be redeployed partly in making these structural changes. However, it is interesting that significant reduction in employment came only in the 1990s, confirming that the initial price caps were lax, and that even when these were tightened the industry still retained considerable inefficiencies. And we have noted that the lowest prices offered by competitors to residential consumers were as much a result of BG's historical contract commitments as of real efficiency savings.

How the residential market develops depends on a number of factors, both in the regulatory regime and more widely within the industry. One concerns the universal service obligation, the requirement that all consumers within 25 yards of a gas main should have access to a supply. Competition will erode present cross-subsidies, so that those who are expensive to supply because of location or payment method are likely to

Table 6
Characteristics of Households Consuming Small and Large Amounts of Gas
(percentage in each group)

	Annual gas consumption		
	≤100 therms	>1,500 therms	All
Poorest quintile	26	17	18
Richest quintile	21	32	21
Pensioner household	31	13	24
Single parent	6	6	4
On income support	16	13	12
Disabled	7	7	9
Sample size	264	218	5,301

Source: Hancock and Waddams Price (1995).

see prices rise. In particular, average charges for small users may increase, causing difficulties for some low-income consumers. Table 6 shows the relation between gas use and income. The regulator has made arrangements to impose a levy on all suppliers if some are left with a disproportionate number of high-cost groups, but it is unclear whether it is likely to be implemented. There is a clear danger that the incumbent will exaggerate the costs and numbers of such consumers, recouping the alleged cost from competitors through a levy which can act as a barrier to entry.

The solution to the distribution problem is not straightforward. It should be a transitory difficulty, in that once the present cross-subsidies are eroded there would be no incentive or justification for further rebalancing. But if these 'vulnerable' consumers are supplied by rump monopolists (the previous incumbents) with high inherited costs and little pressure to reduce them, it may be a continuing static problem. The danger is that this vulnerable group becomes a means for the incumbents to argue to the regulator for continuing special treatment in which they are permitted to pass on their inefficient costs. The separate caps on each tariff implemented from 1997 provide more protection for individual consumers than an aggregate price cap, but may prevent efficient rebalancing and be appropriate only as an interim measure. This would seem a prime example of a case where regulators and the social security agencies should work together for a consistent outcome — ironically, the privatization and fragmentation of government renders this increasingly difficult and unlikely. The interest of the Minister for Energy in the redistributional implications of Transco's increasing cost reflectivity in summer 1997 is an encouraging sign of the Labour government's acceptance of some central responsibility for these issues.

The equity issue is not properly a regulatory issue, but if other government agencies take no action it may become an issue for the industry through public and political pressure. Moreover, the regulator has emphasized the importance of preventing undue discrimination, and the implementation of this clause is likely to be crucial. If the Director General continues to interpret this as all consumers contributing to unattributed costs in proportion to their allocated costs, this will mean further rebalancing in favour of customers using large amounts of gas and paying by direct debit. It will also focus attention increasingly on how costs are allocated, and provides incentives for companies to report a cost structure which, after application of the regulator's rule, yields a profit-maximizing price pattern. To the extent that they are successful, the price pattern will also become more efficient but not necessarily more equitable. The regulator will be drawn increasingly into reviewing the detailed structure of costs, as is already happening with Transco's charges for transportation.

What the first few years of privatization showed was that both the gas regulator and the general regulatory authorities in the form of the MMC, the OFT, and the government were determined that effective competition should be introduced. Their policies proved much more effective in changing the industry than the transfer to private ownership. Liberalizing the gas industry has revealed substantial cost savings, despite Denis Rooke's promise to his staff on the day of privatization that 'nothing will change'. Prices have fallen more in markets open to competition than in those which have remained monopolies, and consumers in south-west England have been offered substantial discounts. But this may be an accident of stranded contracts rather than a true indication of future potential savings.

Continued competition in the gas market will offer more choice to most consumers, but will expose those groups who have benefited from cross-subsidies in the past. Some of these households are on a low income or vulnerable for other reasons, and there is a danger that aggregate benefits will be gained at the expense of those who can least afford the sacrifice. The regulatory regime has yielded significant benefits over the past decade; its immediate challenge is in the distribution of future benefits.

6

Telecommunications

MARK ARMSTRONG*

1. Introduction

In the United Kingdom, telecommunications was the first of the utility industries to be privatized and liberalized, and it perhaps provides the richest case study of the benefits, and the difficulties, of introducing competition into such industries. In this chapter the theory and practice of competition in telecommunications is discussed with an eye to recent public policy towards the industry in the UK.[1]

The chapter has two main sections. In section 2, some background to the industry is provided, including a discussion of the components of the industry (section 2(a)), some salient economic features of the industry, including elements of natural monopoly, sunk costs, network externalities, social obligations, and the prevalence of customer inertia (section 2(b)), and the section concludes with a summary of the state of competition in the UK and current regulatory policy towards the industry (section 2(c)). Because the industry is so complicated, it is useful to sketch some more formal models of competition, and in section 3 two broad kinds of competition are analysed from a theoretical perspective. These are the cases where competition takes place in the sectors where technology makes entry most straightforward, such as in some services and in long-distance telecommunications (section 3(a)), and where there is competition for directly connected customers, which is relevant for entry

* Nuffield College, Oxford. I am grateful to the Economic and Social Research Council for research funding (grant number L114251026), and to Geoffrey Myers and John Vickers for many helpful comments. However, I am solely responsible for the views and remaining mistakes contained in the chapter.

[1] For other non-technical accounts of the economics of the telecommunications industry, see Armstrong *et al.* (1994, ch. 7), Cave and Williamson (1996), and Grout (1996). (The paper by Cave and Williamson focuses on the behaviour of individual firms in the UK.) For a discussion of the industry in central and eastern Europe, see Armstrong and Vickers (1996*b*). For a survey of the important recent developments in the United States, see Council of Economic Advisers (1996, ch. 6).

by cable television companies and mobile telecommunications (section 3(b)). Although this discussion is somewhat abstract, connections with current concerns in UK policy are highlighted. Finally, some concluding comments are made in section 4.

2. The Telecommunications Industry

(a) *A Description of the Industry*

The basic distinction to be made in the telecommunications industry is that between *network operation* and *service provision*. Broadly speaking, network operators provide the links and exchanges which enable communication in some form to take place between one point and another, whereas service providers take this ability to communicate and use it to provide various communication services to end-users. Naturally, both network operation and service provision can be — and are — undertaken by the same firm.

A telecommunications network is made up of a mixture of exchanges and transmission links. Typically, the network is organized as a kind of hierarchy: a link joins a user's telephone to a local exchange (often via a 'remote concentrator'); local exchanges are connected to trunk exchanges by higher capacity transmission lines; trunk exchanges are mutually connected by a system of high capacity trunk links; and, finally, certain trunk exchanges are connected to the international network via satellite or cable. The link from a user to the local exchange (or to the remote concentrator) is known as the 'local loop' and, because it is used by nobody else, it need have no greater carrying capacity than required by that single user. Transmission links can use either cable or radio transmission. Within the network operation sector itself, there is a distinction between *fixed* and *mobile* networks. Users of a fixed network can only use services on that network from a fixed location, using apparatus connected to a given socket, whereas users of a mobile network can — to a greater or lesser extent — use services on that network from any location in the region. It is necessary to use a radio-based transmission link for the final connection to a user on a mobile network, although radio-based links can also be used throughout a fixed network (even in the local loop).

There is a great variety of services which may be provided over a modern telecommunications network.[2] The most obvious of these is basic voice telephony whereby two people engage in a (two-way) conversation, which remains the most common use to which a public

[2] For a comprehensive catalogue of the various services, see Oftel (1996a, ch. 3). Note that Oftel documents are available on the internet at www.open.gov.uk/oftel.

network is put. Other services could be termed 'enhanced' services, and include: electronic mail; premium rate services; on-line information services (such as those providing share-price data); internet services; various kinds of data transfer (including airline ticket booking systems and the cash-dispensing networks of banks); video conferencing; and, finally, television services. With regard to this last category, note that it is perfectly possible to send standard television signals down a telephone network—either simultaneously to a large number of users ('broadcasting') or individually tailored to a given user's demands ('video-on-demand')—so long as the network, and especially a user's local loop, has sufficiently high capacity.

In sum, the four main sectors of the telecommunications industry are:

A local fixed network operation;
B local mobile network operation;
C long-distance (including international) network operation; and
D service provision over combinations of the above networks.

We will discuss competition in each of the four sectors throughout the remainder of the chapter.

(b) *Economic Features of the Industry*

Regarding the impact on the potential competitiveness of telecommunications, the three most relevant economic features of the industry are: (i) the cost structure of telecommunications technology, including elements of natural monopoly, sunk costs, and the substantial per-line cost of connection to a network; (ii) network and other externalities (including social factors); and (iii) customer inertia (and other kinds of barriers to entry). These are discussed in turn.

(i) Natural monopoly

An activity is said to be a natural monopoly if it is most cost-effectively carried out by a single firm rather than by several. Of the four broad sectors listed in section 2(a) above, the sector which has the most widespread natural monopoly cost conditions is local fixed network operation. This is largely because of *economies of density*, whereby it is cheaper per person to build a local network connecting, say, 5,000 people in a given area than it is to connect 500. (The reason is partly because the cost of a local exchange can be spread over more local users, and partly because the greater use of remote concentrators and the like means that a lower proportion of the local network is made up of costly dedicated cabling and ducting.) Clearly, economies of density imply that it is more cost-effective to have a single local network in a given local area than to have several. There are also economies of density in the mobile sector — again because of economies of scale in providing switching at the local level — but far less so than for fixed networks because of the inability to 'concentrate' several local connections together in a single channel. (See Cave and Williamson (1996, section III) for a more detailed discussion of the structure of costs in telecommunications networks.)

Related to the discussion of natural monopoly is the existence of fixed connection costs to both fixed and mobile networks. It is very costly to have more than one telecommunications cable going into a given premises — laying a cable involves digging up the pavement and so on, and on average costs several hundred pounds — and so the local loop could be viewed as an extreme natural monopoly for wire-based networks.[3] Similarly, in order to be able to make or receive calls on a mobile network a user needs a mobile handset, which currently costs upwards of £200 to manufacture.[4] The fact that there is a substantial cost for a user to connect to a network implies that the vast majority of users will be connected to only one fixed network and/or only one mobile network. (Because of the very different characteristics of fixed and mobile network operation, however, it may well be efficient for a user to be connected to both a fixed and a mobile network, despite the duplication of connection costs entailed.) This means that for however long a user is connected to a given (fixed or mobile) network (network 1, say), that network has a *monopoly* over providing access by others to that user. In particular, users connected to another network (network 2) must somehow gain access to the local loop of network 1 if they are to communicate with users on that network. Notice that this is true no matter how many competing networks there are, and so the local network operation sector has the peculiar feature that increasing the number of competing firms does not overcome all monopoly problems. This suggests that regulation will continue to play an important role in the industry for the foreseeable future.

On the other hand, there are probably no other significant areas of natural monopoly in the industry. For instance, traffic on many trunk

[3] To this direct cost of laying new cables should be added the negative externalities caused by the noise and disturbance of digging up pavements and so on. If additional cabling is occurring in any event — say, in order to supply cable television — then the incremental cost of supplying telecommunications services over the new network might not be large, and so there might not be excessive duplication. Another means with which to avoid costly duplication is to use a radio-based link (either mobile or not) which involves a much lower sunk cost which is specific to the location.

[4] Note that, with current technology, a given handset can only be used to connect to a single mobile network, and a user who wished (for some reason) to use two mobile networks or change network operator would have to purchase two handsets.

routes is heavy, and once economies of scale in providing capacity are exhausted, the extent of natural monopoly is likely to be limited in the trunk network. This is especially so if competing networks can easily obtain rights-of-way and can, for instance, lay fibre-optic cable along railway lines or electricity transmission lines. Thus, except for remote areas, there is no reason to expect major natural monopoly cost conditions in long-distance network operation. (However, there will be *some* duplication when there are multiple trunk networks, since two or more sets of trunk exchanges and other traffic management systems will therefore be required.) Similarly, there is little evidence of natural monopoly in international network operation.

Turning to service provision, there again seems little reason to believe there is significant natural monopoly in this sector. To take a simple example, it seems equally efficient to have two or more 'chatline' service providers as to have one, since all that is required to offer this service is an exchange which allows many-person simultaneous conversation (and the ability to bill customers for the service). Similarly, there is no obvious reason why a customer should not be able to choose from several competing cable television service providers to supply programmes down their network, nor why there should not be several internet service providers, and so on. Even with the basic voice telephony service, it does not seem inefficient to have several firms offering this service over the same network (and we will see below that this happens in the mobile sector in the UK). In addition, it is not obvious that there are significant economies of scope between network operation and service provision. (That is to say, there is probably no major cost saving to be had from a single firm being both a network operator and a service provider.) However, there may be some small economies of scope in providing a variety of different services to a given customer, since in that case only a single bill need be sent out.

In addition to problems caused by natural monopoly in parts of the industry, some sectors involve durable investments which are sunk. For instance, if a network operator has already laid a cable into someone's house which cost, say, £500 in 1990, and which had a useful life of 30 years, and a cable television company lays a new cable and supplies both television and telecommunications services to that household, then the original cable no longer generates revenue for the original company and the asset is 'stranded'. Sunk costs are perhaps less of an issue with mobile networks, although they are still important for investment in radio transmission towers and so on, since there is no location-specific investment, and they are also less important for the radio-based fixed-network technologies. However, a major difference between all aspects of network operation and service provision is that the latter typically does *not* require a large degree of sunk investment. This may well be relevant for public policy towards the two sectors in that the former is more vulnerable to *ex-post* changes in the regulatory and licensing regime than the latter, and so may require a more favourable treatment *ex ante* in order to protect investment incentives. We will see in section 3(a) that this provides one explanation for some aspects of recent policy in Britain.

(ii) Network externalities

A network externality is said to exist for a service if users of the service benefit when more people use it.[5] The obvious example is basic voice telephony, where any customer benefits from being able to communicate with a larger number of other users of the service.

This feature of the telecommunications market, together with the fact that it is costly for a user to be connected to more than one network—see (i) above—explains why *network interconnection* is so important with regard to competition policy. If there were two networks which were *not* interconnected—i.e. it was not possible to set up a link from a user of one network to a user of the other—then a firm supplying the voice telephony service over the smaller network would be placed at a severe competitive disadvantage, in that all else being equal it would have to charge a lower price for the service to counteract the lower utility from being able to call a smaller number of other people. It is only with full network interconnection—so that people on one network have the ability to call, and receive calls from, people on all other public networks—that a new entrant has any chance of being able to attract its first customers. Moreover, it is not enough simply to require that networks provide access to their customers for other networks, but the terms of that access ('call termination charges') are crucial. As was discussed in (i) above, access to a customer by others is a monopoly held by that customer's network, and in many cases that network will, if free to do so, set a socially excessive price for such access.

The possible wider social benefits of having an extensive and accessible network—for example, provision to sparsely populated areas and the ability to obtain emergency services—are another kind of positive externality in the broad sense. As in some other utility industries, public policy has often attempted to obtain these wider benefits by requiring firms to offer geographically uniform prices; so, for instance, the charge

[5] This terminology is perhaps slightly confusing. The term network externality is used by economists in many different settings—including video formats and newspaper readership—and not just telephone networks (see Tirole, 1988, section 10.6). Moreover, in the telecommunications context what matters is not the number of customers using a given physical network, but the number using the same service (which may be provided over several networks).

for connection to the network is the same regardless of cost differences across the country. Other instances of social obligations include providing public call boxes in rural areas and providing affordable, specialized services to people with disabilities. Another major example is a requirement that a firm provide special tariffs for 'low users', i.e. for people whose use of services does not cover the fixed costs of connection. A strong case can certainly be made for providing subsidized access to telecommunications for some groups of users. However, we will see later that the common practice of funding such loss-making services by cross-subsidies from other markets in the industry (rather than out of general public funds, say) makes the introduction of competition more complicated.

(iii) Customer inertia

Some barriers to entry are common to all industries with sunk costs and capacity constraints — as is the case with network operation in telecommunications — and we do not discuss these here in detail.[6] What is more particular to telecommunications is the prevalence of *customer inertia*, which implies that entrants may have difficulty in attracting customers unless there is pro-competitive regulation. The two main potential sources of inertia are the lack of *number portability* and the lack of *equal access*.

Number portability is said to exist if customers can keep their telephone number if they choose to change the network to which they are connected.[7] Thus, at least until recently, a BT customer choosing to switch to the local cable television operator would have to change number. If customers have to change telephone number they typically face direct financial costs, such as changing printed notepaper and, in the case of businesses, repainting signs and vehicles, and the possible lost business if potential customers cannot obtain the new number. Such costs, which may be quite substantial for some users, mean that customers will, all else being equal, need a compensating discount if they are to be attracted by a rival network. Therefore, a lack of number portability is a major barrier to entry for new network operators. For fixed networks at least, the technology exists to allow number portability, albeit at a cost, and it

---

[6] For a full discussion of entry barriers, see Tirole (1988, ch. 8).

[7] More precisely, there are several kinds of number portability, and here we focus on *inter-operator* portability where a customer can keep their number if they change operator. In the fixed network operation case, there is another kind of portability which occurs when customers can keep their number if they move house (and maybe stay with the same operator). For a full discussion of number portability, see MMC (1995b).

is important for regulators to determine whether number portability should be introduced and, if so, who should pay for the service.

Equal access is a term usually associated with long-distance and international telephone traffic (although in principle it could apply to other services as well), and refers to a situation where there is no systematic bias in favour of one trunk operator over another. For instance, in the early years of Mercury's competition with BT (see section 2(c) below) there was unequal access, in that if a customer connected to BT's local network wished to use Mercury's long-distance services they would either have to dial a long access code, or buy a special 'blue-button' telephone to dial this code automatically. This naturally biased users against making calls on Mercury's trunk network, and provides another example of a major entry barrier. Full equal access would exist if, say, whenever a user (connected to any local network) made a long-distance call, they were required to dial the *same* length of access code for each long-distance operator. Such a system, which is used extensively in the USA, would result in a more level playing field between operators.

(c) *The Industry in Britain*

In this section a summary of the current situation in the UK is presented, grouped under the headings (i) fixed network operation, (ii) mobile network operation, and (iii) service provision. (Because it has been so deeply linked with fixed network operation, however, the basic fixed voice telephony service is discussed under heading (i) rather than (iii). Similarly, mobile service provision is discussed in (ii).) The Office of Telecommunications (Oftel) is the industry regulator and is responsible for enforcing the regulatory rules contained in the licences for network operators, as well as proposing new licence conditions. In order for new licence conditions to come into effect, they must either be agreed with the licensee, or the Monopolies and Mergers Commission (MMC) is called in to arbitrate. Policy towards entry into the industry (i.e. the awarding of new licences) is usually made by the Department of Trade and Industry, although Oftel has an advisory role here as well.

(i) Fixed network operation

British Telecom (BT) was privatized in 1984, and until that time it held a monopoly over virtually all aspects of network operation and service provision. BT was privatized intact as a vertically integrated network operator and service provider. Mercury was licensed as a national network operator in competition with BT in 1982, although its main services were not launched until 1986. The government announced in 1983 its 'duopoly policy', which was that Mercury would be the *only* other fixed nationwide network operator to be licensed until 1990. Mercury competed with BT in two broad ways: it tried to attract large users to be directly connected to its network — so that such users would have a wire (or microwave) link to its network, thus bypassing BT's network at the originating end — and it tried to attract smaller users to use its network for long distance and international calls while remaining connected to BT's network at the local level.[8] Although it was very successful in gaining market share for directly connected users in a few business sectors (such as the City of London), it generally was not able to make many inroads into the local network market. (Current market shares are given below.)

Just after BT was privatized, the first cable television franchises were awarded, although because of the duopoly policy these networks were initially prohibited from offering telecommunications services in their own right. When the duopoly policy expired, the government opened up the network operation market more fully, and several new operators entered from 1991 onwards. As far as residential customers are concerned, perhaps the most significant of these were the cable television companies who were now permitted to offer telecommunications as well as television services.[9] The cable companies use the long-distance and international network of Mercury wherever possible. A significant decision made at the end of the duopoly policy was that BT and Mercury would *not* be permitted to carry television services over their telecommunications networks until at least the year 2001. This policy decision appears to be intended to assist the entry of the cable television companies into the hitherto monopolized local fixed telecommunications market (the fear being that if BT were allowed to enter the television sector, the cable companies would not survive as suppliers of either television or telecommunications services).[10] However, BT (and Mercury) is permitted to offer 'video-on-demand' services, and if the technology can be developed sufficiently this could pose some threat to the cable companies. Finally, the duopoly policy in respect of international network operation was retained until 1996, and until that year BT and Mercury were the only firms permitted to run full international networks out of

[8] Using the notation in section 2(a), the former strategy involved entry into sectors A, C, and D, whereas the latter involved entry into just C and D.

[9] Other entrants include the nationwide networks, Energis and Ionica, the regional operators, Scottish Telecom, Norweb, and Torch, and the specialized business sector operators, COLT and MFS.

[10] At the end of the duopoly policy, BT was also barred from using radio links in its local loops. As with television, the aim was to encourage entry by independent local operators who were permitted to use this new technology. (Ionica is an entrant using fully radio-based local network connection.) In fact, BT has recently been licensed to use radio links in its fixed network in rural areas.

the UK. However, in June 1996 the government announced that it was ending this duopoly and, to date, nearly 50 licence applications have been submitted (see Oftel, 1996*f*, p. 13).

According to Oftel (1996*g*), in December 1995 there were about 29m exchange lines in Britain, of which BT supplied 94 per cent, Mercury supplied about 1 per cent, and the cable operators about 5 per cent. About 22m of these lines are for residential subscribers, and of these BT again had a market share of 94 per cent, Mercury had almost none, and the cable operators had around 6 per cent. Although the total number of residential exchange lines continues to rise, the number of residential subscribers to BT is falling owing to the increasing number of people switching to cable services. At this time, less than 4 per cent of residential subscribers use indirect access over BT lines for rival long-distance and international services (such as those offered by Mercury). Measured in terms of revenues, BT's market share for all calls was 92 per cent for local calls, 81 per cent for national (long-distance) calls, and 70 per cent for international calls, and if we just consider the residential market then BT's market shares were 94 per cent for local calls, 90 per cent for national (long-distance) calls, and 83 per cent for international calls. Thus, in terms of national market share, BT remains dominant in fixed network operation, especially for residential subscribers, more than a decade after its privatization. It should, however, be borne in mind that the cable companies are very limited in their coverage, and they currently are able to serve only about 5m (or a quarter) of all UK homes. It is estimated that where alternative telephone services *are* available from cable television companies, about 20 per cent of households have chosen to change from BT to the local cable company, thus showing that BT is vulnerable in markets where there is effective competition and that BT's subscriber base can be expected to fall further as cable companies continue to 'roll out' their networks.[11]

Network interconnection has been a thorny issue since the start of network competition, and controversy shows no sign of abating. Because BT has such a large proportion of subscribers, the vast majority of calls on all networks are made to BT subscribers. Therefore, regardless of whether or not a competing network has directly connected subscribers, all networks require BT to deliver most of their calls. In addition, since Mercury's smaller customers were connected to its network via BT's local network, Mercury required BT to originate as well as deliver these customers' calls. Finally, it is important to remember that a minority of calls from BT's customers are to users on other networks (including mobile networks), and so BT needs other networks to deliver some of its

---

[11] See Oftel (1995*a*, Annex C, p. 12).

own calls. All of these call origination and termination services are termed *interconnection services,* and it is the payment for such services which has proved so contentious.

One reason for the difficulty is that different firms often have conflicting interests: BT would like interconnection payments to be high and other networks want the opposite. The problem is compounded by the fact that, especially early on, BT's retail prices were often rather out of line with its underlying costs (as discussed in section 2(a) above). This has at least two dimensions: BT was (and still is) required to set geographically uniform prices for connection, quarterly rental, and call charges, even though the costs of providing services to users in different parts of the country vary substantially; and on average the connection and quarterly rental charges historically did not cover the fixed costs of running the network, and usage charges were correspondingly set above the marginal cost of using the network. These points imply that if BT's interconnection charges were set equal or similar to its marginal cost of providing interconnection, then entrants — who were *not* required to serve far-flung or low-usage customers — could pick and choose which customers and which routes to serve. Such 'cream-skimming' entry has two principal problems: (i) because of the distorted price signals, an entrant could find it profitable to serve certain markets even if it were less efficient than BT; and (ii) such entry could mean that BT loses its most profitable markets, leaving it in the long run unable to fund its loss-making services to rural and low-usage customers. Therefore, while BT is constrained to offer retail prices that do not always reflect its costs, a policy of setting interconnection charges equal to the associated costs is not obviously desirable.

In the duopoly policy era when BT faced only limited competition, these concerns did not need to be faced, and BT was required to offer interconnection to Mercury at terms which at the time were judged to be broadly in Mercury's favour. However, after the duopoly policy ended it became imperative to have a clear policy on interconnection pricing. At the time of writing some details of future policy in this area remain unclear, but Oftel — see Oftel (1996*b,f*) — proposes that from 1997 until 2001:

- BT be allowed more retail pricing flexibility which it could use to make its charges somewhat more cost-reflective. (In any case, since Mercury's entry BT had been permitted to make its tariffs gradually more cost-reflective.) The three main constraints are that the average bill of the 80 per cent of residential customers who use the telephone least should decrease by 4.5 per cent per annum in real terms (which in practice means that BT cannot increase the quarterly fixed charge by much for these low-usage customers), that BT continues to offer a special subsidized tariff for very low users, and that BT should continue to charge geographically uniform prices for network connection, line rental, and calls.

- BT's charges for call termination – which we argued in section 2(b) was the main long-run bottleneck sector – be regulated separately from other interconnection services. (The precise level of the charge has yet to be determined, although it is likely to be based on some measure of average incremental cost together with a contribution to common costs.)

- Most of BT's other interconnection services (such as call origination) be put into a single basket whose average charge must fall by a certain amount in real terms per annum (by how much is yet to be determined). BT will be permitted some flexibility in setting relative charges within the overall price cap, subject to individual charges lying between certain 'floors and ceilings' (yet to be determined). However, like its retail tariff, BT is constrained to set geographically uniform interconnection charges.

- As regards the call termination charges made by other networks, Oftel favours the principle of 'reciprocity', by which is meant that if a competing network is of a 'broadly similar' type to BT's, then that network should set its own call termination charge roughly equal to that which BT is required to charge. It is not yet clear what a network operator whose network is not broadly similar to BT's – and here the mobile operators are the leading example – is to be permitted to charge (although Oftel (1996b, p. 38) states that the current call termination rates charged by Cellnet and Vodafone may be 'too high in relation to cost').

Thus, recent Oftel policy has been to make BT's retail tariff somewhat more cost-reflective. Because of this, Oftel does not intend to incorporate into BT's interconnection charges an allowance for cross-subsidies in BT's retail tariff. Until 1996 Oftel had the authority to impose additional interconnection charges on entrants, which were intended to act as a correction factor to BT's distorted retail tariffs, such additional charges being known as 'access deficit contributions'. This policy has now been abandoned, and interconnection charges will no longer contain any such 'opportunity cost' factors. (In section 3(a) below we discuss the notion of opportunity cost and its importance when retail tariffs are out of line with costs.)

However, in important respects BT remains for the foreseeable future constrained to offer a tariff which continues to involve cross-subsidies, including a requirement to set geographically uniform charges and to offer a 'low-user' tariff.[12] Because of this, BT incurs a loss in serving some users and some remote areas. Oftel has recently estimated the gross cost of these social obligations provisionally to be between £60m and £90m per annum, although it argues that some of these costs should be offset by some rather nebulous *benefits* of providing social obligations (such as 'enhancement of corporate reputation')—see Oftel (1995*b*). Although again some details remain to be worked out, Oftel's policy towards the funding of these social obligations is to set up a fund equal to the costs of the obligations financed by all telecommunications firms in proportion to each firm's revenues from providing basic telecommunications services. The fund would be paid to whichever firms incurred costs in providing social obligations, i.e. principally BT. The policy will, to some extent at least, ensure that entry by rivals into profitable markets does not place in danger BT's ability to fund its social obligations.[13] However, since prices remain distorted away from underlying costs to some extent, the introduction of the fund will not remove the danger of inefficient entry, since entry may still be overly encouraged in markets with high price/cost margins and stifled where margins are low. In addition, since both its retail and interconnection tariffs are required to be geographically uniform despite differing costs across the country, there remains the danger that entrants may be able to 'cherry pick' the most profitable routes and regions.

In section 2(b) we discussed how measures to reduce customer inertia might be an important element of competition policy. As regards policy towards number portability, it is only recently that portability has been required from BT, and until 1996 any person who changed network operator had to change their telephone number. (Given that this was so, the competitive impact of the cable television companies described above is especially impressive.) In 1995, BT and Oftel could not agree on how portability should be introduced—and which networks should bear the cost of portability—and the issue went to the MMC for arbitration. The details of the issue are complex, but very broadly the MMC recommended that BT should bear most of the ongoing costs of providing number portability, but that it should be permitted to make a one-off,

---

[12] For instance, Oftel (1996*e*, p. 6) states that it 'proposes no change to the principle of accessibility on the same terms throughout the UK to services falling within the definition of universal service'.

[13] This arrangement only partially overcomes the funding problem because contributions to the fund are proportional to revenues not profits. To take an extreme case, if BT lost *all* its profitable markets to competition, then it would definitely make a loss on its social obligations because it would still have to contribute to the fund which financed these obligations.

per-customer charge to a network which wanted the service (the figure of £12 was suggested).[14]

As regards policy towards equal access, in contrast to policy in the USA, Oftel has not until now required that any such policy be introduced, nor does it appear that it will be in the future. Indeed, Oftel (1996e, p. 11) states that in 1995 it

> consulted on whether indirect access facilities should be extended by the introduction of 'equal access' arrangements. . . . Oftel has recently indicated that it considers the cost–benefit analysis it is required to make of such a change does not justify introducing equal access arrangements.

However, indirect access has nevertheless become somewhat easier in recent years, and currently a subscriber to Mercury's (or another indirect competitor's) trunk network need only dial an additional three or four digits compared to a BT subscriber.

(ii) Mobile network operation

Turning next to the mobile sector, the government followed another duopoly policy in this sector, and two mobile network operators, Cellnet and Vodafone, were licensed in 1985.[15] (The mobile sector was virtually non-existent in Britain before this time.) BT had, and still has, a controlling interest in Cellnet. In contrast to the fixed sector, mobile network operators were prohibited from retailing their services directly to the public, and instead had to wholesale their airtime to service providers. However, Cellnet and Vodafone were permitted to own or control service providers if they wished (and such service providers are termed 'tied service providers'). Since there was a danger that mobile operators would favour their tied service providers over independent service providers (ISPs), there were conditions in their licences which aimed to prohibit such behaviour. During this period, substantial profits were made by the two operators, but there was very vigorous competition at the service provision level. The idea behind the split between network operation and service provision was to try to introduce as much competition as possible subject to the constraint that there were only two operators. Given the limited competition upstream, it is plausible that a greater variety of packages of services would be offered to end-users under vertical separation than with integration. (It is not clear, though, why the same logic did not also apply to the fixed sector in the duopoly era.)

[14] See MMC (1995b, ch. 2).

[15] For more detail on the UK mobile sector, see Cave and Williamson (1996, section VI).

In 1991 the mobile duopoly policy came to an end, and two further operators were licensed: Mercury One-2-One (MOTO) and Orange. The government has announced that no further operators will be licensed until at least 2005. In contrast to the earlier period, all four operators are now permitted to retail services directly to the public, and MOTO and Orange have chosen to do this almost exclusively. The result has been that the ISPs have been squeezed severely in recent years, and it is possible that this sector could more or less vanish in the medium term — see Oftel (1996c). In contrast to the fixed sector, retail and interconnection charges for mobile telephony have never been controlled.

The number of subscribers to mobile networks has grown explosively, from around a million in 1990 to nearly 6m in 1996 (see Oftel, 1996c). In 1996, market shares of the four operators in terms of numbers of subscribers were Vodafone 43 per cent, Cellnet 42 per cent, Orange 8 per cent, and MOTO 7 per cent. Thus the market appears to be very unequally divided. However, the two newer operators are succeeding in gaining a large fraction of new subscribers (together they gained 42 per cent of the new connections in the first quarter of 1996).

(iii) Service provision

Here we discuss the provision of services over (fixed) telecommunications networks. Basic voice telephony has been mentioned above, so here we concentrate on enhanced services together with some international voice telephony. The market for most enhanced services is highly competitive. According to Oftel (1996a, p. 12), BT currently has a market share of around 50 per cent in this market which generates revenues of about £1 billion per annum. (Note, however, that Oftel does not include television services in its list of enhanced services.) However, BT's market power varies greatly within the sector, and for many data-based services BT has very low market share.

Perhaps the most important question with regard to enhanced services is the price BT is permitted to charge ISPs for the use of its network. Should ISPs be allowed to use BT's network at the same, low rate as rival network operators, or should they pay BT's full retail prices for the service (or something in between)? Should BT have discretion over what it charges ISPs, and if so, should it be allowed to make the charge depend upon the particular service which is to be offered? We discuss this point below in section 3(a), but Oftel's current policy (see Oftel, 1996d, p. 9) is that:

- ISPs offering basic international voice telephony *are* permitted to use BT's network at the same, low rate as are other network operators;

- all other ISPs do *not* have a right to these low charges, although BT 'should be allowed' to set charges which are lower than retail charges for end-users. However, it appears that BT does not have to offer discounts to ISPs if it chooses not to;
- there is a 'presumption against price discrimination between different types of ISP depending on the use to which' BT's network is put.

The anomalous position of international voice provision is said by Oftel to exist because of the recent duopoly of BT and Mercury in international network operation, which has only just expired, and the consequent need to encourage further competition in that sector.

3. Competition in Telecommunications: Some Theory

As is clear from the preceding discussion, the telecommunications industry is enormously complex, and there is a wide variety of kinds of competition involving various combinations of the four main sectors (fixed local network operation, mobile network operation, long-distance network operation and service provision). In this section we focus on just two stylized kinds of competition: one where there is competition only in those sectors without strong elements of natural monopoly, such as long-distance network operation and the provision of services; and one where there is competition for directly connected customers—see Figures 1 and 2 respectively. This pair of strategies, discussed below in sections 3(a) and 3(b) respectively, perhaps represents the two broad competitive strategies, which are not necessarily exclusive, that could be encouraged by a country's regulator.

In Figure 1, there is a single network operator which has all customers connected to its network (Firm M). This firm also operates a long-distance network and offers various services over the network. However, it faces competition in these two areas. Its rivals, if they are to be able to compete at all, need access to Firm M's customers. Rivals in the long-distance market—who are assumed only to offer the basic voice telephony service—need Firm M to originate and deliver calls, whereas rivals in the service provision sector need end-to-end conveyance from firm M (as they have no transmission links of their own). One important feature of this form of competition is the large asymmetry between Firm M and its rivals: rivals need to purchase vital inputs from M but not vice versa.

In Figure 2, by contrast, there are several networks with directly connected customers, and for simplicity let us suppose that the only service they offer is basic voice telephony. In addition, suppose we can

Figure 1

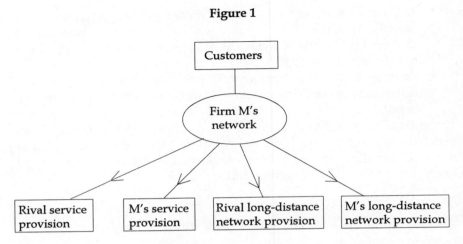

abstract away from long-distance network competition issues by assuming that each local operator has its own long-distance network. This model could apply in a highly stylized way either to the case of competing fixed networks (such as the cable companies/Mercury versus BT in Britain), or to competition in mobile telephony, or both. If, because of the large cost of connection to a network, we assume a user belongs to just one network, then in order to be able to offer its customers the ability to call all people, a network has to be able to gain access to other networks' subscribers. Thus, in this case, the market is more symmetric, at least in one sense: *each* firm has a monopoly on vital inputs needed by other firms.

(a) *Competition in Service Provision and Long-distance Network Operation*

(i) Competition in service provision

Consider first a very simple kind of competition. Suppose there is a service—say it is the service whereby calling a number a person can listen

Figure 2

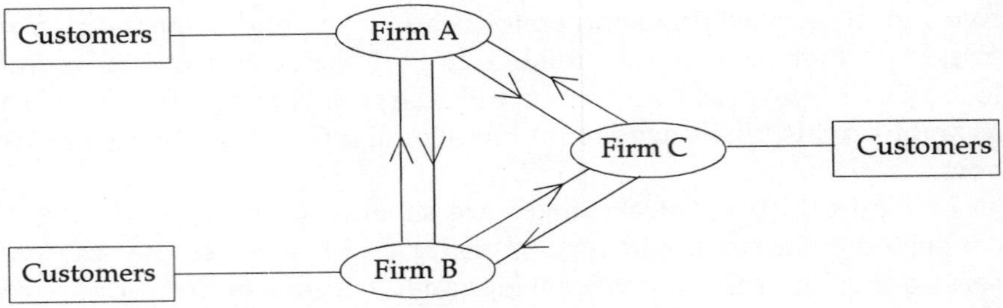

to today's weather forecast—which Firm M does not offer but which could be offered by many identical ISPs. (We suppose there is a competitive market in this service in order to abstract from issues of market power in its provision.) Suppose also that the provision of this service has no cross-effects on the demand for any other service offered by Firm M. Suppose it costs Firm M an amount b to provide the network services needed to supply a unit of the 'weather' service, and that it costs ISPs an additional amount c to provide a unit of the 'weather' service given that they have the necessary access to M's network. Therefore, the total unit cost of providing the service is $b + c$. Let a denote the unit charge made to ISPs for using M's network. Then, because there is a competitive market for providing the service, the equilibrium price for the service will be $a + c$. The question, then, is how should a be set?

One answer is obtained if we assume, for some reason, that Firm M's retail prices are taken as given when choosing a. Using the standard welfare measure of consumer surplus plus M's profits (ISPs make zero profits because of competition), it follows that we want the price of the 'weather' service (which is $a + c$) to be equal to its total cost, $b + c$—i.e. that $a = b$. This would *not* be true if there were cross-price effects on other services offered by M—see below. Therefore, this argument suggests that when they offer services which do not substitute for M's own services, ISPs should have access to M's network at marginal cost.

However, this answer followed from the unpalatable assumption that the choice of access charge a was made in isolation of the other pricing decisions for M. For instance, if M were allowed to charge more for access, then the profit could be used to reduce the price of M's own retail services if they are above marginal cost. It is extremely unlikely that all of M's services will be set equal to marginal costs for at least two reasons: (i) because of natural monopoly cost conditions in local network operation, pricing all services at marginal cost will cause M to run at a loss; and (ii) 'social' considerations will usually call for some prices to deviate from underlying costs. Therefore, using John Vickers's language from chapter 2 of this volume, there is a 'tax' on each of M's retail services paid by final customers. Given that this is necessarily so, why should ISPs be exempt from paying these taxes too?

Suppose, then, there is a break-even constraint on Firm M and that the marginal benefit to society if M's budget constraint is relaxed by £1 is denoted by $\lambda > 0$. (For small changes in M's budget, this can be taken to be a constant.) Therefore, if the profits of selling access to ISPs for the 'weather' service are used to relax M's budget constraint for other services and the access charge is a, total welfare is given by $q(p)(a - b) + v(p) + \lambda q(p)(a - b)$, where $v(p)$ is consumer surplus from the 'weather' service if its price is p and $q(p)$ is consumer demand for the service (where

$dv/dp = -q$), and $p = a + c$. This implies that the optimal access charge satisfies:

$$\frac{a-b}{p} = \frac{\theta}{\eta} > 0 \tag{1}$$

where $\eta > 0$ is the elasticity of consumer demand for the service and $\theta = \lambda/(1 + \lambda)$. This is just a standard Ramsey expression, and states that the access charge a should be set *above* the marginal cost of providing access, and the mark-up should be higher the less elastic is the demand for the service. In particular, even if there are no 'opportunity cost' terms present — and we will come to these shortly — then it is optimal to make the access charge depend upon the use to which the network is put (see chapter 2 in this volume, section 4(d)). Of course, detailed information about demand will not always be available, but that does not imply that the access charge should therefore be set equal to its cost.

Now consider another service which *does* act as a substitute for one of Firm M's services, international voice service provision.[16] The way an ISP would provide this service would be for it to lease lines between the home country and a set of overseas countries from a international network operator (possibly Firm M itself), and use M's network to originate a customer's calls and to transport the call to the point of connection to the leased lines. Suppose again there are many identical ISPs in this market, that their cost per unit of providing the service is c, given that they have the necessary use of M's national network, and that M's cost per unit of originating the calls is b. Suppose also that the ISPs' service is not *perfectly* substitutable for M's own international service. For instance, it may well be that the ISPs' service is inferior in that lengthy dialling codes are needed, a large minimum number of calls is required to be paid for in advance, and/or the service may be frequently congested. Finally, suppose that the ISPs' service has no cross-price effects on the demand for any other of M's services.

Since the ISP market is competitive, the price of the rival international service is $p = a + c$, where a is the access charge. Let M's price for its own international service be denoted by P and let its total unit cost of providing the service be C. With the two prices P and p, let the demand for the ISPs' service be $q(P, p)$ and the demand for M's international service be $Q(P, p)$. Each of these is decreasing in the own-price and, because services are substitutes, increasing in the rival's price. Finally, let $v(P, p)$ denote consumer surplus from international services, so that $v_p = -q$. (Here, subscripts

---

[16] The following is a simplified version of Armstrong *et al.* (1996), which builds on Laffont and Tirole (1994) and is also described in chapter 2 of this volume (section 4(b)).

denote partial derivatives.) If we consider again the case where the access charge a is chosen given M's retail prices (including P), then aggregate welfare in the international sector is $v(P, p) + Q(P, p)(P - C) + q(P, p)(a - b)$. The access charge that maximizes this is given by

$$a = b + \sigma[P - C], \tag{2}$$

where $\sigma = -Q_p/q_p > 0$ is the *displacement ratio* discussed in chapter 2 of this volume (section 4(c)) and measures the degree of substitutability between the pair of services. The term $\sigma[P - C]$ is M's 'opportunity cost' of providing a unit of access to ISPs, i.e. it is M's loss in profit caused by rivals supplying one further unit of the service. Expression (2) is a general version of the so-called *efficient component pricing rule* (or ECPR) which is discussed in chapter 2. If the two international services are very close substitutes, so that each unit of ISP supply more or less results in one unit less demand for M's own service, then s is almost equal to one and we obtain the 'margin rule' (as discussed in chapter 2, section 4(a)):

$$a = b + [P - C]. \tag{3}$$

In this case, and whenever σ is substantially greater than zero, the ideal access charge could be much higher than the direct cost of providing access if there is a substantial profit margin in M's international service business (as often is the case in practice). On the other hand, if the pair of services were only weak substitutes, then σ is close to zero and the access charge should be set close to its direct cost (as in the 'weather' example).

Again, though, this analysis ignores the fact that profits generated when M supplies access could be used to lower all of M's retail prices. When this factor is taken into account, the optimal access charge is simply given by (2) plus a standard Ramsey term:

$$a = b + \sigma[P - C] + \frac{\theta}{\eta}, \tag{4}$$

where $\eta > 0$ is the own-price elasticity of demand for the ISPs' service. Thus this discussion provides another reason, in addition to differing demand elasticities, for optimal access charges to differ according to the use made of M's network: opportunity costs may differ. In sum, according to this theory, the optimal mark-up of the access charge over the associated cost should be greater for (i) services with less elastic demand, (ii) services which closely substitute for the incumbent's own services (provided such services are profitable), and (iii) services in sectors in which the incumbent makes high profit margins.

(ii) Competition in long-distance network operation

In formal terms, the analysis here is virtually identical to that of competition in services. There is a group of firms which are able to provide long-distance network operation services, but who need firm M's local networks to pick up and deliver calls. Provided the group of firms is competitive—and so market power among the entrants is not important—the optimal access charge for using M's local networks is again given by expression (4) above, where b is M's combined cost of picking up and delivering calls to rivals' long-distance networks, σ measures the degree of substitutability between rival operators' and M's long-distance services, $[P - C]$ is M's profit margin in offering long-distance services, and η is the elasticity of demand for the rivals' service. (This formula can easily be adapted to the case where there is only a single rival to M in the sector, as was the case in the UK duopoly policy era.)

As with international service provision, it makes sense to suppose that the long-distance services are not perfect substitutes, although it is less clear that rival services are necessarily inferior to M's. For instance, the lack of 'equal access' in Britain (see above) means that (indirectly connected) users of Mercury's long-distance service have to dial additional digits to access the rival network, and this implies that such users will need a discount if they are to be tempted to change operator. On the other hand, Mercury offered its customers itemized bills well before the service was supplied by BT, and so this aspect of the service was superior to BT. However, in the UK the disadvantages must have outweighed the advantages since Mercury obtained only a modest market share despite offering significant discounts compared to BT's long-distance tariff. In the absence of strong evidence to the contrary, though, it seems plausible that the two firms' services are *fairly* close substitutes, and that σ is reasonably close to one.

(iii) Discussion of recent Oftel policy towards access charges

As described in section 2(c) above, current Oftel policy towards BT's access charges to ISPs is that, roughly speaking, BT is permitted to charge ISPs the same rate for using its network as it charges end-users. This entails a substantial mark-up over marginal costs, and we argued that this could be justified (see expression (4) above). However, from a theoretical point of view, this does not imply that all ISPs should pay the *same* mark-up as end-users; indeed, we argued that those offering services which significantly substitute for BT's own services should, all else equal, pay a higher access charge than those providing services that did not. It is clear, though, that Oftel is unlikely to possess the accurate information needed to implement the rule (4), and therefore it may be a fair compromise that ISPs should pay BT for the use of its network at roughly the same rate as end-users.

The only exceptions to this rule are independent international service providers, who are allowed to use BT's network at the much lower charges that BT is required to offer rival network operators. Superficially, at least, this policy runs directly counter to the above theory, since these ISPs provide a service which *is* closely substitutable to BT's international service and, moreover, BT has large profit margins in this sector. These factors suggest that international ISPs should, if anything, pay *higher* access charges than other ISPs, rather than less. However, the international sector has some peculiar features to do with the need to secure bilateral agreements with overseas operators, and it is perhaps more difficult to promote competition in network operation in this sector than elsewhere. Because of this it may be that prices are too high in this sector, and the policy of allowing ISPs to use BT's network at generous terms is one indirect way to reduce these prices. In any event, this sector has recently been liberalized and the anomalous position of the international ISPs may soon cease.

Turning to the position of long-distance competitors such as Mercury, Oftel policy is to grant competitors access to BT's network at a significant discount compared to end-users. Just as with the international ISPs, at first glance such a policy appears to contradict the principles described above: Mercury's trunk services are reasonably close substitutes for BT's (σ is close to one) and BT historically had made substantial profit margins on long-distance calls. Therefore, the simple theory suggests that long-distance operators should be granted *less* generous terms than many ISPs. However, this ignores one fundamental difference between the two types of competition, namely that entry into network operation involves considerable sunk cost investment. (Mercury needed to install a large-scale fibre-optic trunk network which had little alternative use.) Because of this, Mercury's profitability was vulnerable to *ex-post* changes in the regulatory regime over time and, for instance, new trunk operators could be licensed, or BT's prices could be regulated more tightly than anticipated. These dangers could make Mercury reluctant to invest at a desirable rate over time and countervailing policies were needed. One of these was the government's duopoly policy which guaranteed that Mercury would face no further entry into its market for 7 years; a second was to offer Mercury access to BT's network at generous terms. Perhaps for the same reason, other entrants in network operation have been granted favourable access terms compared to ISPs (and compared to the theoretical ECPR).[17]

[17] Direct evidence that Oftel believes that using the ECPR would stifle network competition is contained in Oftel (1996e, p. 31): 'Oftel's view is that the ECPR has some useful properties but that these are outweighed by its disadvantages, notably the possibility that it could, in the present state of the market, discourage the development of effective competition.'

(b) *Competition for Directly Connected Customers*

Here we discuss the type of competition illustrated in Figure 2.[18] Suppose there is just one service (basic voice telephony) and two firms competing for directly connected customers, networks A and B, say. Because of fixed connection costs, each user is connected to just one network, and the two networks must be interconnected if all users are to communicate with each other. In principle, there are several possible kinds of tariff structure: network A could make its charge for calls differ according to whether the destination was on network A or network B (a kind of price discrimination), or network A could charge the same price regardless of the destination network. We suppose that the latter tariff policy is required, largely because regulators seem unlikely to allow widespread price discrimination of the former kind between similar networks, especially on the part of a dominant operator.[19]

Because of the no-discrimination rule, each operator simply offers one price to its subscribers which is the charge for making a call to any destination. Denote the prices offered by the two networks by p_A and p_B respectively. For maximum simplicity, suppose that each network can choose one of just two prices, a 'high' price, p_H, and a 'low' price, p_L. Consumers observe the two announced prices and decide which network to join. Suppose that the networks offer services which are not perfect substitutes, and that even if one network offers a lower price than the other, the high price network may still attract some subscribers. To be specific, suppose there are N subscribers in total, and that all of these people will join one or other network (i.e. prices are not so high that some people are driven away altogether). The demand structure is perfectly symmetric, and if both networks offer the same price (high or low), half of the subscribers join each network. If one network offers a low price and the other a high price then the low price network obtains N_L subscribers and the high price network obtains $N - N_L$, where $N_L > N/2$. Moreover, once a person has joined a given network they make a number of calls which depends only on that network's price (and not the price of the rival network): this number of calls is q_L if the price is p_L and $q_H < q_L$ if the price is p_H. The final piece of the demand system is to describe how many calls a subscriber makes to users on their own network and how many they make to the rival network. Here we make the simplest assumption,

[18] The following is based on Armstrong (1996b) and Laffont *et al.* (1996).

[19] One exception to this rule is that some cable companies in Britain offer free local calls to other subscribers on the same network but not to BT's subscribers in the area. BT is permitted to make its call charges differ according to the destination network if that network is very dissimilar from BT's; in particular, BT's charges for calling mobile subscribers greatly exceed its charges to fixed subscribers. (In fact, at present BT's charges for calls to mobile subscribers are not regulated at all.)

namely that the fraction of calls to their own network is just the fraction of all subscribers on their network. Thus if both networks offer the same price they each have half the total population as subscribers, and any subscriber makes half their calls to people on their own network, and half to the rival network, whereas if a person is on a low price network and the other network offers high prices, then that person makes the fraction $N_L / N > 1/2$ of their calls to people on their own network.

Turning to the cost side, suppose that both networks are identical and there are just three components to network operation: a fixed cost F for a subscriber to connect to a network; a (constant) unit cost for originating a call of c_1; and a unit cost for terminating a call of c_2. The total cost of transmitting a call entirely within a single network is just $c_1 + c_2$. The networks are assumed to negotiate over the common charge for terminating a call on the other network, denoted t.

With this notation we can write the total profit of a network if both networks choose the low price as:

$$\pi_{LL} = \frac{Nq_L}{2}\left\{p_L - c_1 - \frac{c_2 + t}{2}\right\} + \frac{Nq_L}{4}(t - c_2) - \frac{NF}{2}.$$

Here, each network has $N/2$ subscribers, each of whom make q_L calls, half of which are to subscribers on the same network (which cost $c_1 + c_2$) and half of which are to the other network (which cost $c_1 + t$). In addition, each network makes profit from terminating calls from the rival network: there are $Nq_L / 4$ such calls and the network makes a margin $t - c_2$ on each of these. This expression simplifies to

$$\pi_{LL} = \frac{Nq_L}{2}\left\{p_L - c_1 - c_2\right\} - \frac{NF}{2}. \tag{5}$$

and so the profits do not depend on the interconnection charge t, the reason being that the number of calls made from network A to B is precisely equal to the number made from B to A and interconnection payments cancel out.

Similarly, if both networks charge a high price, each makes profit

$$\pi_{HH} = \frac{Nq_H}{2}\left\{p_H - c_1 - c_2\right\} - \frac{NF}{2}. \tag{6}$$

If the firms choose different prices, the low price firm makes profit

$$\pi_{LH}(t) = N_L q_L \left\{p_L - c_1 - c_2\right\}$$
$$- \frac{N - N_L}{N} N_L (q_L - q_H)(t - c_2) - N_L F \tag{7}$$

and the high price firm makes

$$\pi_{HL}(t) = (N - N_L)q_H \{p_H - c_1 - c_2\} + \frac{N - N_L}{N} N_L (q_L - q_H)(t - c_2)$$
$$- (N - N_L)F. \tag{8}$$

Notice that when the networks charge different prices they do care about the level of the termination charge, since there is a net outflow of calls from the low price to the high price network (because subscribers on the low price network make more calls than the others).

Finally, suppose that networks make more profit from setting high prices than low — i.e. $\pi_{LL} < \pi_{HH}$ — but overall welfare is higher with low prices than high. (So p_L could be thought of as the 'competitive' price and p_H the 'collusive' price.) The question is: if the firms are free to choose the termination charge t, how will they do this? Since firms prefer high prices, they will agree to choose t so that

$$\pi_{LH}(t) < \pi_{HH} \tag{9}$$

because in this case the collusive price p_H can be sustained. (If network A, say, chooses p_H then so will B, since by 'deviating' to the low price it will make lower profits by (9).) From (7), (9) is satisfied if t is chosen sufficiently large, and we deduce that if firms are free to choose the termination charge they will set a *high* charge because this will sustain the collusive retail price. The reason why high interconnection charges are able to do this is that they make undercutting a rival's retail price very costly, since the low price firm has a net outflow of calls to the high price rival, and this results in very costly interconnection payments. Thus we see that the firms in this symmetric setting should be able to reach agreement on interconnection charges since their interests coincide; this is in stark contrast to section 3(a) where firms had conflicting interests.

On the other hand, because the regulator would prefer the two firms to set low prices, if the termination charge is regulated it should be set in order to make low prices an equilibrium, i.e. t should satisfy:

$$\pi_{HL}(t) < \pi_{LL}. \tag{10}$$

From (8), this occurs whenever t is set sufficiently *low*.

This simple model can easily be extended to the discussion of non-symmetric cases, for instance, when there is a regulated incumbent facing an entrant and there is no number portability (so that the entrant must offer a discount on the incumbent's tariff if it is to be able to attract any customers at all). In such a framework it is no longer the case that the interests of the two firms coincide, since typically there will be a net inflow of calls to the incumbent's network — the incumbent will have to deliver more calls from the entrant than vice versa — and so, as in section 3(a), the incumbent will generally prefer a higher interconnection charge than the entrant.

In any event, this model suggests that even when there is competition for directly connected customers the need for regulation of interconnection remains. Therefore Oftel's suggestion that 'there may come a point . . . where competition alone is sufficient to restrain prices and formal price controls are not needed' (Oftel, 1996e, p. 7) is still a matter for debate (although the statement may well be true for retail price regulation provided that interconnection charges are suitably controlled).

4. Conclusions

This chapter has discussed some aspects of competition in telecommunications, both from a theoretical perspective and in the context of recent regulatory policy towards the industry in the UK. Several important topics have, however, been omitted. In the UK context, one crucial issue is how to control anti-competitive behaviour on the part of a dominant firm towards its rivals. One important form of anti-competitive behaviour, of course, is the setting of excessive access and interconnection charges, and we have analysed this topic at length, but there are many other kinds of potentially anti-competitive conduct, including other ways of raising rivals' costs and various methods of predation, and this topic deserves a chapter on its own.[20]

In section 2, those economic features of telecommunications that make competition policy so complicated were discussed. Perhaps the two most salient aspects were: (i) the fixed costs of a subscriber being connected to a network (both for fixed and mobile networks); and (ii) network externalities between subscribers. These two factors taken together imply that network interconnection has enormous significance for policy. It is possible to think of other industries that have the property (i), including the other network industries (gas, electricity, water, and so on), as well as those that have property (ii), such as postal services, but hardly any have the two together. The regulation of network interconnection was discussed in section 3(b) above, and it was argued there that for however long technology has the feature (i), regulation of interconnection was likely to be necessary to achieve desirable outcomes. Moreover, this could be true even if network operators were symmetrically

[20] For an account of Oftel policy in this area, see Oftel (1996c).

placed in terms of market share, rather than the current situation of dominance by one firm.

Another implication of property (i) is that, for fixed networks where the local loop investment has already been sunk by the incumbent firm, competition seems easiest to achieve in those sectors *not* involving new investment in the local loop, such as long-distance competition (with indirect access) and competition in services. This type of competition, where the incumbent firm continues to provide local connection to subscribers (especially residential subscribers), does not require wide-spread duplication of the local loop.

Some aspects of access pricing in this setting were discussed in section 3(a), and we argued that, where the information is available and where the incumbent's retail prices were regulated, access charges should usually be set to exceed the direct cost of access, and the price/cost mark-up should be greater if the incumbent incurs significant opportunity costs (i.e. lost profit) from entry, and if the rival service has inelastic demand. (This rule is known as the ECPR.) However, such detailed information is unlikely to be available, and so a policy whereby the incumbent's network charges are closely related to its charges to end-users (with some modest discount to allow for economies of scale in providing the network services) is perhaps a reasonable compromise. In addition, the ECPR rule ignores the sunk-cost aspect of long-distance competition compared to most service provision, and this difference may justify a discount on access charges for long-distance operators compared to service providers. This is very broadly consistent with current Oftel policy on access pricing.

Although a policy of encouraging competition in sectors other than local network operation has the benefit of avoiding much costly dupli-cation of infrastructure, it has the drawback that the incumbent firm with its near monopoly of directly connected subscribers may be able to distort competition in other, potentially more competitive parts of the industry. One example of this is the lack of 'equal access' for rival long-distance operators, whose customers must dial additional digits or purchase special telephones to gain access to the rival network. Regula-tory policy to overcome each and every one of these advantages will be complex, costly, and imperfect, and this drawback may help justify the encouragement of competition in local networks, despite costly duplica-tion. (Of course, there may be benefits of having multiple local operators in addition to stimulating long-distance competition, such as having increased choice of local network services.) However, even where local network competition is introduced, it seems likely that regulation of retail or interconnection charges will remain necessary for the foresee-able future.

Early policy in the UK—which was determined by government rather than Oftel—seemed to focus on the strategy of encouraging the former 'indirect' kind of competition, at least for residential users, and Mercury secured only a modest number of directly connected subscribers. However, since the end of the duopoly policy, Oftel and the government's policy has become very definitely one of encouraging competition in the local loop, despite the additional infrastructure investment such a policy entails. For instance, some local loop competitors to BT are permitted to operate in markets barred to BT (cable television companies are, of course, permitted to supply television services whereas BT is not), and some are permitted to use technology barred to BT (Ionica is permitted to use radio links for the local loop whereas BT, for the most part, is not). Moreover, BT's rivals at the local level are now likely to be allowed number portability from BT at advantageous terms. Indeed, Oftel now seems to believe that 'indirect' competition has only a limited role to play in serving customers' needs, and its reluctance to introduce 'equal access' is an illustration of this.[21]

Oftel's current policy, then, represents a pessimistic view of the ability of regulation to make 'indirect' competition effective and vigorous, and that the benefits of local competition outweigh the substantial costs. Probably no other country has taken such pro-active steps to ensure the viability of local competition, and so, as is also the case with electricity, Britain is engaged in an experiment in industrial policy. It will be some years before we can judge whether this experiment has been successful.

[21] For instance, Oftel (1996e, p. 11) states: 'Oftel considers that greater competition in the international and national markets will have little impact for most residential customers, since they generally take all their calls as a combined package of local/ national/international calls from their local access provider. Indirect access would allow residential customers to take advantage of greater competition in these markets but the take-up in the residential market has been low. . . . Residential customers will, therefore, in most cases only be able to take advantage of the greater competition in national and international calls when they have effective competition amongst alternative local access providers.'

Also, Oftel (1996a, p. 10) states: 'Although competition from and between service providers can provide increased choice for consumers, this is not an adequate substitute for competition between networks. Only competition between networks can deliver competition in the supply of network services which are a necessary input into basic retail or enhanced services for consumers. Without network competition, even vigorous competition between service providers will not prevent customers from being disadvantaged by inefficient and/or expensive provision of such network services.'

7

The Water Industry

SIMON COWAN*

1. Introduction

The water industry is the most monopolistic of the utilities that have been privatized in the United Kingdom. Duplication of the networks of water mains and sewerage is generally undesirable and there is, at present, no competition in supply using common networks. Nevertheless, the UK government and the industry regulator are keen to expand the role of competition. Many issues that have been prominent when competition was first introduced into telecommunications and energy markets are also present in the water industry. A major theme of this chapter is that direct product-market competition is unlikely to be as prevalent and as successful in water as it has been in other regulated markets. In the remainder of the introduction I describe the characteristics of the industry and its regulation. For further details see Armstrong *et al.* (1994, ch. 10).

Ten regional companies in England and Wales supply both water and sewerage services. The water and sewerage companies (WaSCs) are the successors to the publicly owned regional water authorities established in 1974. Under the principle of 'integrated river basin management' (IRBM), all water-related activities (abstraction, treatment, distribution, sewerage, sewage treatment and disposal, and environmental regulation) within the catchment areas of major rivers were performed by one authority. When the WaSCs were privatized in 1989 the function of regulating water pollution was transferred to the National Rivers Authority, while the companies remained vertically integrated in all other activities.[1] The legacy of IRBM is that the WaSCs' areas are relatively large and there is little cross-border trading between them. Within the

---

* Worcester College, University of Oxford. I would like to thank Mark Armstrong, Andrew Glyn, Dieter Helm, Tim Jenkinson, and David Newbery for helpful comments. They are not responsible for any errors.

[1] The National Rivers Authority became part of the Environment Agency in 1996.

regions of the WaSCs, however, there are companies that supply water (but not sewerage services) in designated areas in place of the local WaSC. At the time of privatization in 1989 there were 28 water-only companies (WoCs), supplying about a quarter of the total population of England and Wales. This has since been reduced by mergers to 8.[2]

The industry is regulated by the Director General of Water Services (the DG) who heads the Office of Water Services (Ofwat). He is obliged under the Water Industry Act 1991, 'to secure that companies are . . . able (in particular by securing reasonable returns on their capital) to finance the proper carrying out of [their] functions'. The reference in the legislation to reasonable returns on capital is unique to the water sector. The DG is also required, among other duties, to ensure that the interests of customers in rural areas are protected, to ensure that tariffs are not unduly preferential or discriminatory, and to facilitate, but not promote, effective competition.

Water companies are allowed to raise average prices each year by RPI + K, where RPI stands for the percentage increase in the retail price index and K is a company-specific number that reflects the increases in the costs of meeting environmental and quality obligations and the scope for operating cost efficiency. Prices have generally grown in real terms because of the large capital expenditure programmes of the companies. The RPI + K formula, known as the 'tariff basket', takes account of the multi-product nature of the industry by dividing the outputs into five categories, namely, metered and unmetered water, metered and unmetered sewerage, and trade effluent. About 90 per cent of domestic households have no meter and are charged according to the rateable values of their properties.[3] The weighted average increase in the prices of these five items can grow by no more than RPI + K, with the weights given by the previous accounting year's share of that item in total revenue. The tariff basket thus allows rebalancing between different prices, subject to the condition that tariffs should not show undue preference or discrimination.

The market values of the water companies' assets at the time of privatization were below the replacement cost levels, and prices are not determined by these asset values. Instead, the regulator sets the price so that an efficient company can expect to earn a reasonable return on an updated version of the initial market value of the assets. This automatically gives incumbent firms an advantage over competitors who have to

[2] There is also a very small water-only company, Cholderton, which is usually excluded from industry statistics.

[3] Rateable values were used as the basis of local authority taxation in England and Wales until the ill-fated poll tax was introduced in 1990.

build new infrastructure, because they will have to pay the full replacement cost to purchase those assets.

The rest of the chapter assesses the role for competition in water. In section 2, I describe the types of competition that are relevant. Section 3 discusses the current framework for product-market competition. Section 4 considers the recent plans to boost the role of competitive forces in the water industry. Section 5 assesses the development of competition so far. Conclusions are in section 6.

2. Types of Competition

The appropriate approach to regulatory policy is to define precisely where the natural monopoly element is, to focus regulation on this area — noting that natural monopoly conditions can change over time as technology and demand alter — and to encourage competition everywhere else. In electricity, gas, and railways the standard argument is that the supply of services over the network is competitive while the network (wires, pipes, track) is naturally monopolistic. In water, the implicit assumption at the time of privatization in 1989 was that the whole of the business is naturally monopolistic and that the role for competition would be very marginal.

There is some empirical evidence to justify the assumption of natural monopoly. A sufficient condition for natural monopoly conditions to hold is that there are unexhausted scale economies. Econometric analysis suggests that operating expenditure in both water and sewerage services rises less than proportionately with output, so marginal costs are below average variable costs (see MMC, 1996c, Appendices 4.2 and 4.4). Further evidence comes from Ofwat (1996a), which assesses unit costs, including capital costs, and notes that the dry conditions in 1995 increased the demand for water and sewerage services and thus reduced unit costs.

Of course this evidence does not imply that competitive forces cannot operate in the industry. Five types of competition can be applied to the water industry:

(i)   yardstick competition;
(ii)   competition for the market;
(iii) contracting out of services;
(iv)   capital-market competition;
(v)   product-market competition.

Yardstick competition uses the fact that the industry is geographically separated. The idea is to relate firm A's allowed price to firm B's unit cost level, thus giving A the incentive to be efficient and cut costs, which in turn lowers the allowed price of B. Such regulation works better the greater the correlation between the exogenous shocks (or cost drivers) that affect the costs of the firms. A simple way to perform yardstick competition is to use a regression of unit costs on the exogenous factors driving costs (see Shleifer, 1985), although in practice it has not been possible to apply yardstick competition in a mechanical way.

A complication in the application of yardstick competition is that firms might merge. In particular, the boundaries of the WoCs are rather arbitrary and mergers between them might be expected to produce efficiency gains. Proposed mergers between most water companies must be assessed by the Monopolies and Mergers Commission (MMC), which is required to take account of the fact that a merger will reduce the number of different water enterprises and thus reduce the DG's ability to conduct yardstick competition. Until recently, the tendency of the MMC has been to note that the merger will reduce the ability of the DG to make comparisons, conclude that it is therefore not in the public interest, but to allow it as long as most of the estimated gains in efficiency are passed though to customers in the form of lower prices. In 1996, however, the MMC reported on the two competing bids by WaSCs for South West Water and recommended that neither takeover should proceed — see MMC (1996c, d). It concluded (MMC, 1996c, p. 4), that 'no remedy, even in the shape of very significant price reductions, would be sufficient to compensate for the loss of [South West Water Services] as a comparator'. In his evidence to the MMC, the DG argued in favour of diversity of ownership 'to secure the greatest variety of management styles and techniques' (MMC, 1996c, p. 14). The fact that this was the first proposed takeover of a WaSC by another WaSC worried the MMC, as this would reduce the number of independent companies providing sewerage services from ten to nine. Previous mergers had not affected the number of companies providing sewerage. The MMC did not, however, believe that the cost to the regulator of losing a comparator could be quantified reliably. Similarly, in 1997 the proposed takeover of Mid Kent Water by SAUR and General Utilities was blocked on comparative-efficiency grounds.

Franchising of services is an option when product-market competition is not feasible. Usually it is combined with public ownership of the main sunk assets. In the UK franchising has, of course, been used for train services. In the water context franchising is used in France and in many developing countries which want to increase the role of the private sector in infrastructure (see World Bank, 1994), but it has not been used in the water industry in England and Wales.[4] Franchising is easiest to operate when the franchisee does not have large investment obligations, because franchisees do not need to worry about not recovering sunk investments when the contract is reassessed. This condition did not hold in the case of the water industry in England and Wales in 1989.

Closely related to franchising is contracting out of services. Throughout both the private and public sectors, organizations now focus on their 'core competencies' and contract out parts of their activities, sometimes to in-house teams. In the case of the water industry, activities such as information technology, billing and revenue collection, and maintenance have been contracted out. The advantage to the company of contracting out is clear—if there is sufficient competition to provide the designated service then cost efficiencies can be achieved. In the public sector, compulsory competitive tendering and market testing has become commonplace. Whether it is appropriate for regulators of private-sector firms to require them to put various functions out to tender is another matter—the private incentives of the firms are generally in line with the regulator's objectives, and the style of UK regulation has been not to try to second-guess management decisions on the appropriate way to run the business. Ofwat wants to encourage further market testing and competitive tendering, but at the same time to make sure that contracts with in-house teams and associate companies are more transparent.

Competition in the capital market can be thought of as a private-sector version of yardstick regulation. Littlechild (1986) reported to the Department of the Environment (DoE) on the prospects for water privatization and emphasized that the ability of investors to make comparisons between different companies in the same sector would be an important incentive mechanism for firms. A firm that was inefficient would see this reflected in its share price and would be vulnerable to takeover. Of course if there are other constraints on takeovers, such as the desire to maintain enough independent firms to be able to do yardstick competition, the forces of capital-market competition will not work.

As far as direct product-market competition is concerned, it would be inefficient to have competing networks of mains and sewers given the current state of technology and demand. The fact that the existing mains networks are naturally monopolistic does not, however, imply that *additions* should be owned and operated by incumbent firms, as long as they link in to the networks appropriately. Duplication of single pipe-

---

[4] Franchising was considered when the privatization of Scottish water services was being considered in the early 1990s—see McMaster and Sawkins (1993)—and a contract to build and operate a sewage treatment plant in the north of Scotland under the Private Finance Initiative (PFI) was awarded in late 1996. Further PFI schemes are being considered in Scotland.

lines might be economic if there is sufficient demand or if there are gains from product differentiation, i.e. the provision of water of different quality. The geographically fragmented nature of the industry means that there can be cross-border competition. Competition in telecommunications, gas, and electricity has relied to a large extent on the shared use of naturally monopolistic networks, and such competition in supply via common carriage is an obvious possibility in the water industry. In the following sections I discuss the possible role for product-market competition in more detail.

3. The Framework for Product-Market Competition since Privatization

The framework for competition in water was established by the Water Act 1989, which introduced the concept of an *inset appointment*. The provisions were amended in the Competition and Service (Utilities) Act 1992 (the 1992 Act). A company can apply for an appointment to provide water (or sewerage) to a customer located anywhere within the area of an existing company. Originally, the only customers eligible for inset supply were *new* customers, including green-field development sites and existing customers who received a private supply of water. The 1992 Act extended the potential customer base by allowing existing *large* customers to receive inset supplies. There are about 600 large customers, defined as those likely to be supplied with at least 250 megalitres of water a year. Such customers must agree to the proposed inset appointment. A company with an inset is appointed for an indefinite period and has the same duties as other water companies. Ofwat (1995b) and Pethick (1996) provide more details. The 1992 Act also allowed cross-border competition for domestic customers. Companies asked by domestic customers from another area for a supply have an obligation to meet it, provided the customers pay for the pipelines needed. This provides a source of potential competition without the requirement to go through the complex process required for an inset appointment. So far, there has been no actual cross-border competition, though there has been some interest shown by groups of households. In this section the focus will be on inset competition.

Ofwat (1995b) suggests that there are four possible sources of supply associated with inset appointments: new sources (or new sewage treatment works); a direct connection to another system (typically the neighbouring system); a bulk water supply from the previous supplier at the boundary of the site; and common carriage. An inset appointee who has a bulk supply does not own the raw water, treat it, nor arrange for its transportation to the boundary of the customer's site. Instead, these activities are carried out by the incumbent supplier, who charges the inset appointee a wholesale price covering the relevant costs. The inset appointee thus acts only as a retailer. Under common carriage a supplier would own the water, treat it, pay for its transportation through another company's network, and supply the final customer. Common carriage will be discussed in more detail in the next section. The costs of building new connections mean that, in practice, the main source of water for inset appointments will be bulk supplies. If the entrant and the incumbent cannot agree the terms of the bulk supply, then the DG can determine them. He is required to make sure that the company that is asked to provide a bulk supply can cover its costs (including capital costs) and is able to meet its supply obligations, while at the same time facilitating effective competition. The DG intends to use long-run marginal cost to determine bulk supply or sewerage charges when the parties do not agree.

The difficulty about requiring incumbents to make bulk supplies available to competitors is apparent in the Mid Kent takeover bid. This small WoC was subject to a hostile joint bid from two neighbouring companies, General Utilities and SAUR, and the bid was referred to the MMC. The takeover was motivated by the desire of the two predators, who are short of new water sources, to obtain access to Mid Kent's water resources. Mid Kent argued that it could share its resources with the two companies via bulk supplies, but General Utilities and SAUR prefer full integration. The predators argued that bulk supply arrangements are unreliable, because Mid Kent has little incentive to share its resources with them. Similar difficulties can be expected when inset appointees seek bulk supplies from incumbents.

The extension of inset appointments to allow large customers to be targeted has induced 20 companies to introduce 'large-user tariffs' designed to meet any potential competition. These tariffs were introduced in 1995. Most companies allow customers to choose between the standard two-part tariff and one with a higher fixed charge and lower charge per unit of water. One company offers more than one alternative two-part tariff, and several companies have non-linear tariffs with declining prices for successive blocks of consumption and no need for customers to choose *ex ante* which tariff to be on. The effect of all of these schemes is that there are quantity discounts for large users that vary from about 1 per cent to about 30 per cent for a customer with a 300 megalitre demand.

The tariff basket form of price control allows firms to rebalance their tariffs and one effect of the introduction of large-user tariffs has been slightly higher prices for other customers. This rebalancing can be justified by the fact that large customers were previously paying too much and were effectively cross-subsidizing smaller customers. The DG wants to ensure that tariff rebalancing does not go too far, and intends to remove large customers from the tariff basket formula. This would mirror the reductions in the scope of price control in telecommunications, gas, and electricity as competition has progressed. It should be noted that the tariff basket formula does *not* allow other charges to be raised when a customer is lost because of competition, so there is currently an asymmetry in the effect of potential and actual competition on other customers' charges.

Ofwat (1995*a,b*) discusses the principles that should apply to large-user tariffs. It argues that marginal or per-unit charges for large customers should not be lower simply because more water is consumed, presumably because large-user discounts represent a form of price discrimination that is thought to be undesirable or at least contrary to the legal duty of the DG to prohibit 'undue' discrimination. Instead, Ofwat argues that there should be a cost-based justification for discounts. One source of lower costs might be the fact that large customers have relatively stable demands and thus do not contribute to peak costs (Ofwat, 1991). Ofwat (1995*a*) suggests a further source of cost differences. It is cheaper to supply large users taking water from large pipes before the water passes into the local distribution system. The price of delivering such wholesale or bulk water should not reflect the 'retail' costs of the bypassed local distribution system.

Two principles discussed by Ofwat seem reasonable. First, tariffs should be structured to avoid giving incentives to waste water. Such an incentive would exist if the payment schedule jumped down at some point, i.e. if there were a region where a small increase in consumption would lead to a reduction in the total bill paid. Medium-sized gas customers on the standard tariff have at times wanted to burn gas unnecessarily to qualify for lower 'contract' prices. The second principle is that any large-user tariffs should be published and should be made available to all customers in similar circumstances, rather then negotiated individually. Again there is a close parallel with experience in the gas industry. The first MMC report on British Gas (MMC, 1988) required it to price according to a published schedule instead of offering individual confidential contracts, to make entry by competitors easier.

Three main types of inset appointments can be expected. First, there will be cases where a bulk supply is not required because the long-run marginal cost of the incumbent is significantly above that of the entrant, who is a neighbouring company. If the saving to the customer caused by switching to the entrant's (lower) large-user tariff exceeds the cost of building and operating a new pipeline, the customer will want to change supplier and, as long as both large-user tariffs reflect marginal costs, the change will be socially desirable. Second, the incumbent might not offer a large-user tariff — they are not obliged to do so and at present about a third of companies do not. They are, however, obliged to offer bulk supplies, and Ofwat will aim to ensure that these are priced at long-run marginal cost. An inset appointee could offer two types of supply to the customer in this case. It could either provide its own water and build a connection or obtain a bulk supply from the incumbent at marginal cost and then retail the water to the customer using the existing infrastructure. This form of competition is likely to force incumbents to develop their own large-user tariffs to avoid the loss of retail margins that such competition would entail. The third possibility is that the large-user tariff does not reflect marginal costs but the bulk supply rate does, so an entrant can come in, obtain a bulk supply at marginal cost and sell at a profit to those customers on the large-user tariff whose costs of supply are below the tariff rate.

At present, only two inset appointments have been announced. The new water supplier for Buxted Chicken, based in Suffolk, will be its sewerage supplier, Anglian Water, replacing Essex and Suffolk Water. The customer will be charged on Anglian's large-user tariff, and Anglian will lay a pipe from its area. The Anglian large-user tariff is always cheaper than the rival tariff for all relevant volumes.[5] For a volume of 300 megalitres a year the customer would save £49,244 annually by going on to the Anglian tariff, which is equivalent to 25 per cent, although the costs of the new pipeline must be offset against this saving. Anglian also plans to offer sewerage services to a greenfield site in Yorkshire. About 20 further applications for inset appointments are being considered.

4. Plans for the Development of Competition

In April 1996 the DoE issued a consultation paper *Water: Increasing Customer Choice*, and Ofwat issued *The Regulation of Common Carriage Agreements*. The UK government had decided that competition in water should be on the policy agenda in response to the drought of 1995 and public concern about the remuneration of top managers. The DoE paper made proposals in four main areas: common carriage, inset appointments, cross-border supply, and connections. I first discuss the DoE's views on the last three areas.

[5] The Anglian tariff has a fixed charge of £7,920 and a marginal price of 46.25 pence per cubic metre supplied, while the Suffolk tariff has a higher fixed charge of £25,450 (for a 6-inch meter) and a higher marginal price of 58.93 pence per cubic metre. See Ofwat (1997a).

On inset appointments the DoE suggests three changes to liberalize the market further. First, more large customers will be able to have inset supplies. The existing rule applied only to individual sites with annual demands of 250 megalitres, and the proposal is to allow adjacent premises belonging to the same organization to qualify for an inset appointment. Second, inset appointments need not be for indefinite periods. The idea is that the DG would be able to make an appointment for 5 or 10 years and nominate in advance another company to take over if the existing one did not want to continue at the end of the period. This will require careful thought about the terms on which any assets involved in the inset appointment are transferred. The inset appointee will have an option of withdrawal and the successor company has an obligation to take over if this option is exercised. The successor company is likely to seek payment of some sort for being the counter-party to this option if it incurs extra costs. Third, incumbents will be obliged to offer terms for bulk supplies or sewerage connection. This says nothing about the nature of these terms (which can be imposed by the DG in the event of disagreement) but it would speed the process of concluding agreements.

The 1992 Act allowed cross-border competition for domestic customers only, and DoE (1996) recommends the extension of this to non-domestic customers. Industrial, commercial, and agricultural customers situated near the boundaries of water companies are likely to be more interested in this type of competition than domestic customers. The third proposal of DoE (1996) is that competition in making connections to the network be encouraged by giving customers the right to make the connection, subject to various quality standards. The costs of connection by the incumbent are recovered from the customer and hence there is little incentive for the work to be done efficiently.

The main focus of DoE (1996) is on common carriage. Under the proposals, entrants will be given a statutory right to use an existing water company's network to supply large customers. Since the waters of the entrant and the incumbent will mix, both will have the same quality obligations. The waters will also have to show similar non-health characteristics, such as the degree of water softness. Although the most likely source of entrants will be existing water companies, the proposals allow new suppliers to obtain direct supply licences. Entrants will not have the full set of obligations of existing water companies; for example, they will not have an obligation to supply all customers in a particular area.

Incumbent firms will have a duty to provide potential entrants with details of the terms on which they would be willing to accept use of their pipelines for common carriage. Agreements between the two parties are expected to cover the volume and type of water supplied, connection and metering, payment of charges to the incumbent for connection and transportation, top-up and stand-by supplies, and the circumstances, when the incumbent can interrupt the entrant's supplies. If agreement cannot be reached, then the DG will be able to determine the matter.

DoE (1996) suggests various safeguards against adverse consequences from common carriage. The DG will be able to intervene to prevent a common-carriage proposal if it would significantly increase the risk of supply disruptions, and he will be allowed to terminate or vary the terms of a common-carriage agreement in the last resort on grounds of water quality. On pricing, DoE (1996, p. 10) notes that the price the entrant should pay for access to the incumbent's network should reflect the 'cost of . . . usage' and should therefore avoid cross-subsidy between the customers of the entrant and the incumbent. The DoE notes that the existing water licences prevent (i) undue discrimination, (ii) tariff rebalancing as a result of loss of customers, and (iii) offering certain customers low prices to deter entry. The DG will be given powers to prevent common-carriage agreements that would lead to adverse price rises for other customers.

Ofwat (1996b) discusses in more detail the terms of common-carriage agreements. One issue concerns leakage. Transportation and distribution of any commodity are typically subject to losses, and water leakage rates in the UK are relatively high. The entrant would have to supply more water than its customers consumed in order to allow for leakage. Ofwat recommends that the leakage adjustment should be the lower of the incumbent's actual leakage rate and the industry weighted average rate.

The main issue for common carriage concerns the access terms. Ofwat (1996b, p. 5) says that the access charge for the use of the incumbent's system should cover the transportation of the entrant's water to its customers. In setting this charge in cases where there is disagreement between the entrant and incumbent, the DG will use information on the incumbent's charges for its own customers' use of the system. These are currently volume-related but, within a customer class, they do not depend on distance. British Gas had similar internal transportation charges before competition for larger gas customers arrived. Ofwat states that one possibility is to require the incumbent to avoid discrimination between the use-of-system charges that apply in its common-carriage agreements and the use-of-system element of its own final supply charges.

5. Assessment of Competition in the Water Industry

In this section the existing framework of competition and the proposals to extend it are assessed. I discuss large-user tariffs and inset appointments, the 1996 common-carriage proposals, and cross-border competition.

(a) *Inset Appointments and Large-user Tariffs*

The main effect of the 1992 extension of the customer base for inset appointments was the introduction of large-user tariffs by about two-thirds of companies. Willig (1978) showed that offering optional two-part tariffs can cause a Pareto improvement, as long as all customers are final consumers and the existing tariff is retained as an option. The two-part tariffs offered by the majority of water companies, however, do not satisfy these two conditions. Customers who can benefit from the quantity discounts are most likely to be industrial and commercial firms. Quantity discounts will make these firms more competitive in their own markets against smaller rivals who cannot take advantage of the lower tariffs and who thus suffer lower profits because of the introduction of quantity discounts. In addition, Willig's result relies on the standard tariff being fixed, and in the water case the existing tariffs were raised (slightly) when the large-user tariffs were introduced, while still satisfying the price caps. Of course, it would be surprising if the tariffs caused Pareto improvements — if they did, the companies would almost certainly have introduced them much sooner. The general conclusion from the introduction of the tariffs is that, while the large customers clearly gained, their smaller rivals and other water customers have been made marginally worse-off.

A standard result in the non-linear pricing literature is that the largest customer pays a marginal price equal to marginal cost (whether the firm's objective is profits or welfare).[6] Without more information on costs, it is not possible to say whether this property holds in practice. The DG has stated that he believes that there is no need for further rebalancing of large-user tariffs. His concern is that further reductions in prices might be designed to deter entry. Ofwat has asked companies to provide information on long-run marginal costs, i.e. it wants to apply the incremental cost test derived from contestability theory to check that prices are not unreasonably low and thus do not act to deter entry. A complication here is that because of the large gap between the market value of

---

[6] Two recent papers show that this result need not hold if the welfare function is non-standard or if the firm is regulated. Sharkey and Sibley (1993) show that with self-selecting two-part tariffs, if the surpluses of consumers have weights that increase with customer size, the optimal marginal price for the largest customer is below marginal cost. Armstrong *et al.* (1995) show that when the firm's average revenue is regulated the marginal price at the top will be below marginal cost, because this relaxes the constraint and allows prices paid by smaller customers to be raised.

assets and the replacement cost value, current cost rates of return are well below the marginal cost of capital. If the asset base used to determine the price floor is the market value, then entrants are unlikely to be able to compete when supply requires new sunk assets. But using the full replacement cost value of assets will force prices to large customers to rise.

The DG views quantity discounts without a cost-based justification as undesirable. While such pricing may be discriminatory in a legal sense, it is often more efficient than uniform pricing. Existing large-user tariffs are currently simple in structure. Thackray (1995) notes that we should expect them to become more sophisticated over time. In particular, there will be efficiency gains from varying the marginal prices across the year and, when metering technology allows, across the day. Different prices for interruptible and non-interruptible services would also be efficient.

The first example of actual product-market competition through an inset appointment was for a customer located near the boundary of two companies' areas. I discuss the efficiency of such competition in the subsection on cross-border competition. In section 3, two other types of inset appointment were considered. The first type is where the incumbent does not offer a large-user tariff but does offer a bulk supply. Rivals might take a bulk supply from the incumbent and capture its retail margin by setting the final price below the incumbent's level. Why would the incumbent give rivals such an opportunity? In general, it wants to offer a large-user tariff that is related to the bulk supply price and which allows no room for profitable entry. The effect of the threat of inset appointments in these cases is likely to be that the remaining companies will offer large-user tariffs, rather than any actual entry. The other type of inset appointment is where there is a large-user tariff but it is priced above marginal cost, while the bulk supply tariff is at marginal cost. Again there is room for profitable entry, but only because the two tariffs are out of line. The incumbent has an incentive in the long run to ensure that such competitive opportunities do not exist. While the threat of inset appointments through bulk supplies is powerful, the number of actual appointments using this mechanism is likely to be low.

(b) *Common Carriage*

Without a national water grid, competition through common carriage can only take place at a regional level. Several benefits might accrue from such competition. First, retail margins might be cut, although these have already been reduced for those companies that have large-user tariffs. Second, such competition will put pressure on the upstream businesses. The costs of abstracting and treating water might fall. Finally, differentiation is possible—customers may want innovative contracts, e.g. for interruptibility, that the incumbent retailer does not offer.

Whether such gains are worth the extra costs involved in establishing common-carriage competition is very unclear. The costs of abstraction, treatment, and retailing to large customers are small relative to the costs of transportation. In any case, incumbents already have an incentive to abstract water efficiently, since there is no automatic pass-through of these costs in the price formula, and many take raw water supplies from neighbouring suppliers. The regulatory burden of assessing access prices for 28 companies' networks, as well as their retail tariffs, will be large. Initially, it is only large customers who can be supplied through common carriage, and they have already achieved significant gains from potential inset appointments and large-user tariffs. Common carriage is not likely to be a major feature of the water industry in the future.

(c) Cross-border Competition

There has been no cross-border competition, though the single inset appointment shares similar economic characteristics. This type of competition is driven by the fact that the tariff within a water company's area is based on the average costs of the whole area. In particular, rural customers pay the same charges as urban customers, in spite of the greater costs of serving the former. Again there is a parallel with gas, where, before the introduction of competition in the early 1990s, British Gas had a uniform tariff throughout the country. At the boundaries of two water companies, variation in tariff levels will induce some customers to switch suppliers, even though they have to pay the costs associated with new pipelines.[7]

Whether such competition will take off is doubtful. First, the regions of the WaSCs are based on watersheds, which naturally tend to be on high ground. Few customers are both located in these boundary regions and able to pay the costs of new pipelines. The counter-argument to this is that there are many WoCs located within the regions of WaSCs with boundaries that are more arbitrary. Second, it is not clear that the new supplier will want the new customers. If the boundary is in a rural area then it is likely that both companies are serving customers at a loss, because tariffs do not reflect distance. Although the target company has a *duty* to supply customers seeking cross-border supplies, there are many ways to avoid taking them on. A simple way would be to quote an excessive charge for connection across the boundary. This might be a reason behind the proposal to allow competition in connection. Another

---

[7] This is precisely analogous to the popular pastime of crossing international borders purely to take advantage of differences in indirect tax rates.

way would be to introduce a distance-related tariff that raises the cost to neighbouring customers of switching.

It is also questionable whether cross-border competition *should* be encouraged. Consider a customer with inelastic demand for water. Such a customer wants to switch suppliers if the reduction in *price* exceeds the (annualized) pipeline cost. This move is socially efficient if and only if the saving in *operating costs* exceeds the pipeline cost. When this latter condition holds the customer is supplied in the least-cost way. The problem is that prices and costs can be such that the customer wants to switch but, when the cost of the pipeline is included, society is now using more resources to supply the same quantity of water. The pipeline cost is a real switching cost. We should note, however, that if tariffs properly reflect marginal costs then all switching that occurs is efficient, because the saving in the bill will exactly equal the saving in operating costs. Existing tariffs, distorted by geographical averaging, are likely to lead to some cases of inefficient switching across boundaries.

6. Conclusions

With only a handful of data points available, assessing the prospects for product-market competition in the water industry is not straightforward. Potential inset appointments have led to quantity discounts in companies' tariffs. The common-carriage proposals are currently subject to consultation. The expense of transporting water, particularly across the watersheds that define many boundaries, will mean that common carriage and cross-border competition will probably have little effect. If competition is driven by the distortions in tariff structures, it is possible that some customers have a private incentive to switch to a new supplier which is not the appropriate signal from society's point of view.

Perhaps the main effect of competition will be on tariff structures. Water tariffs are now related to volume in a non-linear fashion, and large customers have gained real benefits, mainly at the expense of the water companies offering the quantity discounts, but also in part at the expense of other water customers. If access charges for common carriage are distance related, then retail tariffs within each company's area are also likely to exhibit this feature. Similarly, it seems plausible that tariffs will have seasonal components to capture the greater resource cost in summer. These developments will enhance efficiency by making tariffs reflect relative costs, but they will also create awkward political problems of winners and losers.

8

The Rail Industry

W. P. BRADSHAW*

1. Introduction

The sale of the railways in Britain is the last big network privatization. A major distinction between railways and the other utilities — gas, electricity, water, and telecommunications — is that their product is not homogeneous. Rail transport and travel are provided in a market which provides highly competitive substitutes, many of which are subject to lighter or, indeed, no regulation. The tax treatment of some of these substitutes also gives rise to distortions. Rail travel has few of the monopoly characteristics to enable it to extract rent from users, and survival of railways depends on substantial and continuing subsidy. Also, coming late in the programme of privatization meant that the experience of regulating other utilities was taken into account in the restructuring of the railways. The Rail Regulator was in place well before the transfer of operations to the private sector took place, and he was able to play a formative role in the development of the new arrangements.

Competitive pressure on railways is a long-standing feature of the industry. They began losing their share of passengers and freight by the second quarter of the 20th century and the process has accelerated very dramatically since 1960.

This is a worldwide experience. Development of road and air transport has affected every railway activity. There are now very few markets where railway fares and charges can be raised without a more than proportionate loss of revenue. Moving commuters into large cities, where road congestion and lack of parking space inhibits the use of cars, represents the remaining area of the captive market of railways. Even this may be eroded by the development of information technology with its potential for remote working and doing business.

* Centre for Socio-legal Studies, University of Oxford. I would like to thank Derek Morris for his useful comments on an earlier draft.

Table 1
Railway Market Share

| | Passenger kilometres | | | Freight tonne kilometres | |
	Total (billion)	Share (%)		Total (billion)	Share (%)
1935	34	31		27	43.7
1938	35	27.6		28	41.2
1947	39	27.6		34	49.1
1952[a]	39	20.7		36	45.6
1952	39	18		37	42
1957	42	17		34	37
1962	37	12		26	25
1967	34	9		21	17
1972	35	8		21	15
1977	34	7		20	12
1982	31	6		16	9
1987	40	7		17	9
1992	38	6		15	7
1995	37	5		1994 13	6

Note: [a] Source and method of calculation changes in 1952.
Source: Gourvish (1986) above the line, Transport Statistics below the line.

Regulation of the monopoly powers of railways, enacted in the 19th century, continued well beyond the point where road transport had eroded the market dominance of the railways. Various interest groups and politicians sought to maintain regulation of railway charges and it was not until 1962 that railway freight charges and passenger fares outside London were deregulated. Although the formal regulation of passenger fares and freight charges ceased after the 1962 Act, since that time ministers have always been involved in decisions about general fares increases.

Other obligations, such as common-carrier status, the maintenance of unprofitable lines and services, and disclosure of the details of commercial contracts lingered on well beyond the point necessary to protect the commercial interests of users. In much of Europe the arrangements for funding unprofitable services, which are deemed to be socially necessary, are not clearly defined, although in Britain the Public Service Obligation (PSO) arrangements provided under the 1974 Transport Act provided a mechanism for funding loss-making services considered to have a social value. However, the calculation of that social value was essentially political in nature, as were decisions to reduce the amount of subsidy available and instructions to railway management to secure economies as best they might—without making politically embarrassing reductions in services.

Throughout Western Europe rail services are subsidized. Efforts have been directed at attempting to separate services which meet a social need (e.g. local commuting and rural services) from those which might be regarded as 'commercial' (EEC Regulation 1191/69). Such a division was made in Britain in the 1980s when government ruled that InterCity and freight services should operate without subsidy.[1] The effectiveness of such decisions rests on the ability to separate the costs of providing those services which are commercial from those which are social. This is difficult when the infrastructure is shared and when one train may perform both social and commercial functions in one journey. Even greater difficulties emerge when attempts are made to accommodate external costs into the decision-making process. The noise, pollution, congestion, and accident costs of road transport provide a series of second-best arguments for subsidizing railway services. To these must be added the fiscal distortions arising from the tax reliefs available to company-financed motorists or duty-free allowances to air travellers. The problem of defining the purpose of subsidy and the allocation of such resources to purchasing a combination of services which delivers the best environmental and social mix is an area requiring much further study. On the other hand, it is clear that if road users were confronted with a set of prices at the time of use which reflected the external costs imposed on other members of society the costs of road use would rise.[2] Rail fares and charges could then be increased and the need for subsidizing the railway would diminish.

The practical problem facing politicians seems to be that there is a general public will to maintain railway services and, indeed, a desire that railways should be used more, particularly by freight. But railway travel

[1] A Ministerial Direction issued in October 1986 redefined the Public Service Obligation grant to exclude InterCity services from 1988–9 and set rates of return to be earned by this business and the freight activities of British Rail.

[2] The debate about the extent to which various classes of road users meet their full costs is complex. The issue is addressed in the Eighteenth Report of the Royal Commission on Environmental Pollution, ch. 7, which also makes the point that, unlike the method of costing applied to Railtrack, the road system is not valued as a capital asset so no provision is made for depreciation or an appropriate rate of return (para 7.8). Another recent study by Maddison et al. (1996) suggests that the aggregate marginal external costs of road transport outweigh the taxes paid by road transport by a factor of three. However, Newbery (1995b), in a paper which argues for road pricing for the use of congested roads, says that the current level of charging for road use is about right in terms of revenue collected, but that the distribution among various road users is unfair. The government, in its 1996 White Paper, Transport. The Way Forward, argues that 'the main efforts for the future need to be devoted to developing and introducing good price signals, ensuring as far as possible that transport costs include environmental and other economic costs' (para 8.12).

is perceived as being expensive[3] and, in some cases, it is.[4] If, therefore, it is not politically possible or indeed environmentally desirable to close the railway, then politicians are left with the problem of which railway services should be subsidized (and why) and how that subsidy should be spent most efficiently. The fundamental problems are: What do we want the railways for? How much of railway output is it worth society buying? How do we take account of the market failures and distortions in the whole of the transport market in the process of providing subsidies? How can the efficiency in the provision of railway services be maximized, bearing in mind the characteristics of high fixed costs, very low marginal costs, and the profit-maximizing behaviour of providers? Finally, there is the question: What place does competition have to play within the railway industry in solving these problems? This chapter addresses the role of competition in securing efficiency in the delivery of railway services, particularly in lowering the level of state subsidy provided.

2. The 1993 Railways Act

In the 1993 Railways Act the government decided that competition had a vital role to play in increasing railway efficiency. It did not, however, attempt to answer the other questions, apart from setting a minimum timetable of trains, and standards of punctuality, reliability, and overcrowding. The controversy at the very outset of the franchising process over the proposed withdrawal of the sleeping car service on the West Highland Line revealed both the highly political nature of such decisions and the lack of rigour in determining the revenues and costs involved in the provision of the train.

(a) *Structure of the Industry*

The Railways Act split the responsibility for the ownership and operation of the infrastructure (track, stations, signalling, electrical supplies for trains, and management of timetables) from the operation of train

---

[3] Recent research among samples of the population about the cost of rail travel to Gatwick from some stations on the Reading–Gatwick Line has shown the perceived cost to be approximately 50 per cent above the actual cost (Becke, 1996).

[4] Return fares between London and Edinburgh range from £34 for a standard-class Super Apex ticket booked in advance, to £196 first class. This compares with £5 7s 6d (£5.37½p) (third-class return) at nationalization in 1948, equivalent to around £100 in today's money, while a first-class return in 1948 cost the equivalent of £150 (Doe, 1996).

services. The passenger rolling-stock was also separated and ownership of the fleet was divided among three leasing companies. This division broke up the vertically integrated structure of the industry which is a common feature of railways throughout the world and has been so since the early days of the industry. This vertical separation did not have the support of railway professionals.[5] The government's reasons for making the change were that the separate ownership of the infrastructure was necessary to allow competition between different operators of passenger trains and freight trains using the same tracks. It was argued that only if the track were in neutral ownership could competing users be confident of impartial treatment in the allocation of paths in the timetable and fairness in respect of day-to-day decisions concerning precedence in running. It was further argued that, as one of the government's priorities was to secure suitable levels of investment in rail infrastructure, this required a strategic view of a kind that only a track authority could provide and that Railtrack would focus infrastructure investment on parts of the network where it was most needed. It was felt individual franchisees would find difficulty in meeting the capital investment requirements in particular franchise areas. The existence of a national track authority would ensure that safety standards and procedures were coordinated in a clear and systematic way. Finally, the track authority would ensure the efficient coordination of operational timetabling across the whole network (Hansard, 2 February 1993, col. 163).

In choosing a model for rail privatization which provided for vertical disintegration with an independent track authority and competition between operators, the government rejected three other possible models of reform. Apart from the privatization of British Rail (BR) as an entity, two other options were canvassed. One was a return to a number of geographical passenger companies responsible for all aspects of operation. The majority of journeys are made within such boundaries but arrangements would have been needed for cross-boundary passenger and freight services. The other model (the business-sector option) was to transfer the then existing BR businesses, InterCity, Network SouthEast, Regional Railways, and freight, to the private sector, together with the

[5] In an address to the Railway Study Association, Ed Burkhardt, President of Wisconsin Central, the purchaser of most of BR's freight business, is reported to have said: 'Open access is made possible by the railway industry structure in the UK, which sees infrastructure separated from operations—a structure devised by government theorists keen on competition, who seem to have missed the fact that railways have only 6 per cent of the market and trucks have all the rest. In my view separation of infrastructure from operations is a poor idea which only drives up costs. I've never appreciated an integrated railway so much as by having to deal with one that isn't.' (*Modern Railways*, January 1997)

infrastructure over which they exercised control as prime users. The transfer of BR as an entity had little appeal because of the lack of transparency concerning the use of subsidy and the belief that such a model did not provide for innovation and enterprise or sufficient incentives to increase efficiency. The geographical model was the simplest option. It allowed for local initiative and yardstick comparison of performance. It was rejected because it would have created territorial monopolies. It is debatable as to whether the much more complex nature of the model eventually chosen, with its high transaction costs, will deliver benefits from competition which will offset the simplicity of the geographical option. The business-sector option, which built on the then existing BR organization, had little to commend it in terms of innovation, or competition, but was probably put forward in an attempt to avoid yet another upheaval in the BR organization.

3. Introducing Competition

The notion that different operators would compete in the same railway market on the same tracks is novel. It requires not only an impartial mechanism for managing the timetable and operation, but also rules concerning the payment each operator should make for access to the track and other facilities, and also for payment of penalties for delays, whether caused by the operator or the owner of the infrastructure. Another set of rules is needed for those operating stations and, particularly, selling tickets and answering inquiries to ensure prospective travellers are informed about the range of competitive services available. The Rail Regulator created under the Act has thus spent enormous effort in creating a rule-based system to govern relations between the infrastructure owner, Railtrack, and the train service providers. As created at privatization, the owners of the rolling-stock (ROSCOs) are virtually monopolists because all available passenger rolling-stock was allocated among the franchised companies on long-term contracts. Franchisees had to accept the terms already in place and there is effectively no spare rolling-stock available, although any improvements in scheduling efficiency and maintenance procedures may create some marginal resources. Competition in supply will only arise when new trains are built. In addition, the ROSCOs are outside the scope of regulation.

The decision to use franchise bidding as a means of transferring railway operations to the private sector is interesting. Franchising in the Chadwick/Demsetz model is the means of securing the supply of a service in monopoly-type industries by means of competition among potential suppliers. But franchising railway services appears to be subject to a number of the difficulties pointed out by Vickers and Yarrow (1988, section 4.6.1), particularly specification and administration. The specification of the service to be provided by franchisees is the task of the Franchising Director. In the metropolitan conurbations this responsibility is shared with the passenger transport executives (PTEs). There is also statutory consultation with local authorities and other interested parties. The service specified in the tender documents, called the passenger service requirement (PSR), is the minimum which the successful franchisee must offer. For the more commercial services, the PSR has tended to specify a minimum frequency of one train an hour on principal Intercity routes and has anticipated that bidders will want to offer a more frequent service for business reasons. First and last trains and off-peak, evening, and weekend services are specified. Outside the former Intercity network—and following a case in the High Court, and further guidance from the Secretary of State—the PSR has tended to reflect the pre-existing BR timetable.

In any franchise bidding contest the specification of the service tends to be the preserve of the tendering authority and may be said to be driven by administrative and political reasons rather than the market. The administrators are particularly concerned to be seen to be fair to all bidders and, in the case of railways, because of the need to secure the cooperation of the PTEs, would also reflect their wishes. In the bidding process, those tendering were encouraged to offer services in excess of those set down in the PSR, as well as ancillary services at stations, passenger information, rail-link buses, and investment in new rolling-stock. It is also a condition of the franchises that performance standards are met and many franchisees offered, as part of their bids, to improve existing standards of punctuality and reliability. Because these 'quality' attributes were part of the contract and were offered as part of the competitive bidding process, it is necessary that the Franchising Director monitors standards of service and ensures that improved quality, where it was offered, is actually delivered in the event that there is some overlap between enforcement action by the Franchising Director, e.g. in levying fines on an operator who cancelled more trains than was allowed in the Franchise Agreement, and by the Regulator, who is pursuing an Enforcement Order against all the passenger train operators collectively for failure to provide a National Rail Telephone Enquiry Service in accordance with their licences. There will be further complications surrounding asset handover when franchises come to an end (franchisees do not own rolling-stock or fixed assets, but uncertainty about being able to realize the unexpired value of any capital expenditure which they may have made will make it less likely that they will invest on a substantial scale). There is also the problem of incumbent advantage when rebidding takes place. During franchise bidding there have been sufficient bidders to ensure competition. However, particularly with the short franchises, behaviour is likely to be conditioned by the need for incumbents to position themselves either to re-bid successfully or to exit from the process with a substantial profit in hand.

Having decided to dispose of the 25 train-operating companies (TOCs) into which the passenger operations of British Rail were divided, by franchise bidding, the government was faced with a dilemma. Franchising of railway service operation was an activity of which the market had no previous experience. Achieving satisfactory bids meant that franchisees required a fairly comprehensive set of reassurances. The prospect that, within their franchise areas, where they were expected to bid against others for the right to enjoy the market, they might face possible 'cherry-picking' entry within the same market by potential 'open access' non-franchised operators, or even by neighbouring franchisees, was not attractive. The Franchising Director, the officer responsible for the process of letting the franchises, therefore sought and obtained agreement from the Regulator to moderate competitive entry for an initial period during which the franchisees would have an oppor- tunity to establish their businesses.[6]

Direct competition between competing operators over the same track in the passenger market is therefore mainly an issue for the future. Any competition which does develop in the next 4 years will take place in the few cases where there is a choice of route, e.g. London–Birmingham, or where franchises overlap for part of their routes, e.g. London–Reading or London–Gatwick Airport. One issue is whether franchisees, having obtained a territorial monopoly through a process of franchise bidding, will tacitly agree not to compete with neighbouring operators, as may be the case with the large groups which have emerged to dominate the bus industry.

In order to sell the various component parts of the railway industry at a reasonable price, the government's advisers felt it necessary to sell the new companies with guaranteed contracts in place. In most cases these stretch ahead for a number of years and give what amounts to a guaranteed income stream to the purchasers. For example, ROSCOs have leases in place for all of their rolling-stock.

There is virtually no spare rolling-stock available, so that competition on the supply side will require either manufacturers or the ROSCOs to come to agreements with operating companies. Such competitive supply

[6] A full discussion of the reasons why the Rail Regulator decided to moderate competition during the early years of privatization is contained in ORR (1994b).

will take time to develop. Since the initial stages of franchise bidding, longer franchises have been offered, closing somewhat the gap between the relatively short length of franchises compared with the long life of the rolling-stock itself. The franchise for the West Coast Main Line, from London to Glasgow via Birmingham and Manchester, where a major upgrading of infrastructure and a new fleet of rolling-stock is required, was awarded to the Virgin Rail Group for a period of 15 years. Short franchises make it difficult for TOCs to fund the provision of new rolling-stock without some form of residual guarantee from the Franchising Director which would, in effect, be a Treasury guarantee. Since the original sale of the three ROSCOs, the smallest, Porterbrook, has been sold on to Stagecoach, the franchisee of South West Trains, thus recreating a degree of vertical integration.[7]

The track, signalling, and other infrastructure facilities are owned by Railtrack but the associated maintenance, renewal, and design work, is divided among 20 suppliers. These companies have been sold with contracts in place. As these initial contracts run out there will be increasing competition for work and several mergers have already taken place among suppliers.

The repair of rolling-stock, other than regular routine maintenance which is the responsibility of the TOCs, is the work of 'heavy maintenance suppliers'. Seven companies have been sold with contracts in place. In addition, there are workshops, some of which were sold into the private sector when British Rail Engineering Ltd (BREL) was privatized in March 1989, which provide for major overhauls and refurbishment programmes.

Competition in the supply of engineering services to Railtrack and to the owners of rolling-stock will develop as contracts run out and as new tasks are identified for which no existing contract exists. It is principally in these areas, many of which are still fairly labour-intensive, that it is hoped that significant reductions in railway costs will emerge.[8] This will partly depend upon how much genuine competition there is in the bidding, as it is likely that many of the original purchasers of the engineering businesses will merge to form vertically integrated companies offering design, renewal, and maintenance. This may tend to establish areas of geographical influence. So far as work on the track is

[7] This sale of the company, sold by the government for £528m, at a price of £825m has been approved by the competition authorities subject to various undertakings.

[8] Railtrack's Annual Report (1995/6) states: 'We intend to take full advantage of the increasingly competitive market for maintenance and track renewals. Work carried out by the infrastructure maintenance companies will be exposed progressively to competitive tendering from the expiry of the first contract in 1999, and at an earlier stage for the work of the track renewal companies.'

concerned, it is unlikely, in view of the strict regulations which are in place, that efficiency gains will be made by cutting corners at the expense of safety both of users and of staff.

It is certainly possible that supply-side competition in actually providing and maintaining the fixed and rolling assets of the railway will prove a powerful means of reducing railway costs and improving quality. For this to happen it will probably be better if the purchasers concentrate on defining the outputs required rather than the means by which these are achieved. A long-term failing of railway administrations has been the tendency for over-large technical departments to specify in very great detail the equipment to be supplied. In the new railway the opportunity exists to spell out a functional specification of what the equipment is expected to achieve, leaving the supplier with the scope and the risks associated with design and manufacture. It is also desirable to leave the supplier with the risks associated with under-performance and responsibility for ongoing maintenance. Thus the contract for supply of new rolling-stock for the Northern Line of London Underground specifies the number of trains required for service each day, leaving the supplier to decide how many trains to build (allowing for those undergoing maintenance) and to provide and staff the maintenance facility. A similar approach has been adopted by Chiltern Railways, which has selected AdTranz to supply four new trains , but has taken responsibility for the maintenance of the whole fleet. It claims that a small compnay cannot afford to maintain much engineering experience in-house. There were relatively few orders placed for new rolling-stock or for fixed equipment on the railway following the announcement of the privatization process.[9] The supply industry has therefore shrunk and is not particularly strong. Franchisees have committed themselves to purchasing 2,000 new passenger coaches over 7 years, but this quantity is described as being insufficient to reduce the high age profile or to increase carryings (Gillan, 1997). However, more orders are now being placed. It is important, if real economies are to flow from the new system, that there is genuine competition in supply-side bidding.

4. Marketing of Railway Services and Pricing

Although there will be little scope for 'on rail' competition between the TOCs, there is substantial scope for innovative pricing. British Rail

[9] There was a gap in new orders for replacement or supplementation of the BR passenger rolling-stock fleet between October 1993 and September 1996 (*Railway Gazette International*, 1996, p. 614).

discouraged local pricing, believing that it was better to focus on nationally advertised products such as Savers, Super Savers, Apex, and various forms of Railcards. This tendency arose partly from constant criticism in the media and from user groups about the confusion which it was alleged arose from there being too wide a variety of fares. Despite the fact that BR bowed to this criticism, many markets are local in nature and yield-management techniques suggest that a more devolved, disaggregated fares strategy is warranted. It is now evident that many TOCs are looking to various mechanisms for filling empty seats and we are likely to see a variety of franchise-specific and more local promotions aimed at filling these and at building consumer loyalty. In addition, various value-added services, ranging from free drinks and newspapers to family carriages and other features, are appearing. What we are seeing is competition in ideas for maximizing fare yields. Companies are constrained from raising fares by the fare caps which are part of the franchise agreements. The Railways Act requires the Franchising Director to include in the relevant franchise agreement a provision for ensuring that the prices of fares are reasonable. Standard class return fares, single fares for short distance journeys, 'Saver Fares', and many season tickets are constrained.

For 3 years from 1 January 1996, price rises are limited to the retail price index (RPI) and for 4 years beyond then to RPI–1. There will be limited scope to offset rises in one fare by reductions in others. In the commuter markets around London, Edinburgh, Manchester, and Cardiff, the price caps will include most fares, including season tickets, which will be regulated by reference to a tariff basket. Fare rises may be adjusted up or down to reflect performance and upwards if agreed investment programmes result in improved quality of service (OPRAF, 1996). Increasing yield within these caps is, therefore, a very important part of franchisees' business strategies. Filling empty seats on existing trains involves no extra outpayments by the TOCs to Railtrack for access to track and stations, so is a more attractive expansion strategy than running extra trains, which requires considerable outpayments.

5. Labour Costs

As well as having a centralized fares policy British Rail also had very centralized wage bargaining arrangements. This also suited the trade union movement, which is organized on a national basis, but it produced wage rates which were often uncompetitive in urban areas but were more than adequate elsewhere. Very few railway staff worked on part-time contracts. Out of 138,000 employed in 1992/3 only 1,500 were part-timers. Work patterns were inflexible in an industry which is subject to great peaks in demand. For example, few railway staff work split shifts, where staff work for a few hours in both the morning and evening peaks. This pattern of working is common practice in the bus industry. Train staff do not stay away from home overnight, which is the practice of many long-distance lorry drivers.[10] There are strict demarcation lines between duties so that, for example, drivers neither collect fares nor refuel their trains. All companies involved in railway work of any description will want greater flexibility from the work-force and may be willing to pay substantial premia to achieve this. Great Western Trains, one of the first franchisees, has negotiated a new pay package with its train drivers. A guaranteed salary of £20,200 replaces a basic wage of £11,692 plus many allowances. Included in the deal is a 37-hour week and more rest days and holidays. However, 55 drivers' jobs out of 301 will go.[11] Drivers will drive single-manned up to 125mph instead of 100mph. The trade unions will be suspicious and are keen to retain national bargaining arrangements. It is interesting that in the bus industry, where national bargaining was abolished prior to deregulation and privatization in 1986 with the break-up of the National Bus Company, the trade unions are now seeking to re-establish national negotiations with FirstBus, one of the big merged companies. There will be competition in the railway industry among all employers to establish changed service conditions and payment systems which are appropriate to each business. Successful companies will be those that secure good deals with the unions and avoid strikes. The Regulator has a role to play in ensuring that contracts and particularly performance regimes operating between contracting parties are not drawn in such a way as to force those trying to change working conditions to capitulate at the first threat of strike action. As a result, strike action is treated as *force majeure* in terms of contract compliance, provided the train operator has observed industrial relations procedures.

[10] From 29 September 1996, Great North Eastern Railway, which operates the East Coast Main Line, secured the agreement of drivers, against the advice of their trade union, to reintroduce lodging turns, where they stay away overnight, a practice which was discontinued about 30 years ago. English Welsh and Scottish Railway has achieved similar changes in the freight business, with salaried status and a 7-day working week.

[11] LTS Rail has negotiated a restructuring deal reducing the number of drivers from 146 to 108, which also increases the number of days off per man from 85 to 126 p.a. The length of the working day is extremely flexible within a range of 4–12 hours (*Rail Privatisation News*, 14 November 1996).

6. Freight

In the market for carrying freight and mails, the government decided that the businesses of British Rail should be split into six parts. It has subsequently sold the four largest companies, including the three companies into which Trainload Freight had been divided prior to sale, and Rail Express Systems, which carries mail, to one purchaser, Wisconsin Central, now trading as English Welsh and Scottish Railways (EW&SR). During the process of sale, Wisconsin was able to convince ministers that rail is in an extremely weak position in most of the freight commodity markets in which it operates and is certainly so in those which are totally dominated by road transport. Wisconsin argued that there was little scope for 'on rail' competition and that such economies of scale as do exist in rail operations should be preserved. In a paper to the Scottish Railfreight Conference (19 April 1996) Ed Burkhardt, President of Wisconsin Central, estimated that the costs of running the trainload freight operation in three parts would have been 20 per cent higher than those of a single undertaking. The government accepted these arguments and there is, effectively, only one domestic rail freight operator in Britain. However, small 'open access' operations have been established by two companies, National Power and Direct Rail Services. The possibility of open access remains available to other potential entrants.

Wisconsin Central has reduced operational costs substantially both in North America and New Zealand, and expects to make economies in Britain by using new locomotives, 250 of which have been ordered from North America, and by achieving freight rolling-stock costs in Britain nearer to those found in the USA. Ed Burkhardt surmised that these differences in the costs of procurement arise because the British market has been protected from international competition. He also foresaw 3,000 operational job losses. He is looking for much reduced track-access charges, particularly for additional traffic. EW & SR provides the trains used by Railtrack for track maintenance. He pointed out that Wisconsin uses 100 maintenance wagons for 2,500 miles of track. The British infrastructure maintenance fleet numbers 20,000.[12]

7. Bus Companies and the Railways

Prominent among those companies which have been successful in bidding for railway franchises have been bus companies. This has given rise to concerns about 'public transport monopolies' being

[12] *Modern Railways*, June 1996, pp. 382–6.

created.[13] In one case the President of the Board of Trade has accepted undertakings from National Express, the successful bidder for the franchise for the Midland Main Line, after the Monopolies and Mergers Commission (MMC) ruled that the takeover of the rail service by a company offering competing coach services was against the public interest. The MMC concluded that the takeover of rail routes by National Express would reduce competition in the leisure market on five routes and lead to higher fares for both rail and coach passengers and a lower standard of service.[14] Joint ownership of bus and rail services is something which the market finds to be a natural extension of transport businesses. In the 1920s the main railway companies in Britain became extensive operators of bus services and, more recently, in Sweden it has been a bus operator which has successfully bid for franchises against the state railway. There appear to be economies of scope in joint operation and there are those who argue that integration of public transport services is more likely to occur when joint ownership is in place. The argument is sometimes extended to say that public transport as a whole (buses and trains) has to work closely together to meet the competitive challenge of the car.

8. Regulatory Issues

Although railways may appear at first sight to be a mature industry, the changes made in Britain pose quite new challenges. Coupled with growing road congestion and rising demand for travel and movement of goods, there may be significant opportunities for growth and profit. Competition in the supply side ought to reduce the costs of providing infrastructure and rolling-stock. Wage reforms will reduce labour costs. More focused marketing will increase revenue. But the rule-based structure of the industry together with performance regimes may constrain enterprise. It may also lead to profit-maximizing behaviour which

[13] Strathclyde Passenger Transport Authority decided on 30 August 1996 to raise with the Monopolies and Mergers Commission the fact that four of the pre-qualifiers for the Scotrail franchise were bus companies with substantial businesses within the PTA area. The Clerk and Legal Adviser to the Authority commented that it was not in the interests of the Authority that a single operator should gain control of significant sections of public transport within the area (*Rail Privatisation News*, 5 September 1996, p. 3).

[14] MMC (1996*e*). About 90 per cent of coach passengers and 40 per cent of rail passengers on the routes are leisure travellers. The undertakings given by National Express restrict increases in coach fares to the RPI and commit it to maintaining services at the present level unless 'there is a significant reduction in passenger numbers'.

will reduce the level of activity in the industry below socially desirable levels. It should be the task of a future government and of the Regulator to confront these problems as a matter of urgency.

There seems to be little community of interest between Railtrack and the train operators in promoting the use of the railway which is one of the statutory objectives of the Regulator.[15] Railtrack may, indeed, have perverse incentives, where a less busy railway may mean that more land is available for exploitation for its property value.[16] The performance incentive regime, under which facility owners and train operators compensate one another for delays, may be so harsh that it creates an incentive to under-use the potential capacity of the network, so that excessive margins exist to allow for delays (while no attention is paid to delays on parallel roads). The timetable, the key document in exploiting the capacity of the network, remains a private document in Railtrack's hands. This may inhibit competition in devising alternative scheduling arrangements leading to better use of available capacity and of rolling-stock and train crews.

9. Franchising and Subsidies

Whatever is done to bring competitive bidding into the provision of engineering services and to open the timetable to all parties, Railtrack will remain a monopoly and it will be difficult for the Regulator to be certain that its cost structures are efficient or that its capital expenditure programme is the most appropriate. In setting the track access charges for the period 1995–2001, the Regulator had to take a view of the cost of maintaining the rail network and replacing the assets in modern equivalent form. This assessment took into account the need to overtake a backlog in investment, particularly in stations and on the West Coast Main Line. Railtrack has since published two Network Management Statements, one in 1995/96 and one in 1997. These statements have failed to satisfy the Regulator concerning the investment programme — whether it was appropriate and the extent to which Railtrack was obliged to carry out the programme. He has described the access contracts between the TOCs and Railtrack as being insufficient for the effective regulation of

[15] 1993 Act: 4.1.(b) 'to promote the use of the railway network in Great Britain for the carriage of passengers and goods and the development of that railway network, to the greatest extent that he considers economically practicable'.

[16] The Regulator has determined that 75 per cent of Railtrack property income, over and above the amounts allowed for in the access charges (some £1 billion over the 6 years of the review), may be retained by the company for the benefit of shareholders (Annual Report of the Rail Regulator, 1995/6, para 53).

the company's investment and stewardship duties. The Regulator has thus sought an amendment to Railtrack's network licence, giving him powers to monitor the investment programme. The company conceded this, rather than contest the issue before the MMC. There still remains the problem of the information available to the Regulator on which to make his judgement, it being much easier to measure promised inputs in terms of expenditure, and more difficult in respect of performance output (Winsor, 1997). There must, therefore, be a strong argument for splitting up Railtrack, perhaps initially causing it to divest its Scottish operations and also its freight lines and associated facilities. Such a break-up would provide valuable information to the Regulator and would better inform the debate about the level of track-access charges which are appropriate both in the freight market and in the more peripheral regions.

Franchises are extremely rigid, with a PSR specifying first and last trains and minimum frequencies, which often closely reflects the existing timetable. This close specification of the service is an administrator's view of what the market requires. Whether it really reflects market potential is open to question. It seems unlikely that an administratively determined specification will continue to adjust to meet changing demand patterns. It is presumably to provide an incentive to franchisees to adjust services to meet demand that the threat of contestability through open access is posed. A genuine threat of entry would certainly cause incumbents to be alert to the danger of leaving gaps in service provision. Efforts were made to make competition a realistic possibility where a route is served by two franchises, e.g. Ipswich–London by Great Eastern and West Anglia/Great Northern. Here, the Franchising Director was keen to maintain competition by making separate awards. He warned bidders that, if one operator secured both franchises, additional paths would be provided and offered to other operators.[17]

No reference is made in franchise agreements to the generation of passenger-kilometres or weighting these in accordance with social values. Franchises cannot be renegotiated during their currency (except in one case). Neither can these be extended if performance targets are exceeded.[18] Most franchises were originally expected to last for 7 years. It was the intention of the White Paper that this should be the case so that franchisees should be 'kept on their toes' by the prospect of more frequent exposure of franchised services to competitive tendering (De-

[17] *Railway Privatisation News*, 5 September 1996. This could result in the waste of very valuable capacity unless the paths were used.

[18] Section 29 (3) of the Railways Act 1993 allows for a provision to be included in the franchise agreement to enable the franchise term to be extended by a further specified term. So far, such a provision has only been included in the franchise for Network South Central.

partment of Transport, 1992, para 27). However, it was quickly recognized that short franchises have the disadvantage of making it difficult to invest either in new rolling-stock or in providing new and improved stations or other fixed assets. Short franchises may also encourage short-term management strategies which seek to extract the maximum of cash from the business prior to exit by the franchisee. Many later franchises, especially in cases where investment is needed, are longer, typically 15 years.

If competition is to secure the optimal outcome for the taxpayer, who is now paying a substantial additional sum for the provision of railway services,[19] then government should define what output it is seeking to purchase. While government has rejected the recommendation made by the Royal Commission on Environmental Pollution of the adoption of targets for modal transfer,[20] the use of such targets could be useful particularly if they indicated which journeys are worth subsidizing and why, and set down some rationale showing the price at which additional marginal journeys might be purchased.[21] For freight there appears to be an argument that new flows should be admitted to the system at marginal cost, providing that existing users are not subject to discriminatory pricing. The President of Wisconsin Central, the owner of the freight business, in an address to the Railway Study Association in November 1996, said that the freight track-access pricing system is not workable and if he cannot get the regime changed he will look to government to secure changes.

10. Issues to be Addressed

Once government has articulated some clear objectives as part of its environmental and transport policies, it will fall to the Franchising Director to issue franchises which encourage investment and other behaviour facilitating the achievement of these objectives. Here, it will be important for the Franchising Director and Rail Regulator to resolve the conflicts which will arise between the desire of the Regulator to allow

[19] Payments to BR by the Treasury under the PSO arrangements and by the PTAs under Section 20 of the 1968 Act in 1992/3 amount to £1,067m. In 1995/6 payments rose to almost £2 billion.

[20] See the government's response to the Transport Debate (HMSO, 1996, ch. 13).

[21] The Franchising Director was instructed by the Secretary of State to begin to develop criteria to enable him to evaluate the benefits to be obtained from the provision of loss-making services. A consultation paper, 'Appraisal of Support for Passenger Rail Services', was issued by the Office of Passenger Rail Franchising in November 1996.

competitive open-access passenger operations on the one hand and, on the other, the need of the Franchising Director to secure the best deal for the taxpayer, which will include achieving high levels of investment, without recourse to the public purse. There is a real danger that cream-skimming competition could undermine any long-term strategy. While direct competition, as long as it is sustained, may bring benefits to those able to take advantage, evidence from the bus industry suggests that such competition will only arise on the busiest routes and at the busiest times and may lead to fewer services at other times as cross-subsidy is reduced.

The price cap on Railtrack's access charges is due for review, to be completed by July 2000. As well as considering issues such as breaking up the company in the interests of transparency, the opening up of the timetable as a public document, the effects of the performance regime on network management, and the proportion of property receipts to be devoted to reducing track-access charges, the Regulator may wish to consider whether the formula should contain a volume element where Railtrack has an incentive to increase the use of the network. All these issues would be greatly clarified if government makes clear its objectives in subsidizing the railway, perhaps in some new guidance issued to the Regulator by the new government.

The Regulators' Perspective

9

The Generation and Supply of Electricity: The British Experience

S. C. LITTLECHILD*

1. Introduction

It is now 7 years since the restructuring and privatization of the British electricity industry. To a greater degree than in the privatization of the other utilities, electricity privatization was accompanied by an intention to introduce competition in those parts of the industry where competitive forces could apply. This intention was reflected in the government's 1988 White Paper, *Privatising Electricity*, in the statutory framework, in the restructuring of the industry, and in the accompanying regulatory regime.

Green and Newbery (1997, and updated in chapter 4 of this volume) have provided a useful discussion of how competition has developed in the generation and supply of electricity. This chapter extends and updates their discussion, with more detailed information on market shares, and also compares experience in England and Wales against that in Scotland. The chapter concludes with a brief look ahead to the introduction of competition in supply for all customers in 1998.

2. England and Wales

(a) *Partial Restructuring*

At Vesting, the assets of the Central Electricity Generating Board (CEGB) in England and Wales were split four ways. National Power and PowerGen were given the thermal plant, Nuclear Electric the nuclear stations, and National Grid Company (NGC) the transmission system and the pumped-storage plant in Wales. The 12 regional electricity boards, responsible for

* Director General of Electricity Supply, Office of Electricity Regulation

Table 1
Market Shares of Output in the England and Wales Generation Market (%)

	89/90*	90/91	91/92	92/93	93/94	94/95	95/96	96/97	7/96–6/97
National Power	48.0	45.5	43.6	40.9	35.0	34.0	31.5	24.1	21.9
PowerGen	29.7	28.4	28.2	27.0	26.0	25.9	23.1	21.5	20.7
Eastern	0.0	0.0	0.0	0.0	0.5	0.8	1.3	6.6	8.2
Scottish Interconnector**	1.6	1.7	2.3	2.5	2.4	3.0	3.6	3.5	3.4
French Interconnector	3.2	5.9	6.2	6.3	6.2	6.2	5.7	5.8	5.8
Nuclear Electric	16.0	17.4	18.6	21.4	23.2	22.2	22.5	17.3	17.4
Magnox Electric	0.0	0.0	0.0	0.0	0.0	0.0	0.0	6.9	7.3
Pumped Storage	0.5	0.6	0.4	0.5	0.4	0.5	0.7	0.8	0.8
New entrants:									
CCGT	0.0	0.0	0.3	1.0	5.7	6.5	10.4	12.2	13..3
Others***	0.5	0.5	0.4	0.5	0.7	0.9	1.2	1.2	1.2
Total	100	100	100	100	100	100	100	100	100

Notes: *Estimates based on post-Vesting structure; ** includes Chapelcross; *** includes Derwent Cogen and pooled combined-heat-and-power (CHP) and renewables plants. CCGT is combined-cycle gas turbine.

distribution and supply in their areas, became regional electricity companies (RECs).

(b) *Development of Competition in Generation: Aggregate Market Shares*

Table 1 shows the changing market shares in the generation market in England and Wales from 1989/90 to 1996/97. It also includes figures for the year ending June 1997, which are indicative of some of the continuing changes that are not fully revealed by the figures for 1996/97.

The changes since 1989/90 reflect five main developments. First, the interconnectors were able to operate their existing links at full capacity, increasing their output by about two-thirds. ScottishPower and Hydro-Electric also increased the capacity of the Scottish interconnector.

Second, Nuclear Electric significantly increased the output of its stations, typically by reducing the number and duration of outages. The market share of the existing nuclear stations has increased by about a half since Vesting. In addition, Sizewell B has come on stream.

Third, new entrants built new capacity, often in partnership with regional companies. This took some years to have any significant effect, but by 1993/94 the share of such entrants was up to 6 per cent. By the year ending June 1997 entrants accounted for over 13 per cent of the market, not including the new capacity built by Eastern.

Fourth, in view of my concern about their market power, National Power and PowerGen accepted undertakings to dispose of 6,000 MW of existing coal-fired or oil-fired plant so as to increase competition. These disposal undertakings were accompanied by undertakings to hold Pool price constant in real terms during 1994/95 and 1995/96 so that customers should be protected in the period before the disposals took place. The effect of the undertakings on Pool price is discussed in section (f) below. The disposals were completed in 1996 with both companies selling coal-fired plant to Eastern Group, now part of the Energy Group. The Energy Group accounted for about 8 per cent of the market in the year ending June 1997.

Fifth, as part of the nuclear privatization in 1996, Nuclear Electric's plant was split; the newer advanced gas-cooled reactor (AGR) and pressurized-water reactor (PWR) stations, which account for about two-thirds of nuclear output, became part of the privatized British Energy, and the older Magnox stations became Magnox Electric, which remained in government ownership. Nuclear stations accounted for over 24 per cent of market output in 1996/97. (Although this is not shown on the table, Nuclear Electric, even after the split, was the largest single producer in the first quarter of 1997/98.)

As a result of these market changes, the shares of National Power and PowerGen in the market as a whole have nearly halved. Before Vesting, their plant in aggregate accounted for nearly 80 per cent of output in England and Wales. By the year ending June 1997, they accounted for a little over 40 per cent. In contrast, the aggregate shares of new entrants plus the Energy Group have grown from nothing to over a fifth of the market in the 6 years since Vesting.

(c) *Herfindahl Index*

The overall effect of these changes can be summarized using the Herfindahl index, which measures concentration in a market by summing the squares of the market shares of all the participants. The index has a maximum value of 10,000, for a single monopoly supplier, and a minimum value tending to zero for a very large number of suppliers each with very small market shares. Figure 1 shows that, at Vesting, the Herfindahl index for the generation market in England and Wales had a value of about 3,500, or 0.35 expressed as a proportion of the maximum possible value. By 1997 the index had fallen to about 1,500, or 0.15.

The reciprocal of the Herfindahl proportion indicates the equivalent number of equal-sized competitors in the market. The situation at Vesting was thus equivalent to about three equal-sized competitors supplying the generation market in England and Wales; by 1997 it was equivalent to more than six equal-sized competitors. In this broad sense,

Figure 1
Herfindahl Index of Market Share by Output, England and Wales

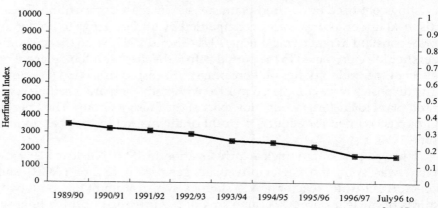

the extent of competition in generation has more than doubled. On the basis of the value of the Herfindahl index, the generation market in England and Wales has moved from what the US Department of Justice classifies as a highly concentrated market to what it calls a moderately concentrated market.

(d) *Market Sectors*

These developments focus on shares of the generation market as a whole. But at least two important qualifications need to be made. First, market shares are by no means the only indication of competition. Many other factors are also relevant, including the ability of players to expand their output, either to initiate competitive challenges or to respond to price increases by others taking market share. Second, for many purposes it is important to consider the extent of competition in different sectors of the market. New entrants have typically run at baseload, using their plant to full capacity at all times of the day and year. The larger incumbent generators have also run at baseload. However, the additional generation required to meet daily, weekly, and seasonal peaks has come almost entirely from the two largest established generators. New entrants do not have the capacity to respond significantly to variations in price or in demand.

To measure the extent of this competition in different sectors of the market, an earlier analysis (Littlechild, 1996) defined baseload output for each generator as the average level of output between the 8 hours from 11 p.m. to 7 a.m., and non-baseload output as the average level of output in the remaining 16 hours of the day, over and above the level of baseload output.

Table 2
SMP Setting (%)

	1995/6	1996/7	7/96–6/97
National Power	49.7	40.5	36.3
PowerGen	32.9	28.3	28.6
Eastern	0.1	14.6	19.2
PSB	13.3	13.5	12.7
Exports	2.7	2.5	2.9
Others	1.2	0.7	0.4
Total	100.0	100.0	100.0

On this basis, National Power and PowerGen in aggregate accounted for 95 per cent of the non-baseload market in 1993/94. NGC's pumped-storage business and the interconnectors accounted for most of the remainder. A year and a half later, National Power's and PowerGen's combined share of the non-baseload market had fallen slightly, as a result of increased non-baseload output by the interconnectors, pumped storage, and independent generators, but was still at 90 per cent.

Similar calculations show that in 1996/97 the 90 per cent share was divided between National Power, PowerGen, and Eastern/Energy Group. The interconnectors (mainly the Scottish interconnector) and pumped storage (now owned by Mission Energy) had continued slightly to increase their share of the non-baseload market, but this was offset by a fall in the share taken by independent generators.

These figures suggest that, although market shares have changed steadily and significantly in the market as a whole, they have not done so in all sectors. There is a very great difference between the extent of competition in different sectors of the market. Further analysis of such market sectors is indicated. For example, the above calculation reflects variations in output by time of day, averaged across the year, but does not reflect variations in output by weekday versus weekend, or by season of the year.

(e) *Shares of Price Setting*

Another measure of market influence is the proportion of time that a company sets the system marginal price (SMP) in the Pool. Table 2 shows that in 1995/96 National Power and PowerGen set SMP over 80 per cent of the time. In 1996/97 their share had fallen to just under 70 per cent and in the year to June 1997 to under 65 per cent, with Eastern/Energy Group setting it nearly 15 per cent of the time in 1996/97 and nearly 20 per cent of the time in the year to June 1997. NGC's pumped-storage business (PSB), now Mission Energy, set SMP just over 13 per cent of the time in

Figure 2
Real Monthly Pool Prices Since Vesting

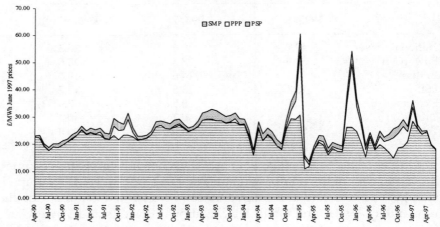

Note: PPP is pool purchase price.

Figure 3
Real Time- and Demand-weighted Pool Prices by Component

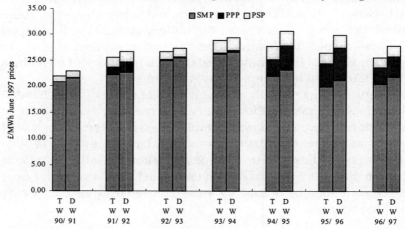

each year. There were similar developments at different times of day. The SMP is now set by four companies, rather than three.

(f) *Pool Prices*

The pattern of Pool prices since Vesting is shown in Figure 2. Figure 3 gives the averages for each year, time-weighted and demand-weighted, by component, in real terms. There have been several significant trends.

First, average SMP and pool selling price (PSP) steadily increased in real terms from 1990/91 to 1993/94. This reflected not only the market

Figure 4
Differential between Time- and Demand-weighted Average Pool Prices

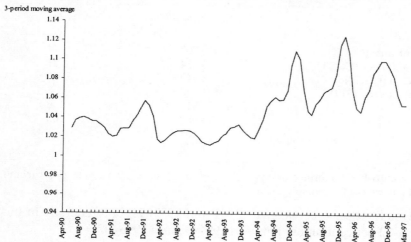

power of the two major generators, but also the artificiality of Pool price in the early years, which in turn reflected the influence of the Vesting contracts. This somewhat limits the force of the argument by Newbery and Green, that the structure of the generation market at Vesting produced higher prices than would have resulted from a more disaggregated and more competitive generation industry. Pool prices in the early years were lower than the figures that they calculated would characterize such a more competitive price structure.

Second, there has been a reduction in average SMP from 1993/94 to 1995/96. This has reflected, among other things, the effect of the Pool price undertakings in 1994/95 and 1995/96, the steadily falling cost of generation from existing plants, the effect of actual competition from new entrants coming on stream, and the threat of further new entry following the reductions in new entry cost in recent years (in turn reflecting lower gas prices, lower capital costs, and improved plant efficiencies). It is a concern that there was an upturn in the SMP in 1996/97.

Third, there has been a significant increase in the level of capacity payments since 1993/94, and also in the unscheduled availability component of energy uplift. These increases have offset the reductions in the transport element of uplift following from the new incentive mechanisms applied to NGC.

Fourth, and partly as a consequence of the last developments, there has been an increase in the ratio of peak prices to off-peak prices (sometimes called 'stretch'). For example, Figure 4 shows that the average demand-weighted Pool price was generally in the range 2–4 per cent above average

Table 3
Composition of New Capacity in England and Wales 1990/91 to 1996/97

	MW	%
New Entrants (CCGT)	6,702	44
National Power (CCGT)	3,174	21
PowerGen (CCGT)	3,040	20
Nuclear Electric (PWR)	1,250	8
Other*	914	6
Total Pooled	15,080	100
NFFO	404	
CHP	1,778	

Note: * Scottish interconnector upgrade, Indian Queens open-cycle gas turbine (OCGT), Derwent Cogen, and Sellafield CHP.

time-weighted price between 1990/91 and 1993/94, but generally in the range 5–12 per cent higher between 1994/95 and 1996/97.

(g) *Changes in Capacity*

Developments in Pool prices have been significantly influenced by the pattern of opening new capacity and closing existing capacity. Since Vesting, about 15,000 MW of new capacity has been brought on to the system via the Pool, and a further 2,000 MW or so via Non-fossil Fuel Order (NFFO) projects and combined-heat-and-power (CHP) schemes, mainly non-Pooled. Most of the new capacity is combined-cycle gas-turbine (CCGT) plant which new entrants and existing generators have built in almost equal proportions. The composition by ownership and plant type has been as shown in Table 3.

Over the same period National Power and PowerGen have taken about 19,000 MW of existing coal- and oil-fired plant off the system. The amount of capacity on the system has therefore generally fallen, over a period when demand has been increasing. Consequently, the capacity margin has fallen. Figure 5 shows the change in capacity in each year including an estimate for 1997/98 based on plans declared to date. Figure 6 shows how the amount of capacity on the system has generally decreased over time.

(h) *Future Developments in Generation*

At present a number of independent generation projects are under construction and due to commission in 1998 and 1999. They total nearly 3,000 MW of capacity. This will increase by about 40 per cent the amount of new independent capacity on the system.

Figure 5
Closures/New Capacity by Financial Year, 1990/91 to 1996/97

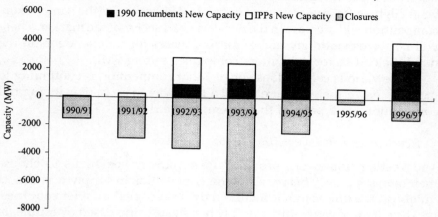

Note: IPP is independent power producer.

Figure 6
Cumulative Closures/New Capacity by Financial Year, 1990/91 to 1997/98

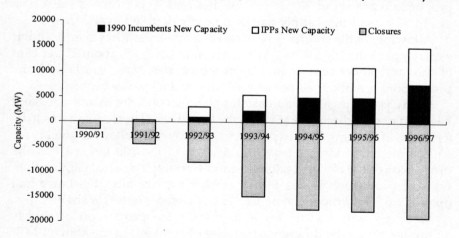

The construction of more new plant is under consideration. Possibilities totalling around 20 GW are reported in the trade press. By no means all of this will be built, but some seems likely to be.

Because neither the plant under construction nor any future plant can guarantee to run baseload, because of the extent of competition there, new CCGT plant is increasingly being designed to run mid-merit, and gas purchase contracts are being tailored accordingly. In addition, a number of open-cycle gas-turbine (OCGT) and diesel plants are being built to provide 'peak lopping' services, thereby strengthening competition at the peak. The total market shares of such plant will therefore not be as high as for previous new entrants. However, by the same token, competition will increase in the non-baseload sector of the market. There will be correspondingly higher market shares for independents in the non-baseload sector, with more companies setting SMP.

These various calculations suggest that competition is continuing to increase. Nevertheless, there is still a long way to go in developing full competition in all parts of the generation market.

(i) Developments in Competitive Supply

The Vesting framework provided for electricity customers to choose their own supplier. This provision for competition in supply was almost unique at the time, but has increasingly been copied in other countries.

The extent of competitive supply has steadily increased over time. In 1990/91, the first year after Vesting, just under 30 per cent of the sites and just over 40 per cent of the sales in the above 1 MW market in England and Wales went to second-tier suppliers (that is, to suppliers other than the local public electricity supplier). Now, in 1997/98, the corresponding proportions are about 60 per cent of sites and 70 per cent of sales. The extent of second-tier supply has thus nearly doubled over 7 years.

Allowing for the shorter time it has been open, there has been a similar experience in the 100 kW to 1 MW market. In 1994/95, about 25 per cent of sites and 30 per cent of sales went second-tier. Now, in 1997/98, the proportions are about 40 per cent of sites and 50 per cent of sales.

In any year, the proportion of sites going second-tier in any size band has been positively correlated with the size of site. There also seems to be a process of learning from experience and this works about as quickly for small sites as for large ones. After 4 years of the 100 kW market, the proportion of 100 kW sites taking second-tier supply is a little higher than was the proportion in the 1 MW market 4 years after the latter had opened up. The proportion of sales, as opposed to sites, is slightly less.

Figures 7 and 8 show for each market the proportion of supply accounted for by the different categories of supplier. In the above 1 MW market, the major generators (National Power, PowerGen, and Nuclear Electric) increased their share to over 40 per cent of the market in 1996/97, although this share has declined in 1997/98. In both markets, RECs operating second-tier are accounting for an increasing proportion of output and sites. Supply is increasingly becoming a national rather than a local activity.

Figure 7
Changing Market Shares of Consumption in the Over 1 MW Market

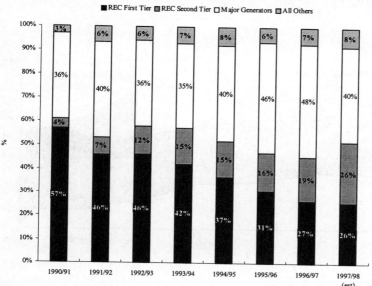

Note: Major generators are National Power, Nuclear Electric, and PowerGen. All others includes ScottishPower, Hydro-Electric, and the independent suppliers.

Figure 8
Changing Market Shares of Consumption in the 100 kW to 1 MW Market

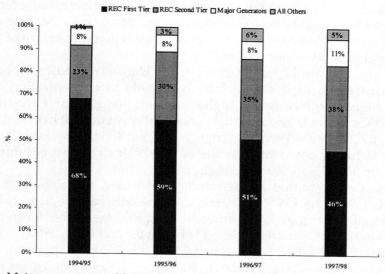

Note: Major generators are National Power, PowerGen, Nuclear Electric, and Magnox. All others includes ScottishPower, Hydro-Electric, and the independent suppliers.

Figure 9
Herfindahl Index for the Supply Market in England and Wales
(by sites)

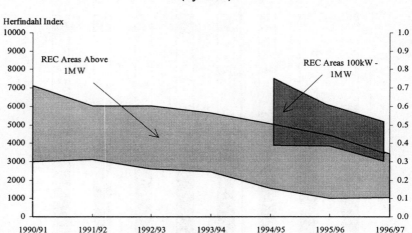

(j) Herfindahl Indices

These developments can again be summarized using Herfindahl indices, shown in Figure 9. If England and Wales is considered to be a single market, the Herfindahl index has remained at about 0.1 in both the 1 MW and 100 kW market, which would normally imply very competitive markets. But a similar index value would have been observed even if there had been little or no second-tier supply, simply because there are 12 RECs, each of which typically accounts for less than 10 per cent of the total England and Wales market.

A more relevant picture is given by the Herfindahl indices in each REC area taken separately. Here, the levels of concentration are much higher, reflecting the higher market shares retained by the local RECs. There is also a greater concentration in the 100 kW markets than in the 1 MW markets. These figures suggest that the market is by no means as highly competitive as the national calculation would imply. There are also significant differences between REC areas.

However, measured by the Herfindahl index, the above 1 MW markets and the 100 kW to 1 MW markets have both become steadily less concentrated over time. Comparing different REC areas, the Herfindahl indices in the 1MW markets varied between 0.3 and 0.7 in 1990/91 but by 1996/97 had fallen to the range 0.15–0.35. Roughly speaking, the extent of concentration in the above 1 MW markets has halved. In the first 3 years of the 100 kW market, the Herfindahl indices fell from the range 0.4–0.75 to the range 0.35–0.55, again a steady reduction in concentration.

Table 4
Real Reductions in Electricity Prices Paid by Industrial Customers,
1989/90 to 1996/97

Size of customer	Reduction (%)	Price in 1996/97 (p/kWh)
Small	−19.4	5.01
Medium	−24.6	3.76
Large	−22.1	2.88
of which:		
Moderately large	−24	3.16
Extra large	−17.8	2.52

Detailed figures for 1997/98 are not yet available, but the aggregate market-share figures suggest a further reduction in concentration as measured by REC-area Herfindahl indices.

(k) *Prices*

In assessing the competitive market, it is appropriate to look at the effect on prices as well as market shares. Figures produced by the Department of Trade and Industry (DTI) show that, in real terms, industrial customers throughout Great Britain have on average experienced price reductions of between 18 per cent and 25 per cent since privatization (see Table 4). These reductions reflect tightening of the price controls on the charges of monopoly transmission and distribution businesses, as well as the nature and extent of competition in generation and supply.

3. Scotland

(a) *Initial Restructuring*

The extent of restructuring was more limited in Scotland than in England and Wales. The South of Scotland Electricity Board (SSEB) and North of Scotland Hydro Electric Board became ScottishPower and Hydro-Electric respectively. They retained their status as vertically integrated companies responsible for generation, transmission, distribution, and supply in their respective territories. The nuclear plant that had been owned by the SSEB was separated into a new company, Scottish Nuclear, which, like Nuclear Electric, remained in government ownership. A series of contracts concerning the operation and output of each plant, collectively known as the restructuring contracts, were put in place between ScottishPower, Hydro-Electric, and Scottish Nuclear. These

Table 5
Market Shares of Output in the Scottish Generation Market (%)

	1989/90	1990/91	1995/96	1996/97
Scottish Nuclear	54	36	43	42
ScottishPower	31	44	38	38
Hydro-Electric	15	18	20	20
AEA	0	2	0	0
	100	100	100	100

contracts required ScottishPower and Hydro-Electric to take all Scottish Nuclear's output and had the effect of giving ScottishPower and Hydro-Electric access to a more balanced portfolio of generating plant than each would have had on its own.

These contracts are of relatively long duration. The Coal Agreement between ScottishPower and Hydro-Electric, that gives Hydro-Electric access to one-sixth of ScottishPower's coal capacity, expires in 2004. The Nuclear Energy Agreement between ScottishPower, Hydro-Electric, and Scottish Nuclear expires in 2005. The Peterhead and Hydro agreements expire in 2012 and 2039 respectively.

(b) *Development of Competition in Generation*

Table 5 shows market shares of output in generation in Scotland since Vesting. Before Vesting, plant subsequently owned by Scottish Nuclear accounted for more than 50 per cent of output. At privatization, Scottish Nuclear's Magnox station at Hunterston was closed and the company's share of generation opened nearly 20 percentage points lower. However, as a result of increasing output from its remaining AGR stations, Scottish Nuclear's share of the market increased by 6 percentage points between 1990/91 and 1996/97, mainly at the expense of ScottishPower's market share.

The total output from Scottish generation capacity has increased significantly (by more than a quarter) over this period. This is partly a result of increased demand within Scotland, but primarily due to the increase in exports through the interconnector to England and Wales. Exports in 1996/97 were more than a fifth of total Scottish generation.

The Herfindahl index indicates the overall change in concentration in generation, as shown in Figure 10. Before Vesting, the index had a value of 0.41 in Scotland. It fell to 0.36 in 1990/91 but has subsequently been essentially flat. Concentration in the Scottish generation sector was thus more concentrated at Vesting than was the generation market in England and Wales and has experienced no significant reduction in concentration

Figure 10
Herfindahl Index of Market Shares by Output: Scotland

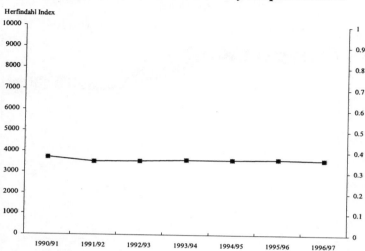

since then. Moreover, there is actually less competition than these figures suggest because all of Scottish Nuclear's output is sold to ScottishPower and Hydro-Electric until 2005 under the Nuclear Energy Agreement.

(c) *Future Developments in Generation*

There has recently been some small movement towards greater competition in generation in Scotland. Fife Energy has indicated its intention to construct a 75 MW plant within ScottishPower's area. Taking into account the size of the Scottish market, and the role of exports, the output of this plant might be expected to account for something over 1 per cent of total Scottish generation and close to 2 per cent of Scottish demand. Of potentially greater significance is PowerGen's plan to construct a 350 MW CCGT plant at Gartcosh in Lanarkshire. That application is currently the subject of a public enquiry.

The possibility of entry into generation has been amply demonstrated in England and Wales. The same cannot yet be said in Scotland. No doubt the particular circumstances of the Scottish market, and the particular structure maintained at Vesting, have influenced developments (or the lack of them) to date.

Competition in England and Wales has benefited from the interconnector between the two systems. Scottish exports to England have provided additional competition in the Pool. The Pool is also a source of potential competition for the market in Scotland, in the sense that suppliers in Scotland are able to purchase their requirements from

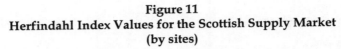

Figure 11
Herfindahl Index Values for the Scottish Supply Market
(by sites)

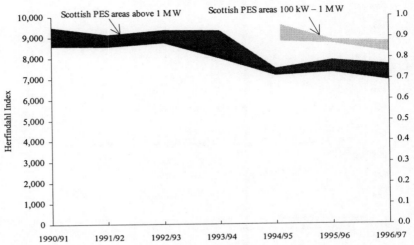

the Pool if they wish to do so. The prices established in the Pool, plus any additional transport costs associated with importing, thus act as a limit on prices in Scotland, at least until such time as imports reached a level that ran up against the limit of the capacity of the interconnector. To date, there have been negligible imports from the Pool into Scotland. Pool prices have, however, provided a useful yardstick against which to measure regulatory judgements concerning the appropriate price of generation in Scotland, in both the price-controlled and the competitive segments of the market.

The development of a fully competitive market in Scotland depends on there being greater variety in the sources of generation on offer to suppliers and, ultimately, to customers.

(d) *Supply Competition*

ScottishPower and Hydro-Electric have each retained a far higher proportion of their home markets than have any of the RECs in England and Wales. In 1996/97 they retained some 85 per cent of the market between 100 kW and 1 MW and 86 per cent of the market over 1 MW. Moreover, of the share of the market taken by second-tier suppliers, the greater part was accounted for by ScottishPower and Hydro-Electric acting as second-tier supplier in the other company's area.

The degree of concentration can again be summarized by the Herfindahl index. Figure 11 displays these index values. Figures for the market in Scotland as a whole are misleading, as in England and Wales as a whole. Once again, it is more sensible to focus on each area separately.

In the above 1 MW market in each of the two Scottish areas, the Herfindahl index was around 0.9 for the first 4 years after privatization. The index has since reduced to the range 0.7–0.8, but this is still more concentrated than if there were two equal-sized competitors. In the market between 100 kW and 1 MW there has been an even more modest decline to 0.82 in one area and 0.88 in the other.

Preliminary estimates for 1997/98 show that, in the market above 1 MW, the market share of second-tier suppliers has stayed relatively constant at 13 per cent of sales, but within that total the share of companies other than ScottishPower and Hydro-Electric has increased from 5 per cent in 1996/97 to 8 per cent. In the market between 100 kW and 1 MW, second-tier suppliers are now estimated to account for 13 per cent of sales as against 8 per cent in 1996/97. Within that total, ScottishPower and Hydro-Electric no longer account for the majority of those second-tier sales: their combined share of the second-tier market has remained constant at 6 per cent. There has thus been reduction in concentration in supply in Scotland but, on the basis of market shares, the extent of this competition in supply is still significantly less than in England and Wales.

(e) *Prices*

In the first few years after Vesting, industrial customers' perceptions were that prices may have fallen further, or to a lower level, in Scotland than in England and Wales. However, in recent years many such customers perceived an opposite tendency. Although they are not published separately, the DTI's figures are collected separately for England and Wales and for Scotland, using samples based on type of industry and on size of customers' electricity demand. However, comparison is not straightforward because the composition of Scottish customers by industry and size is different from that in England and Wales. Moreover, the coverage of the industrial base is rather lower in Scotland than in England and Wales, even on a proportionate basis, and this means that Scottish figures have to be treated with considerable reservation.

Bearing these points in mind, calculations using a common weighting by type and size of customers suggest that, in 1994, Scottish prices were on average about 10 per cent lower than in England and Wales. An important part of the reason for the difference in prices is the different treatment of the costs of nuclear and renewable energy. In 1994, all customers in England and Wales paid a fossil-fuel levy of 10 per cent on their electricity bill to fund the additional costs of nuclear and renewable generation. In Scotland there have been no renewables orders until recently. The additional costs of nuclear generation have been recovered through the contracts between Scottish Nuclear and ScottishPower and Hydro-Electric, which are in turn reflected in prices to franchise customers, rather than to customers in the competitive market. Adjusting downwards the prices in the non-franchise market in England and Wales for the effect of the levy broadly removes the difference between average prices north and south of the border.

Calculations for later years suggest that prices in Scotland were about 3 per cent higher than prices in England and Wales in 1995, but that in 1996 the difference was broadly eliminated.

(f) *Trading Arrangements in Scotland*

Suggestions that prices in Scotland were increasing relative to those in England and Wales (and in some cases were higher), in addition to complaints from customers, suppliers, and others, led me to conclude that the operation of the supply market in Scotland was not consistent with the development of a fully competitive market. During 1996 I took steps to address these concerns and proposed to ScottishPower and Hydro-Electric that they reduce the price at which they, as generators, sell to other suppliers in Scotland. In previous years they had sold at the equivalent of the PSP. During 1997/98 they agreed to sell at the equivalent of the Pool purchase price (PPP) plus the ancillary services component of Uplift (whereas the PSP includes all of Uplift).

Customers and other suppliers naturally welcomed this, and it seems to have contributed to the increase in second-tier supply by other suppliers. The basis on which trading in Scotland should take place in future is at present the subject of further discussion, in parallel with the review of the supply price control.

4. The Competitive Market from 1998

The ending of the franchise in 1998 will complete the transitional period established at privatization for the introduction of competition in the supply of electricity. At present, the industry, and the regulator, are spending a great deal of time and effort in ensuring a robust set of arrangements is in place to make a reality of choice for domestic and other smaller customers. The complexity and costs of introducing these arrangements are considerable, but they have been designed in such a way that customers will face a straightforward process for changing supplier should they wish to do so. Evidence from the competitive market to date does not suggest that a high proportion of smaller customers will switch supplier immediately upon the introduction of competition. But this evidence does suggest that competition, once allowed, tends to grow over time. A similar pattern is likely to emerge in the domestic market after 1998, reflecting the gradual transition of the British electricity industry from monopoly to competition.

It will be important to protect customers during that transition by means of a restraint on the prices charged by the public electricity suppliers. In my view, this assurance can be most effectively provided, while creating conditions suitable for competition, by fixing a set of maximum tariffs to be made available by each public electricity supplier to domestic and the smaller non-domestic customers. These tariff restraints potentially expose suppliers to variations in purchase costs to a greater extent than the pass-through forms of price control that have been used hitherto. This consideration reinforces the need to avoid the exercise of market power by the major generators, including in forthcoming contract negotiations.

There are important relationships between the development of competition in supply and in generation. A significant part of the benefits from the introduction of competition in supply for all customers will derive from the greater pressure this will put on suppliers to contract effectively for their purchase requirements and on generators to meet those requirements at lowest cost. I argued against the proposed takeovers of RECs by National Power and PowerGen, on the grounds that vertical integration between such major incumbents could deter the further development of competition in generation and supply.

Newbery and Green argue that removal of the supply franchise may have an adverse effect upon competition in generation. They point to the possibly reduced willingness of the RECs to sign long-term supply agreements with generators. It is true that 15-year contracts with RECs are no longer the basis for entering the generation market. However, this has been the case for some time and entry has by no means ceased. The removal of the monopoly in supply is forcing suppliers and generators to seek lower costs, to enhance their sales and purchasing skills, and to tailor their contractual arrangements to market conditions. Generators are building and operating plant on a 'merchant' basis, that is, without the security of a long-term off-take agreement for power purchase. Gas suppliers, plant manufacturers, and others are each taking shares of the risks that they can best manage. New entry in the generation market has continued to take place, despite the reduction and imminent expiry of the franchise. It is important that it continues to do so.

5. Conclusions

The various calculations presented in this paper suggest that, in England and Wales, competition is developing steadily in both generation and supply. This has been particularly the case for baseload generation where expansion by smaller incumbents and entry by independents has significantly reduced the market shares of National Power and PowerGen. For non-baseload generation, divestiture of plant to the Energy Group (formerly Eastern) has introduced a third significant player, thereby widening choice for customers and suppliers. However, there is a need for more competitors, particularly in the non-baseload part of the market. Some further new entry is in process, but more is needed.

Market shares retained by RECs in their own areas vary considerably, but, in general, competition in supply is more developed in the above 1 MW market than in the 100 kW to 1 MW market. Over time, in all REC areas, there has been a reduction in concentration in both parts of the market. The increase in competition in supply needs to continue.

In Scotland there has been virtually no development of competition in generation, and the development of competition in supply has been considerably slower than in England and Wales. To a large extent this reflects the structure of the Scottish market at privatization, particularly the strong incumbent positions of the two vertically-integrated Scottish companies and the limited interconnector link between Scotland and England, which has prevented the emergence of a single market in Great Britain. The situation has been held by relating Scottish generation prices to those in England and Wales. More competitive market arrangements would be desirable, but the scope for these is at present limited. In due course, however, new plant will need to be built in Scotland. It will be an important test of the Scottish system whether it can deal even-handedly with new entrants and incumbents.

10

Regulating Telecommunications

FOD BARNES*

1. Introduction

Competition is rapidly taking over from regulation as the main 'control' on the UK telecommunications industry. The benefits of this are becoming apparent: more imaginative pricing packages, better consumer focus, and prices being set by competitive pressure rather than by regulation. This change is underpinned by an increasingly competitive market structure. At the top level there are now over 50 major public telecommunications operators (over 190 licences have been issued), four mobile network operators, and many more providers of telecommunication services. At a more important level an increasing proportion of the population has a realistic choice of suppliers for telecommunications services: as of January 1997 in excess of 35 per cent of residential customers had a choice of two or more local access suppliers, and this is likely to rise to more than 70 per cent over the next 3 years. Business customers are even better off in terms of choice of local access provider. And in addition, nearly everyone has access to a choice of long distance and international telecommunications companies.

The telecommunications market is rapidly becoming, and in parts may already be, competitively supplied. But this has not arisen overnight. The statutory monopoly was removed in 1982 and the market was effectively opened up to any supplier in 1991. The process, which still has some way to go, of getting from the single supplier to effective choice for all is complex and has brought into sharp focus some difficult questions regarding the nature of competition in the telecommunications industry; the type, extent, and application of the appropriate 'rules' within which competition can operate; and the process of regulation itself. It is these problems of transformation with which this chapter is concerned, firmly located in the real world of real problems as experienced by Oftel.

* Policy Adviser to the Director General of Telecommunications. I would like to thank Alan Bell for many helpful comments on earlier drafts. All errors remain mine.

2. The Transitions from Detailed Regulation

There is a clear distinction between competitive markets and price-regulated monopolies: in one, prices are set by the interaction of supply and demand and, within the constraints of the competitive process, companies have freedom over the structure and level of prices, when to change them, and what combination of price and quality to offer. In the other, absolute price levels are set by regulation, relative prices are likely to be constrained, if not set, and quality levels are implicitly or explicitly set by the regulator. Within the UK telecommunications market, if a dominant and highly regulated BT is successfully to make the transition to become one of many suppliers operating in a competitive market, then regulation must also make the transition from deterministic control to no (direct) control. Unfortunately, the market does not suddenly flip from monopoly to competition, so intermediate levels of regulation may be needed as the competitive market—but in which BT has a degree of market power—develops. The following example looks at the problems Oftel has encountered in the withdrawal of detailed regulation within a market—in this case the replacement of detailed and specific price determination by Oftel with pricing flexibility (albeit on a cost base agreed by Oftel) in the market for interconnection services provided by one telecommunication company to another.

(a) *Example 1: What Price per Service?*

Interconnection services are those which are provided by one network operator to another to enable such operators to provide retail products. They typically consist of, for example, call conveyance for part of a call's transmission from the caller to the called party, or services that keep the configuration of networks up to date so that they can successfully convey all the calls that are presented to them. Critically, they consist of the use of *part* of a network, or *part* of a 'service' that would be provided by a network for its own use. The general problem is, therefore, 'what is the price of a small part of a complex network operation?'

The total costs of running BT's network are reasonably well defined, and measurable. The cost of supplying a service that uses part of the network, for a small amount of time, at a particular time, is much more difficult to define and measure. A number of different approaches are possible, all of which are viable, and all of which would result in the recovery of total costs through time. However, they can produce quite different charges for individual services.

The setting of individual component charges for a monopolist by the regulator, according to some deterministic formula based entirely on past costs and an 'arbitrary' accounting cost allocation rule, may not matter very much if there is no competitive supply for those services. (There may be an allocative efficiency loss which has an impact on other sectors of the economy, but they are unlikely to be substantial.) However, the pricing of each interconnection service in this way, reflecting some rather arbitrary, though consistent, allocation of costs, produces a pricing structure that is unlikely to occur in a competitive market. In such a market, prices would be set with reference to both cost and demand conditions.

If competition between operators does start to emerge, the arbitrary basis of the imposed pricing structure is unlikely to lead to efficient entry and may distort that competition. In addition, as competition takes hold, it is appropriate to remove the mechanistically determined price control from the incumbent in order to allow it similar degrees of freedom to the new competitors. (Indeed, the objective should be to remove price control completely once competition is well established.) Given the nature of the determined price structure, sudden removal of price control is likely to result in rapid changes in price structure, even if, in total, prices were constrained by that competition. The degree of market disruption caused by the change in price structure would also be likely to be a constraint on the development of competition (even if only transitory). There is, therefore, considerable benefit to be had if the arbitrary element of price control can be removed before competition has developed sufficiently to allow the complete removal of price control.

The competition rules applying to price behaviour that would be appropriate once price control has been removed completely would be those applying to enterprises in a competitive market—that is, the rules relevant to anti-competitive behaviour. Predatory prices would be ruled out, as would pricing strategies designed to eliminate competitors. Prices significantly above costs would not be possible in a competitive market. Beyond these controls, individual pricing decisions would be within the commercial strategy of the company.

In a market where competition is developing, but not fully established, competition cannot be relied upon to stop excessive prices, but within that constraint there is no obvious reason why the pattern of prices should not be left up to the supplier, subject to the normal rules on anti-competitive behaviour. Retail price control in telecommunications has always been largely based on this approach, with the degrees of freedom for BT increasing through time. This is now the fundamental basis of the network charge control for setting wholesale conveyance charges that Oftel has proposed to BT for the period to 2001 — an RPI - X constraint on a basket of interconnection services with individual prices for conveyance limited to a floor of (total service) long-run incremental costs and a ceiling of 'stand alone' costs. (In this case stand-alone costs include any costs common to conveyance and access—see Oftel (1997) for more details of the proposals.) These would replace the individual determination by Oftel of the price for each network element, and hence the price of each interconnection service.

In practice, the application of such a basket-based price control introduces some additional complications. In particular, it raises the question of the need to ensure that services within the same basket have common cost characteristics. Another dimension is the degree to which competitive price restraint is possible and/or likely and the facility available to BT to change prices of services in the basket to benefit itself at the expense of competitors.

Some interconnection services may never be competitively supplied, at least within foreseeable technological developments. In particular, the final delivery of a call to its terminating point may never be a competitive market as the telephone number used by the caller uniquely identifies the network that has to be used to terminate that particular call at any particular point in time. The caller, who is, in general, paying for the termination, has no possibility of choice over the terminating network to be used (this decision is made by the person receiving the call) so must accept whatever charge is levied. (*In extremis* the caller could not make the call, but this is unlikely to be a significant restraint on charges.) Even where a called party has more than one access supplier (and this is unlikely to apply to residential customers) it is still likely to be the called party, not the caller, who can choose which access provider is used to terminate in-bound calls. Because of this there are no incentives on terminating operators to keep prices low—rather the reverse.

This monopoly aspect of call termination means that it is inappropriate to add this service to a general basket of interconnection services where competitive supply is expected. If it were, the ability to load costs on to that particular service would be likely to distort competition in other services in the same basket, particularly in respect of provision of services from suppliers that did not have a call termination business (for example, those only providing long-distance or international interconnection services).

Problems of a rather different nature arise at the other end of the spectrum, where competition in the provision of one or more services is expected to develop sufficiently for all price controls to be lifted from them within the life of the price control. The appropriate value of the price deflator is dependent on the basket of services its covers. Change the scope of the basket, and the value of X is also likely to need changing (unless the cost drivers of the service taken out have the same characteristics as those of the remaining services). At a minimum, therefore, the removal of a service from price control in the middle of the price-control time period would be likely to imply a change in the value of X. But more importantly, the anticipation of the removal of a service would provide an incentive to play the system with both anti-competitive effects and a negation of the protection of excessive prices for the remaining services. By rapidly reducing the prices of prospectively competitive services while they are still in the basket, market entry is made more difficult and the prices of other services in the basket do not need to be reduced so much; once the service has been removed from the basket, prices can be allowed to drift up (or not be reduced as fast as the underlying costs fall), but now there is no knock-on effect on the required price changes on the services still in the basket. The regulatory price pressure on the remaining (non-competitive) services is thus reduced. To avoid this manipulation of the price control, the value of X would need to be recalculated when a service left the basket, taking into account the actual price changes to individual elements since the basket was first set. This degree of recalculation of X would be likely severely to limit the incentive properties of the RPI – X approach. Thus, these prospectively competitive services also need to be excluded from the general basket, and subject to their own 'safeguard' control until the anticipated effective control through competition takes over.

The third problem relates to the basis on which the total revenue for services within the basket should be calculated, and the precise definition of the individual price floor. Although the latter can be refined as experience is gained in operating this system, the former requires a unique answer in order to set the basket control.

Competitive markets have no respect for the pattern or extent of past investments — prices are related to the costs of the most efficient current producer, and tempered by the anticipated costs of a new entrant with no sunk costs (and by the existence, or otherwise, of barriers to entry). Competitive pressure would also be expected to move prices down towards the incremental costs, but long-term provision of the service will only be maintained if the total costs of the efficient operator are, on average, recovered.

These considerations lead to the conclusion that the total revenue from the basket should at least cover the long-run incremental costs of the production of that basket of services. However, costs common to both interconnection and access (costs recovered from BT's retail customers) would still need to be incorporated. There is clearly no perfect answer, but an answer consistent with any assumptions made in the retail price controls is necessary. Nominal allocation of these common costs on the basis of a mark-up in proportion to direct costs falls into this category, and is what is proposed.

The definition of the floor has been set at the incremental cost, where the increment is all conveyance, as measured for a component of the network (e.g. a single transmission or switching stage). The ceiling is where all the common costs between that component and access, in addition to the incremental costs, are recovered in the price of that component. Thus each component has a floor price and a ceiling (which in some cases may be the same — if there are no shared costs with access for that component) and BT is free to set component charges anywhere in this range for each component, subject to a maximum total weighted price of all components taken together (i.e. the basket).

In practice, the things that are actually sold in this market are combinations of components, so even where a component's price floor and ceiling are the same there is still some flexibility in the price of the actual services sold to other operators.

This degree of flexibility may not be perfect, and other definitions of floors and ceilings could be used. However, the information requirements to establish even the proposed floors and ceilings are quite severe. It is also the case that the degree of flexibility allowed is significant; it will increase the potential difficulty in assessing whether or not BT's charging policy is having anti-competitive effects. On the other hand, the freedom given to BT should have significant beneficial effects for customers. Under these circumstances, experience of controlled walking before attempting to run is necessary to contain the risks of anti-competitive behaviour.

The development of the interconnection pricing regime, and the movement of regulatory controls so that they allow outcomes closer to that likely to arise under a fully competitive market, has a paradoxical implication for the requirements for information. On the one hand, the regulator needs much more sophisticated data on which to base the initial price cap — long-run incremental costs and common costs — and on the other, the degree of precision required in relation to individual prices is *potentially* lower — as long as individual prices are clearly within the relevant floor and ceiling range, the regulator needs to be less concerned about the precise relationship between costs and prices. To a considerable extent the precision needed in the financial management system is in the hands of BT — the closer to the floor it wishes to price, the greater the precision and the more robust the financial data relating to costs needs to be.

(b) *Lessons from Example 1*

The transition from regulation of prices to competitively set prices is, in practice, complex. The regulatory intervention becomes more complex before it gets simpler, and simultaneously becomes more detailed (in terms of disaggregation) but less deterministic and intrusive (in terms of there being only one possible outcome). This process of transition to less intrusive regulation is only possible if there is sufficient financial data, of an adequate quality, to underpin the decision process.

The second lesson is that the practical objectives of regulation may conflict with the transition process. To some extent the transition needs to be anticipated at the time any regulation is being reset. This puts a premium on the regulator being able to anticipate future market developments sufficiently to enable the regulation not to get in the way of possible transitions to competition.

The third lesson is that the anticipation of the appropriate rules once competition has arrived may itself not be straight forward. At least in the initial stages of the process of competition displacing direct price control, the rules relating to anti-competitive behaviour may need to take account of the imbalance in market positions of the players and to reflect the particular nature of interconnected networks and the market structure. This may result in an intermediate degree of flexibility—not determined by regulation, but not the same degree of flexibility that a producer in a fully competitive market would have.

3. Keeping Competitive Markets Competitive

Some parts of the telecommunications industry are already fully competitive: there are large numbers of suppliers and no firm has a dominant position. These market segments do not need regulation of the price control type, but they may still need regulatory action. Two characteristics of these markets seem to set them apart: action in a related (not fully competitive) market can have a direct impact on the prospects of suppliers in the competitive market, and the suppliers may be very different, ranging from the small specialist to those that are just a small part of very large companies which may be dominant in related markets. BT's activities in equipment sales, and Oftel's intervention in this competitive market, illustrate some of the problems involved in keeping competitive markets competitive in the telecommunications sector.

(a) *Example 2: Telephone Equipment*

The days of the universal, any colour you want as long as it is black, telephone are long gone. There are hundreds of shops selling telephones (and other telephony equipment) produced by a multiplicity of suppliers. BT's market position as either a retailer of equipment, or supplier of

'BT badged' equipment varies from strong (market share in the order of 25 per cent) to insignificant, depending on the type of equipment. With the exception of a special rule (Condition 21 of BT's licence) relating to BT manufacturing equipment (which, except for very specialized markets, BT does not do) there are no special regulatory rules applying to BT in this area (and none was needed, even at the time of privatization in 1984).

Generally, the market is working well, and has been from at least the time of privatization. There are no special economic regulatory rules that apply to this activity, and no licence is required. In relation to BT, no direct regulation of behaviour is needed. However, this does not mean that Oftel has been inactive: BT has been, and is still (in 1997) subject to a number of *competition authority*-type interventions to temper its activities in this area. This intervention has thrown up a considerable number of complex issues about the appropriate tests for anti-competitive behaviour and the appropriate level of financial information that should be easily available from BT in order for Oftel to be able to *maintain* a competitive market in equipment supply where a regulated entity with a very strong market position in a related market (i.e. telecommunication services) also wants to be a commercial player.

The general problem confronting Oftel is to set, and maintain, the 'right' rules across the boundary between the fully competitive market—equipment supply—and the not yet fully competitive market—network services—so that the equipment market remains competitive. There are rules which would achieve this objective—for example, an outright ban on BT's participation in the equipment supply market—but probably at some considerable cost to consumer convenience and at the cost of restricting BT's line of business. If behaviour rules can be developed that do ensure that the competitive equipment market can remain competitive, customers should be able to get the advantages of both vertical integration and competitive supply. However, getting the right rules in place has turned out to be a difficult task.

(i) The Telephone Equipment Direction

BT is subject to the Telephone Equipment Direction under Condition 20B.15 of its licence, which deals with subsidy and cross-subsidy of parts of BT's activities. There are two related issues behind this intervention. The first deals with the question of whether BT is subsidizing equipment it has procured from third-party manufacturers in the wholesale market (i.e. BT-branded equipment), thus distorting competition between equipment manufacturers to the detriment of manufacturers and/or suppliers of non-BT-branded equipment. The second deals with the question of whether BT, as a retailer of equipment (i.e. the activities of the BT shops), is subsidizing that activity to the detriment of competition from other retailers.

(ii) BT-branded equipment (wholesale market)

BT-branded equipment is available to provide most equipment that domestic users are likely to attach to their telephone lines (e.g. corded telephones, cordless telephones, small fax machines, and answering machines), and such BT-branded equipment has market shares in the order of 30–40 per cent (corded phones) down to about 15–20 per cent (fax machines). These market shares are significant—and tend to be considerably larger than any other branded supplier, but BT is not dominant.

However, the actions of BT in this area resulted in complaints that BT was cross-subsidizing the supply of BT-branded equipment and distorting the market, to the detriment of non-BT-branded equipment. Accounting data suggested that, measured on an accounting basis, this activity of BT was making persistent losses, and there were no robust data available on an incremental basis.

In principle, the 'problem' of this cross-subsidy is relatively straightforward. Running an equipment supply chain and running a telecommunications network are very different activities, so there is little difficulty arising from shared or common costs. The identification of the relevant costs which BT should cover from this activity is, therefore, relatively straightforward. In practice, quantifying these costs turned out to be difficult because of the inadequacies of BT's management information and accounting system. (The practical problem of actually quantifying costs from the information available at the time it is needed is a theme that will run through this chapter.)

But even if the practical problems are overcome there are, at the edges, still some other problems. For example, the BT brand is relatively powerful, at least for simple telephony equipment. On what basis should BT's equipment supply activities have access to that brand? Should this activity contribute some 'fair' proportion of the costs of brand maintenance? Or should it purchase the brand image on a commercial basis from the brand creator (i.e. the BT network)? Or should it only contribute any incremental costs of extending the brand to equipment? (The particular answer chosen in this case was the 'fair contribution'.)

The equipment direction was issued in September 1995. The first complaint in this area had been received much earlier and, indeed, there already was in existence a direction under Condition 18 requiring BT to eliminate subsidy of a much larger section of its activity (the whole of the apparatus supply business). However, the specific complaints received by Oftel were targeted at a more narrowly focused section of the market

and it was not until the interconnection and accounting separation
(ICAS) licence amendments were agreed with BT in March 1995 that it
became realistic to focus action at the level of detail required. But what
level of detail?

(b) *Regulatory Entities and Market Definitions*

There is no general requirement on wholesalers or retailers to make a
'profit', or even cover their costs, on *every individual* item they sell. There
is no obvious reason why the rules should be different for BT. It would,
therefore, seem to be inappropriate to require BT to make a profit on
every single item of equipment it sells under the BT brand (i.e. as a
wholesaler) or every item it sells retail. But the other extreme, where the
only requirement is for BT plc (i.e. BT's equipment supply and network
operations taken together) to cover its costs in total, is clearly not
acceptable either. If competition is the objective, one necessary division
is clearly between activities that are currently competitive and those
which are not. This isolates the 'monopoly' activities (which can be
regulated) from the competitive markets which are potentially open to
anyone who wishes to supply. But the reality in telecommunications is
that this neat boundary does not really exist. Most telecommunications
markets are not monopoly (or even subject to limitations on the number
of suppliers). Thus, theoretically, it would be open to conclude that it
would acceptable for BT to cover its costs at the aggregated level of, say,
equipment supply and business telephony (both of which are not now
subject to price control) on the grounds that BT is potentially subject to
competition from suppliers who could also operate in both markets.

(i) Market reality

The reality of competition is, however, rather different. Those in competition with BT in the equipment market are not realistically in a position
to enter the network supply business, either in terms of the capital
required to enter such markets, or in the skills to run such a business.
Many of them are very small, in terms of operation and capitalization,
compared to BT. If these companies are to compete with BT in a way that
will guarantee that, if they are more efficient than BT and/or better at
meeting customer requirements, they will be able to succeed, then two
conditions need to be met. First, BT must at least cover all its incremental
costs (including any cost of capital) incurred in participating in these
markets from within that market. Second, any action necessary to stop
anti-competitive behaviour must take place fast enough to avoid, if
possible, competitors going out of business before any corrective action
can be taken.

A secondary consideration is the potential source of the subsidy. In the long term, at least, subsidy is only available from markets where there is some degree of market power. In the transition between 'monopoly power' that needs directly regulating (e.g. by direct price control) to one where competition can be relied on to eliminate the possibility of it being a subsidy source, there is likely to be a period where price control is not necessary, but there is still a degree of market power with, therefore, the possibility of subsidy being provided into other markets. This is especially true where these other markets are characterized by much smaller commercial players offering a much more limited range of products and services.

The reasons why competition in the first market may be 'sufficient' to allow the removal of direct price control but still leave a market player with sufficient market power to generate subsidy, is the practical reality that regulation is far from perfect. Thus, an 'unregulated' (i.e. not subject to a price cap), but less than fully competitive, market may provide a better outcome than regulation in this market, but raise the dangers of anti-competitive behaviour in the other markets. In practice, therefore, the concern to ensure that there is no cross-subsidy from markets where BT has market power into markets where it does not, does not necessarily correspond to ensuring that there is no cross-subsidy from 'regulated' to 'unregulated' markets.

(ii) Timely action

Translating this into action means that the necessary level of disaggregation of the activities at which it is appropriate to apply competition tests and for which financial information is likely to be required for competition purposes, cannot be decided by simply looking at which activities are 'regulated' and which are not. The appropriate level of disaggregation will depend on a number of different, and changing, factors. These factors are more likely to be concerned with market definitions and the particular state of actual and potential competition, than the particular regulatory categories being applied at any point in time. These boundaries are clearly not fixed and change through the actions of both BT and other market players.

In the particular example of the equipment supply business, BT faces a market where many of its competitors are (relatively) small and compete in only part of that market (e.g. simple telephones, but not fax machines). Allegations of anti-competitive behaviour may, therefore, be rather narrowly focused (e.g. that the supply of BT-branded corded telephones is being cross-subsidized) and may be well founded (at least within the narrowness of the market definition). To test these allegations, financial data disaggregated to quite fine levels will be required and, because of the size of the competitors, speed of response will be important if damage to the competitiveness of the market is not to result where the complaint itself is proven.

Unsurprisingly, perhaps, BT's financial information base has not been organized in such a way as to make the extraction of this type of market-based information easy. The equipment direction has had to be underpinned by the development of special investigations into the collection and disaggregation of cost information. What was apparent was that BT, itself, was not aware of the relationships between costs and revenue generation at this level of detailed, market-led, disaggregation. Only at higher levels of aggregation, which could include both activities in which BT held significant market power (and/or where barriers to entry might be high) and activities where BT faced significant competition, could costs and revenues be brought together in a meaningful way.

The difficulty of defining in advance the boundaries of the activities that will require financial analysis means that rigid, regulator-imposed, accounting manuals are unlikely to be adequate for competition purposes. What is required is a system that is flexible enough to allow such information to be generated easily from accounting data as and when required. Complete flexibility is probably unobtainable, but knowledge of the market, market players, and knowledge of likely future technological trends should provide a sufficient basis for creating a manageable financial information system. However, the regulator is unlikely to have this information and, even if he did, the direct imposition of the financial information requirements on such a flexible and on-going basis would be likely to be highly intrusive.

In the course of its normal business in a competitive market BT should, of course, have the relevant information. Thus, the licence condition relating to accounting records (Condition 20B) and the Fair Trading Condition (Condition 18A) both put the onus on BT to anticipate what kinds of information are likely to be required, and to design the external (and internal) financial management and accounting systems accordingly. Although this is making BT change its accounting systems, and could thus be characterized as intrusive regulation, the resulting information system should also be commercially valuable to BT, over and above satisfying its regulatory requirements, and allow Oftel to be less prescriptive on particular issues.

(c) BT, the Retailer of Equipment

BT's share of the retail market for simple (domestic market) telephone equipment (both BT-branded and other) is, in general, less than its share of the equipment market (because BT-branded equipment is sold in non-BT shops). It is a strong position, but not, in general, a dominant position.

A similar set of issues arise in relation to BT as a retailer of equipment, with some additional complications. In its manifestation as 'sale through BT shops' there is the relatively straightforward issue of the allocation of the (shared) costs of the shop between retailing of equipment and the provision of other services relating to BT as a provider of telecommunication services (e.g. bill paying). Apart from the issue of the availability of the necessary information (see above) there are no great concerns arising in the methodology that should be employed in the recovery of these common costs.

There is also an issue of the range of equipment stocked: are BT shops in such a significant position of market power in the retailing market for the stocking policy of the shops to be competition issue? In practice, BT shops (on their own) are not really significant enough to be able seriously to distort competition in the equipment market (the market share of BT shops is significantly below that of BT-branded equipment). The theoretical possibility that BT could distort the equipment market by vertical integration *through the use of BT shops* does not appear to be happening in practice. Thus, in spite of allegations of anti-competitive behaviour in this area, no regulatory action has been suggested or imposed by Oftel.

However, in other manifestations of 'BT the retailer' there are more complicated issues. BT as a provider of telecommunication services has access to potential (equipment) customers in ways which are not available to other equipment suppliers (although they may be to other network operators). This may be as a result of fault fixing or in respect of the supply of new services. As far as the customer is concerned they want services that are likely to require both telecommunication services and equipment. Allowing the network operator (e.g. BT) to provide both will avoid the customer having to deal with two different entities, and allowing the same person to deal with both aspects of BT's activities avoids the customer being shunted around within the same organization. It may also allow a much faster provision or restoration of the service the customer wants — for example by allowing the engineer who installs a new line also to sell the customer a phone. On the other hand, this integration of activities with very different (competitive) market structures could have some distorting effect on the equipment market, because it allows BT (and other network operators) to sell equipment in ways to which other equipment suppliers could have difficulty in responding.

So, in addition to ensuring that the costs are correctly identified and recovered, there may be other restrictions that are appropriate to apply across the boundary between the telecommunications services business and the supply of equipment. But what the correct set of restrictions are is not clear cut. Currently, BT (as network operator) is allowed to supply equipment direct to customers in this way, but the transactions must be kept separate, and billed independently.

A more problematic (but now declining) activity is the rental of 'simple' equipment by BT (i.e. a simple telephone). Here, joint billing is allowed, as without it the additional billing costs involved would be significant for the rental of such a low-value item. Some customers appear to wish to rent this type of equipment, and allowing them to benefit from the economy of scope in billing would appear to be in their interests.

(d) 'Project March' – Usage Interactions between Equipment and Telecommunications Services

The purchase of telephone equipment and the consumption of telephony services are generally separate activities in terms of consumption (usually sequential). However, from a producer perspective there are closer relationships – the consumption of services is dependent on the provisions of equipment. Irrespective of the identity of the equipment supplier, network operators have an interest in the greater diffusion of equipment in order to increase the (subsequent) sale of their services. This interaction introduces a further complication in the interactions between supply of equipment and the supply of services – BT's Project March is an example of this interaction and its potential competitive impact.

Telecommunications networks generally have the characteristic that the marginal call is more profitable than the average call and, if that call is not at the time of peak usage, the marginal profitability may be very high. Some apparatus will increase marginal usage (or at least marginal usage that generates an income) significantly. It is thus in the network operators' interest to get that apparatus installed, and it may 'pay' such an operator (in terms of increased profitability) to 'subsidize' the sale of this equipment.

BT (as a network operator) has made such an offer (Project March – in June 1996) and subsidized the sale of answering machines, the use of which is very profitable for network operators because the machines answer calls which would otherwise go unanswered (and thus not be paid for). It would not seem appropriate for BT (as network operator) to be prohibited outright from behaving in this way. Answering machines provide a useful service for both the called party and the calling party. 'Returning' some of the profit earned by network operators to those installing such machines does not seem unreasonable. However, the conditions of such an offer would clearly be important if it was not to distort competition in the equipment market (between different equipment suppliers and between different retail outlets) and competition between different network operators. In the event, these conditions were subject to Oftel intervention (hence the delay from March to June). The final conditions of the offer were that the subsidy was to be paid on any answering machine bought within the offer period, and the subsidy was to be paid by BT, whatever network the machine was attached to (these were not the conditions as originally proposed by BT).

The reasoning behind the requirement that the payment was to be made on all machines is fairly straightforward: the advantage to the network operator stems from any machine and is not confined to any particular machines (e.g. BT branded machines) nor to where they are bought (e.g. in a BT shop). The reasoning behind the requirement that the subsidy is paid by BT irrespective of network to which they are attached, is less straightforward.

Essentially, there are two reasons. The first is that the major benefit to network operators arises on the network on which the call *to* the answering machine is made, not the network to which the machine itself is attached. It is the caller, not the called party, who pays for the call that would otherwise go unanswered. Because of BT's market position in the supply of telephony services most of these calls will have come from the BT network even if the machine is connected to a different network. The second reason is that, because of the way interconnection charges are structured, the profit on incremental calls is distributed between network operators in proportion to the amount of different networks used in that call—it does not all go to the network that generated that call. Again, under these circumstances, most of the benefit is likely to flow to BT (because it has the biggest network) irrespective of who makes the call, even when this is a return call made by the owner of the answering machine. (It is for this reason that it is economic for BT to run generic call-stimulation advertisements—'it's good to talk'—without worrying too much about the networks the calls are made on.)

(e) *Lessons from Example 2*

The division between equipment supply and the provision of telecommunications services is relatively clear cut. Equipment supply and manufacture are not network industries and behave much more like competitively supplied economic activities (i.e. more like the supply of any household equipment). Nevertheless, defining the appropriate boundaries between and within these different activities, and defining the appropriate behavioural rules across these boundaries, is a complex and dynamic process, related to the particular states of competition in the respective markets and their technological developments. Thus, even here, the company with market power needs to use its knowledge of the markets and technology to anticipate where competition problems are likely to arise (and hence where the regulatory boundaries need to be) and to ensure that it has the information necessary to demonstrate that it is not acting in an anti-competitive manner across these boundaries.

A second lesson is that there are additional issues relating to the operation of a company operating in both regulated and competitive markets, beyond simply having the right financial information available and meeting financial requirements. Where such competitive markets are related to markets with structural or other imbalances, there is a balance to be struck between short-term consumer requirements of convenience and simple rules designed to maximize competition in those competitive markets. There are unlikely to be perfect answers to balancing this conflict and it will be a matter of judgement where some behavioural lines should be drawn to ensure that customers get the best deal in the long term. Where these lines are drawn is also not likely to be stable over the long term, but influenced by the state of competition in the relevant markets.

The third lesson is that there may well be complex interactions between activities in these different markets and competition within each one. The regulatory 'rules' need to be capable of dealing with these interactions in a way that is competitively neutral if customers are to get the full benefit of the opportunities created by these interactions.

4. Future Regulatory Issues

The two examples described above deal with issues where at least the structure, if not the fine detail, has been mapped out. However, there are issues that can now be identified as being likely to be significant, but where even the structure of the possible solutions is largely undefined.

(a) *Example 3: Globalization*

One of these is the impact of globalization (or at least multi-national operation) of producers (and/or at least some kinds of consumer). As the international scope of the market increases, the relationship between different national regulatory structures, and the relationship between national and supra-national regulatory structures, becomes much more important. This impact can be both positive and negative — positive because the regulatory rule structure should match as far as possible the economic market of both producers and consumers, negative when it results in the application of a uniform set of rules that does not take into account the actual differences of different geographical markets. It is also important to remember that, even with the globalization trends in the telecommunications market, the vast majority of services are still produced and consumed within individual national boundaries.

For Oftel these issues have been thrown into sharp relief by the proposed merger between BT and MCI, with the consequent global focus of the merged entity (to be known as Concert). In regulatory terms the result of the proposal to merge has been to require Oftel rapidly to work through what, if anything, this consequent change of focus, and change of organizational structure, means for UK consumers. At the time of writing this task is still incomplete.

Less unexpectedly, the increasing competition of European markets and the moves to treat the European Union as the domestic market (i.e. by having cost-based interconnection agreements between operators in different member states, rather than accounting rates), has meant an increasing focus on the interaction between national UK and European regulation. However, this is not an interaction between regulatory systems in a steady state. Much of the detail of European rules has been developed very recently and, by the nature of the way the European institutions work, the actual outcome is subject to many pressures, some of which may only be tangentially related to telecommunications. More importantly, the detail of the European rules is being developed against a background of very different existing market structures in different member states.

To safeguard the interests of UK consumers under these circumstances, an additional set of skills is required over and above that needed to deal just with an 'isolated' UK. These are presentational and negotiation skills and the ability to recognize the implications of the difference between the current UK market structure and those of other member states.

At least to date, the UK has been largely successful in ensuring that European regulation works in harmony with, rather than against, the competitive market developments in the UK. But this has been achieved only by the recognition that different detailed rules may be necessary to achieve the same overall objectives of competitive markets, depending on the existing market structure. Although this appears to be slightly at odds with the trend within the UK market—where producers are increasingly subject to the same 'rules'—it is consistent with the increasing emphasis on markets, and hence the existing market structure in any particular market, being the main determinant of what kinds of detailed regulatory rules are appropriate. In the transition from a statutory monopoly to significant competition it may be necessary to go through a stage of highly deterministic and detailed controls on the ex-monopolist. Indeed, the process of transition may not start unless there is this level of regulatory intervention. But it would be counter-productive to *reimpose* this level of control on markets, such as the UK, that have already achieved a much more competitive structure.

(b) *Example 4: Convergence*

A second area of activity where the 'answers' are still largely unknown is the 'convergence' of telecommunications technology (driven by the digitization of all content), so that telecommunications networks that were highly differentiated in what services they could deliver (e.g. broadcasting networks or telephone networks) are now much closer to equivalent in terms of the services they can deliver to customers. This is having a significant impact on some of the underlying regulatory structures, which tend to treat different types of networks rather differently, and on some of the assumptions that underlie the regulation of these networks (e.g. the economics of the provision of high bandwidth to customers, or the products that drive consumer acquisition of the means of access to networks). Different ways of providing the same type of services and the provision of totally new types of services are developing rapidly in ways that cut across the existing set of regulatory rules and institutions. Inconsistent regulation across different delivery mechanisms or arbitrary service classifications runs the distinct risk of distorting markets and being unnecessarily restrictive, resulting in economic inefficiency and customers failing to get the full benefit of the technological developments in telecommunications.

General competition law can provide the framework within which these new developments can be tackled and Oftel's experience to date is that this provides a very good starting point. However, although convergence is bringing different types of network closer to equivalence, it is not making them the same. The particular points of bottleneck, or the particular way customers are locked into networks by their purchase of equipment, do still vary (and are likely to continue varying) for economic and technical reasons.

To achieve consistency of regulation across a diverse set of network types is difficult. It is making Oftel look more carefully at the relationship between the particular rules that apply to a specific network type (or even to a specific operator) and the objective, which is usually competition. Consistency of outcome is not achievable by the application of the same detailed rules to all, but only at the level of consistency of objectives. A stark example of this is the almost simultaneous conclusion by

Oftel that little, if any, *ex-ante* regulation of enhanced services (e.g. voice mail or Internet service provision) on switched networks (e.g. 'telephony' networks) is necessary, while at the same time it is developing quite detailed regulation for the provision of enhanced services (i.e. conditional access services) on unswitched networks (e.g. 'broadcasting' networks).

The objective is the same in both cases — to maximize the possibility of diverse services from diverse providers being offered to customers by minimizing the impact of bottleneck control where this exists. The different (regulatory) approaches arise because control of the telecommunications link to that customer is (technically) provided in very different ways, leading to very different locations of the bottleneck. In switched networks the control is basic to the design of network and is embedded at the centre of the network. In unswitched networks this control is an added feature, and is (physically) distributed at the edges of the network (i.e. the 'set-top box' at the customer end and the provision of information encryption services and 'control of the set-top box' services at the producer end).

More fundamentally, convergence is also making Oftel review its existing set of detailed rules to ensure that they are still fit for their purpose and still consistent with the high-level objectives of competition. This is, of course, no bad thing, but it does not make the practice of regulation any easier.

(c) *Lessons from Examples 3 and 4*

There are two main lessons that emerge from Oftel trying to deal with externally imposed change. The first is that, as the centre of focus moves from a national to a supra-national stage, an additional set of skills is required — skills of diplomacy. These may not pre-exist in a regulatory body, but the need for them may arise very quickly (e.g. from a merger). But in addition, the need for these skills (and, indeed, the emerging supra-national focus) is more a reflection of the developments in the producer and consumer markets. Anticipating these developments (by, for example, tracking them in a systematic way) would pay dividends in terms of ensuring that domestic regulation does not get in the way of the commercial benefits of globalization while safeguarding the UK customers' interests.

The second lesson is similar, but in this case involves trying to anticipate the impact of technological developments on the continued appropriateness of the existing regulatory structure and the detailed rules within it. The skills needed here are not so different, but there is an important change in emphasis from the deterministic application of a given set of rules, to the achievement of a consistent set of objectives through the application of more flexible rules. This builds on the changes that pre-date convergence of moving from prescriptive licence conditions ('rules') to effects-based rules (with operational guidelines).

5. Conclusions

Paradoxically the transition from regulation of a monopoly through to the 'unregulated' competitive market is likely to require a phase where regulation (or the application of special rules) is more comprehensive than at either end of the spectrum. However, this is not just a simple process of the rules getting tighter before they are relaxed. The rules in the transition are qualitatively different from those that are adequate to deal with straightforward monopoly problems. The rules become less deterministic, allowing for a greater range of possible outcomes, while still setting special boundaries as to what is, and is not, acceptable behaviour by operators with market power.

Although this is moving the market towards the types of activities that would be expected under a competitive market, it is also increasing the uncertainty of what is still likely to be seen as a regulated market. This, in turn, is likely to increase the apparent discretion of the regulator, because the boundaries of acceptable behaviour may be difficult to define precisely, and in advance. The actual discretion may have, in fact, reduced, in so far as the range of outcomes that could be prescribed by the regulator has reduced to those that approximate a competitive market outcome — a restriction that does not exist under pure monopoly regulation. However, the impact of the (reduced?) discretion has also changed. Under monopoly conditions, the different outcomes tend to change the distribution of prices between different customer groups, but tend to leave the overall position of the monopolist relatively unchanged. In transition the different outcomes still have different impacts on customers, but, more crucially, distribute costs and profits between different competitors, often in a relatively dramatic way. It therefore becomes more important to arrive at the 'right' answer — to ensure that the distribution between market players is fair.

In addition, whatever the actual change in discretion, this process is likely to raise the profile of the issue of the 'accountability' of the regulator — an issue that will also become more important if the regulator appears to come to 'wrong' answers. Thus the transitional period between monopoly and fully functioning competition is likely to make the regulatory processes more difficult, as well as making the regulatory decisions more complicated. This is one of the main reasons for the development of more extensive consultations, the publication of more extensive background information, and the provision of much fuller explanations of why particular decisions turned out the way they did. It is also part of the reasons for more extensive use of expert advisory panels in Oftel.

In most cases, these changes in regulatory processes are made at an informal level—no new 'rules' are imposed on regulation. However, there are exceptions and in Oftel's particular case some of these regulatory processes are becoming formalized in relation to the most obvious manifestation of the transition—the Fair Trading Condition—where, for the first time, an effective right has been given to the subject of an anti-competitive behaviour investigation to require the issue to be looked at by an independent advisory panel, and for its conclusions to be published. In addition, extensive guidelines have been published both to give interested parties a better understanding and as a recognition that this type of condition does allow for a range of behaviours and is itself considerably less deterministic than most licence conditions.

Two conclusions flow from this assessment. The first is that it gets more complicated before it gets easier—for the regulator and the regulated—but, if done right, for customers it should get better all the time. And the pain is worth the goal of increasing the competitiveness of the market. The second is that regulation is not something that can be set in concrete and imposed on the industry. Dynamic industries require dynamic regulation that can change as market and technological change occurs, which in turn means that complete regulatory certainty is both undesirable and unobtainable.

11

Competition in the Water and Sewerage Industry

I. C. R. BYATT*

1. Introduction

Competition takes many forms. Sometimes it involves entry into markets, sometimes new products. It can mean new producers. Sometimes it involves price wars, at other times new methods of marketing. Some analysts, considering how competition works in practice, focus on an industry structure — many firms, oligopoly, or monopoly — and others on barriers to entry and, more generally, whether markets are contestable rather than competitive. How do utilities, and particularly providers of water and sewerage services, fit in? What are the particular issues which might arise if market competition in the provision of these services grows, and what challenges do they pose for both the regulator and the government?

Unlike in the gas and electricity industry, competition in the water industry has been slow to emerge. This has been due to a combination of the natural characteristics of the water and sewerage industry and the limited opportunities afforded by the legislation. As a regulator whose statutory duty is to facilitate competition, unlike the other regulators who must promote competition, I would like to see more market competition.

I have, however, wanted to proceed cautiously. Opening up the industry to competitive forces will unwind current subsidies and may present a number of social issues which will fall to the government, rather than the regulator, to resolve. Water is a scarce resource. It should be used economically and it is important that prices should not give the wrong economic signals to customers. Competition should not drive prices down below the continuing costs of augmenting supply. Defining what these costs are has proved to be difficult and is one reason why competition has been slow to emerge.

* Director General of Water Services.

2. The Characteristics of the Water Industry

Some utility products are physically homogeneous, with easily defin-able characteristics. Drinking water is not. Although it is controlled by high minimum standards, these standards do not include all that the customer is concerned with, in particular, taste. Sewage is not homoge-neous; trade effluent ranges from being difficult and expensive to treat to being something weaker than domestic sewage.

Water is a natural monopoly combining considerable sunk costs in the infrastructure with high transportation costs. It is a rising cost industry, where cheap sources of supply are generally exploited first and where the incremental costs of supply are generally above average costs. There are geographical constraints on supply. Abstractions must be licensed and are carefully controlled.

The companies are vertically integrated covering water resources, distribution, and supply. There is no national grid. Transfers are essen-tially bilateral, although the terms of supply, including the price, can be determined by the regulator.

Although privatization made significant changes to the industry, it did not attempt to change the structure of the industry. Even now, many supplies can be, and are made without the holding of a licence of appointment or the obtaining of the exemption to hold such a licence. It is estimated there are about 50,000 private water suppliers in England and Wales. The nature of these supplies varies from a house with its own water supply to a private limited company supplying a not insignificant number of customers. For example, until 1997 when it was taken over by Severn Trent, the Cheadle Waterworks Company supplied approxi-mately 10,000 customers in Cheadle, Staffordshire.

On the dirty water side, 4 per cent of domestic premises are not connected to an undertaker's sewerage system and many businesses arrange for their own trade effluent disposal or for pre-treatment of effluent before discharging it into the undertakers' sewers.

The water and sewerage industries could even be viewed as two distinct industries, one licensed and regulated by the Director General of Water Services and the other unregulated. The key advantage for the supplier acting under licence is the statutory right to lay pipes across other people's land. This advantage must, however, be weighed against the obligations placed on licence undertakers (including the obligation to provide services if requested) and regulatory costs.

One feature of the water and sewerage industry is that, in contrast to electricity, where there has been a right of an independent producer to sell power to the electricity grid for many years, the water industry has no experience of allowing sharing of the distribution system.

Moreover, only 10 per cent of household customers are metered, although companies which have actively pursued a policy of metering have much higher meter penetration among households. Without a meter there would be no way of checking what water had been delivered to a customer.

3. The Role of the Regulator

The Director General of Water Services has a statutory duty to facilitate competition. It is worth noting that the word is facilitate — rather than promote as is the case for the other utility regulators. In legislating for competition in the water industry, Parliament recognized some of the difficulties in introducing competition into this industry.

The 1989 legislation did not, unlike in electricity, involve any restructuring of the industry to enable competition between alternative producers. It allowed almost no opportunity for market competition between undertakers, nor for customers to choose their service provider. What was possible was for the appointment of a new service provider within the area of an existing undertaker — commonly known as an 'inset appointment'. But new suppliers could only emerge to supply water to a qualifying site. A qualifying site was one which was not connected to an undertaker's distribution main or sewer and was situated 30 metres or more away from the main or sewer.

The scope for market competition was, therefore, very limited and Ofwat received no inset applications in respect of these sites. The 1992 Competition and Service (Utilities) Act widened the scope for competition, albeit in a limited way, through changes to the qualifying rules for inset appointment and by allowing customers to call upon neighbouring undertakers to supply water and sewerage services for domestic use across their boundaries. This right to demand cross-border supplies has rarely been used. This may be for a number of reasons. Customers may be unaware they have a choice, but in many cases it is likely that the pipe-laying costs which could be incurred by the customer in order to change supplier provide a disincentive.

While market competition in the early years of the regulatory regime was thus limited, the regulator could, however, use another form of competition which puts pressure on the costs of provision and stimulates rivalry in the provision of services to customers. This so-called comparative or yardstick competition permeates throughout the regime operated by the Director — and indeed beyond the immediate sphere of the Director's activities.

4. Comparative Competition

Although cautious in introducing opportunities for market competition, Parliament recognized that comparative competition offered great potential benefits.

Under medium-term price control, companies are able to increase their profits by reducing costs. By increasing profits they hope to reward shareholders by paying bigger dividends and driving up the share price. The City—analysts and shareholders—presses the companies to increase efficiency. It has access to considerable information about each company obtained from company accounts, the comparative information collected and published by Ofwat, and from specific presentations by companies. Comparative competition is a powerful mechanism which has led to big increases in efficiency among the water and sewerage companies. These efficiencies can be passed back to customers at periodic price reviews.

The regulatory regime similarly puts pressure on companies to improve service provision and to deal better with their customers. Each year Ofwat publishes comparative information on levels of service. The Customer Service Committees (CSCs) audit the service to individual customers. Companies vie with each other on customer charters. Companies strive to provide better services to customers, not only in the areas measured and reported on by the Director, but also in other areas (for example, increased levels of payments to business customers if standards of service are not met).

Comparisons are used widely in Ofwat's regulatory work both at price reviews and at other times. These comparisons are used to:

- estimate the minimum operating and capital expenditure which should be allowed for in setting price limits;
- make assumptions about the cost of capital and other financial parameters to be assumed in setting price limits; and
- press companies to improve quality of service to customers (for example, higher water pressure, less sewer flooding, faster responses to queries, better arrangements for charging, more appropriately structured tariffs, better transfer-pricing/ring-fencing policies, increased compensation for poor service, better resolution of complaints, improved policies for disadvantaged customers and better policies for sharing benefits with customers either in the form of rebates or by carrying out discretionary investment).

Comparative competition will only work if the regulator can compare a diversity of management styles resulting from a diversity of owners. Potential mergers between water and sewerage companies, therefore, are treated with caution. The Secretary of State has a duty to refer mergers, other than those involving very small companies, to the Monopolies and Mergers Commission (MMC). Small mergers are those where neither the value of the assets of the undertaker, nor the value of the assets of any water or sewerage undertaker already belonging to the person making the takeover, exceed £30m. These mergers may, however, still be referred to the MMC at the discretion of the Secretary of State under the Fair Trading Act 1973.

The MMC must also, in considering any mergers under the Water Industry Act 1991 and whether they operate or can be expected to operate against the public interest, have regard to: 'the desirability of giving effect to the principle that the Director's ability, in carrying out his functions by virtue of this Act, to make comparisons between different water enterprises should not be prejudiced' (section 34(3)(a) of the Water Industry Act 1991, as amended by section 39 of the Competition and Service (Utilities) Act 1992).

In the most recent merger references (the bids made by Severn Trent and Wessex Water for South West Water and by General Utilities and SAUR for Mid Kent Water), the MMC concluded that the proposed mergers would be expected to operate against the public interest. The MMC was considering the proposals in an industry which had significantly altered since 1989. A series of mergers had reduced the number of water only companies to 19 (from 29). Five of these have asset values below the £30m threshold for automatic references, and, of the remaining 14, a number are owned, materially influenced, or controlled by one or other of three major groups, General Utilities, SAUR, and Lyonnaise des Eaux. The particular adverse effects—adverse to the public interest—noted by the MMC were the prejudice to the Director's ability to make comparisons between different undertakers. The MMC considered there were no recommendations it could make to the Secretary of State which would be sufficient to remedy the loss of a comparator and, accordingly, recommended that the mergers should be prohibited.

Comparative competition will continue to underpin the regulatory regime for water. At the same time I would like to see the water and sewerage industry opened up to more competitive pressures.

How might competition through markets supplement competition through yardsticks? The scope for significantly beneficial results from market competition depends on the supply of the raw material. If this is limited, the results of competition will be modest. Creating a market for raw or treated water supplies is dealt with in the sections below on common carriage and abstraction licensing.

5. Inset Appointments—Arbitrage rather than Innovation in Supply

The 1992 legislation widened the scope for inset appointments. Since then the level of interest in these appointments has increased, mainly in respect of sites where the customer is a large user and is already receiving services from an undertaker.

Experience to date is, however, different from that contemplated in 1992. At that time, two possible types of inset appointments were contemplated. The first was where new resources would be developed or new sewerage services would be provided, and the second where a brokerage-type arrangement would be sought. Only one of the applications Ofwat has so far received has involved the development of new sewerage services and infrastructure. [1] No inset appointments involving the development of new water resources have been received. Anecdotal evidence suggests that it is because competition in the water and sewerage industry is currently focused on the large user, chiefly by sinking bore holes or constructing treatment plants on the customers' sites, that there are few benefits, to either supplier or customer, for such arrangements to fall within the regulated industry.

I would like to see applications for inset appointments which involve new sources of water or new ways of disposing of treated effluent. To date, however, the majority of applications received since 1992 concern applications by a third party. Of the 28 applications received since 1992, 23 have related to brokerage arrangements. None, if successful, would have the immediate result of introducing a new entrant with new resources to the market. Only two existing customers have sought to become their own undertaker via the current inset appointment mechanism, and both, in the end, decided not to proceed.

(a) *Brokerage Agreements*

Brokerage applications involve the same sources of supply with a middle man driving down prices towards the cost of supply. Where there has been a dispute about the costs of supply the Director has powers to determine the price. In doing this he is assuming the role of a competitive market. The price the Director determines will reflect his view of the costs involved in supplying the particular customer. In other markets, competitors can match prices and must compete on the basis of other factors such as customer service. Applying the same principles to the water industry, it would be inconsistent for the Director not to allow

---

[1] This relates to an inset appointment application made by Anglian Water Services to become the sewerage undertaker in place of Severn Trent Water for a site formerly known as RAF Finningley, near Doncaster.

the incumbent supplier to match the price he has determined for the inset applicant. It should not be thought of as anti-competitive for the incumbent to match the price determined by the Director. As his determined price is based on costs it is not, therefore, predatory. From the customers' perspective, customers' interests have been protected in the sense that a lower price has been delivered.

Such an argument must, however, raise the question of whether such brokerage applications are ever likely to result in a customer changing supplier. Ofwat does not believe this needs to be the case. It is always up to the parties involved to agree terms. If agreement cannot be reached, terms can be referred to the Director for determination. If after this, both parties (the broker and the incumbent) offer the same price, there are other terms, e.g. levels of customer service, on which companies can compete. In the end, it is for the customer to choose whether to change supplier or not. To this extent the situation would mirror a competitive market.

Inset applications by third parties are nevertheless a valuable process and have led to significant reductions in tariffs to large customers. The price of supplying wholesale (bulk) water is being disentangled from the cost of supplying retail water. Twenty out of the 28 water companies have introduced large-user tariffs in respect of water supply, and three companies have introduced similar tariffs for sewerage services. Securing these lower tariffs involves arbitrage rather than innovation in supply. It has taken place without the granting of many inset appointments and, indeed, without the granting of any brokerage-type inset appointments. Potential competition has done the job without actual entry taking place.

(b) Lessons Learnt from the First Inset Applications

Originally Ofwat thought that inset applications would take approximately 6 months to resolve. In practice they have taken longer. Why? Inset appointments are new, both to the applicant and to the regulator. Care should be taken to get it right. As is to be expected, policy has evolved from considering the various applications.

Ofwat has experienced delay by the interested parties in making information available. I would like to see undertakers placed under an obligation to offer terms on which such supplies and connections would be made. The process to be used when considering an inset application contemplated an exchange of information. In practice, requests have been received from applicants, incumbents, and consultees for their representations to be treated confidentially. This has only made Ofwat's task more difficult.

In future, information received from the applicant and the undertaker which is requested to provide a bulk supply or a mains sewerage connection will be exchanged to allow the opportunity for comment. It should prove an effective tool for testing the arguments of the applicant and existing undertaker. The Director will, of course, consider requests for restrictions on the disclosure of specific information. But such non-disclosure must not be allowed to prejudice the outcome. This increased transparency should increase understanding of the issues and stimulate a debate on costs.

(c) *Successful Inset Appointments*

The first successful inset appointment was made on 28 May 1997 and involved a variation to the appointment of Anglian Water Services (Anglian) to incorporate Buxted Chickens of Flixton, Suffolk, into its area of supply. The site falls within the area normally supplied by Essex & Suffolk Water. Supply to Buxted exceeds 250 megalitres (Ml) per annum and thus qualifies for an inset appointment. Anglian will, from 1 October 1997, supply this customer with water, being already the appointed sewerage undertaker. A second inset application involving sewerage services is currently under consultation (RAF Finningley, see footnote 1).

6. Tariff Implications of Competition

Competition may unwind the cross-subsidies in the water and sewerage industries. The costs of supplying large users are lower than for supplying household customers, where such large users do not use the local distribution system. There may be geographical differences in cost within company areas as well as between companies. Unwinding these cross-subsidies may be desirable from an economic point of view, but as relative prices shift, customers losing the benefit of cross-subsidy find prices rising. This can be particularly awkward when bills are rising for other reasons. The chairmen of the CSCs have regularly raised these concerns with the Director. There are trade-offs between politics and economics which require careful handling.

One particular feature of this existing arrangement allows companies to recoup revenue when they lose tariff customers. In order to avoid lower prices for large users being automatically recouped from other users, I have proposed removing tariffs in respect of large users (those using 250 Ml or more water per year) from the tariff basket (Ofwat, 1997*b*). Charges should still be non-discriminatory. Companies may use special agreements to charge on a different tariff to those published in their charges schemes, provided that they can show that the charges are neither unduly preferential nor unduly discriminatory. At present, however, customers are unlikely to have access to information about undertakers' charges in special agreements. I would like to see more transparency in this area and have suggested that information about these special agreements should be placed in the Ofwat library.

Water is a scarce resource. It should be used economically. This applies to business users as well as everyone else. Prices must not give the wrong economic signals to customers. Prices should promote sustainable development. Where demand is susceptible to price, charges should be based on the resource costs of the water involved, as set out in the draft framework Directive recently published by the Commission of the European Communities.

In February 1997, Ofwat published a paper prepared for it by London Economics (Ofwat, 1997c), setting out the reasons why prices should be related to the continuing costs of augmenting supply including incremental capital costs, that is, to long-run marginal costs. First, as a general rule, the lowest cost resources of water will be developed first. Consequently, new sources of supply will be increasingly costly to develop. Second, the regulatory capital value of the water industry in England and Wales, on which companies can earn a return, is estimated to be about one-tenth of the water companies' estimate of the current cost replacement value of their assets. This gives rise to the so-called capital value discount (Ofwat, 1997c) which could result in tariffs set by the incumbent undertakers being at a level that would undercut any potential new entrant wishing to develop new resources.

Tariffs, particularly for large users, should not be offered by water companies at too low a level—that is, without regard to the continuing costs of augmenting supply. Tariffs set on a full allocation of historical accounting costs would not necessarily send the appropriate signals to both customers and companies to conserve water and for companies to develop new resources. If tariffs were set in relation to the cost of developing new resources then there would be no incentive for new entrants to develop new resources.

I supported the introduction of large-user tariffs on the basis that there are cost savings when compared with supplies to other customers. Undertakers must, however, justify any further reductions by reference to their long-run marginal costs.

This approach will promote efficiency of water use and resource development, including efficient maintenance of the infrastructure. It also provides a framework for managing the development of new sources of supply and the establishment of prices for bulk supply. Setting prices to cover long-run marginal costs will involve development of more sophisticated tariffs. Such tariffs should achieve better demand management and generate the greater revenues necessary to expand the capacity of water company systems.

Sensible tariffs should enable customers and potential suppliers to make better choices about their supply and their consumption. Save the environment and save your pocket. The Aire and Calder project (see Centre for Exploitation of Science and Technology, 1994) gives a good example of how businesses can help themselves—60 per cent of measures to reduce waste had a pay-back of less than one year, 10 per cent had a pay-back of over 2 years. Setting bulk supply prices for inset appointments without regard to the long-run marginal costs would not provide an incentive for the efficient use of resources.

7. The Way Forward?

There are various ways in which the water industry may be opened up to competitive forces. These include the following.

(i) Insets involving new sources of supply

Inset appointments would have wider benefits if associated with new sources of supply. Such sources may be untapped water under major cities such as London and Birmingham where the water table is rising, water from rivers which are cleaned up as a result of the better treatment of waste water, or new boreholes in areas where underground supplies are not depleted. If such sources are to be developed, we should ask whether existing pipes can be used to deliver such water to customers, by people other than the existing company, i.e. by developing common carriage and opening up the network to other suppliers.

(ii) Opening up the network—common carriage

Opening up existing networks to common carriage is transforming the telecoms, gas, and electricity industries. Unlike in the other utilities, there is no statutory entitlement of access to an undertaker's pipes in the water industry. In the case of water there are two big problems to be solved. The first is the issue of quality and whether the standards set can be safeguarded. The second is whether customers will experience changes in taste, and hardness, which will lead them to regard the product as inferior.

A report commissioned jointly by the then Department of the Environment and Ofwat from the Water Research Centre, concluded that the difficulties in safeguarding standards, while presenting challenges, are not insurmountable.

On the second point, I believe that attempts to ensure taste would never change as a result of common carriage are likely to ensure that competition could not take place. Changes in taste and hardness would, therefore, have to be accepted as they are already when supplies are changed within a company's grid.

The responses to the proposals made by the previous government for common carriage were generally supportive and Ofwat has since been approached by potential suppliers interested in using undertakers' pipes. Without statutory entitlement for access to undertakers' pipes, this route is unlikely to succeed without challenge to competition legislation.

The biggest opportunity for developments in this area may, however, lie in the proposals currently being considered by the government for inclusion in a Competition Bill.

(iii) Using Articles 85 & 86

The government is currently consulting on proposals to introduce a Competition Bill. The Bill will introduce a prohibition-based approach to competition law in the UK. There are two prohibitions. First, a prohibition of anti-competitive agreements, cartels, and concerted practices, based on Article 85 of the Treaty of Rome. Second, a prohibition of abuse of a dominant position, based on Article 86 of the same treaty. Breaches are to be judged according to their effect or intended effect on competition (which contrasts with the current 'form'-based approach).

The Director is to have concurrent powers with the Director General of Fair Trading, with decisions subject to appeal to a specially created appeals body, the Competition Commission (a reformulated MMC).

The Bill will markedly strengthen UK competition law. The prohibitions will allow more effective action against anti-competitive behaviour, strengthen investigatory powers, allow interim measures to be imposed, and make available powerful sanctions, including the right to fine a firm up to 10 per cent of its annual UK turnover.

It is likely that the provisions in relation to abuse of dominant position will be the more significant in terms of the development of competition in the water industry, given its vertical structure and regional monopoly position.

The prohibition of abuse of dominant position may well prove to be a key element in the development of common carriage for water.

Potential new entrants to the water industry could ask incumbent water undertakers for terms and conditions to use their distribution networks for moving water. Incumbents could be prevented from abusing their dominant position and, as such, may need to offer terms and conditions for such purposes.

(iv) A market in abstraction licences

The opportunities for competition could be enhanced by suppliers competing for resources. The willingness of the Environment Agency to licence new sources of water (and the re-use of waste water in rivers) is critical. Tradability of abstraction licences (possibly even the auctioning of such licences) could transform the present position by simplifying transfers and stimulating people to find new sources of supply.

New entrants may develop new resources, either by obtaining new abstraction licences or capitalizing on existing water resources. They need not apply for an inset appointment—the ability to make private or unregulated supplies is one significant difference between the water industry and the other utilities.

On 19 May 1997, the Minister for the Environment announced a comprehensive review of the system for abstraction licensing, to include consideration of tradable abstraction rights and charges for abstraction.

(v) Connection work

In the electricity and gas sectors connection work has been opened up to competition and I have recommended that water customers, too, should be able to choose who is to carry out the work. The removal of the water undertaker's monopoly right will require legislative change, but I have welcomed the schemes being developed by some companies, for example, Severn Trent, allowing developers to arrange for the majority of the work to be carried out by independent contractors, albeit under supervision to ensure quality standards are maintained. Other companies are being encouraged to introduce similar schemes.

In conclusion, therefore, the water industry is being slowly opened up to competitive forces. This has already had desirable effects on prices and could be extended.

The challenge is whether we can stimulate new sources of supply without damaging the environment? Will those with access to water or sewerage treatment facilities come forward with applications for inset appointments linked to new supplies of water or ways of disposing of effluent? The government's review of abstraction licensing may lead, in time, to a market for abstraction licences.

While recognizing the importance of competition in reducing prices, I do not want to see prices for supplies for large users fall below the continuing cost of augmenting supply. Maintaining prices in line with such costs would encourage development of new and economical sources of supply and give customers the right incentives to make efficient use of scarce water supplies.

12

Competition in the Rail Industry

JOHN SWIFT*

1. Introduction

Railways were subject to radical restructuring before the transfer of operations to the private sector. The new structure involved:

- vertical separation between the owner and operator of the network (Railtrack) and train operators, designed to avoid the distortion of competition that can arise where a dominant network operator also competes in downstream markets;
- 25 separate passenger train operating companies, providing overlapping services over some parts of the network, and six separate freight operating companies, together with the possibility of entry from 'open-access' operators;
- rolling-stock owned by three competing rolling-stock leasing companies (ROSCOs), again with the possibility of entry to the market by new players, such as rolling-stock manufacturers;
- privatization of other supply companies, involving, for example, competition in the supply of infrastructure maintenance and track renewal services provided to Railtrack; and
- licensing required by, and only by, the operators of 'railway assets'.[1]

As with the electricity industry, which was also restructured before privatization, one of the aims of the new structure was to allow competition between train operators to develop, both to protect the interests of dependent customers and to promote the use and development of the railway network through innovatory improvements in services and through lower fares. For example, the establishment of the ROSCOs was designed to minimize barriers to entry by reducing the capital required

---

* John Swift QC is the Rail Regulator.

[1] 'Railway assets' comprise networks, stations, and light maintenance depots. Thus, while Railtrack and all train operators are licensed, licences are not required by ROSCOs or companies supplying goods or services to operators of railway assets.

by 'open-access' train operators. Separating functions in this way, albeit with contracts between the different players, was expected to encourage innovation and efficiency in the provision of services, with risks being borne by those parties best able to manage them. By focusing subsidy on the franchised passenger train operators, it also allowed potentially profitable companies to be created out of a loss-making industry. But as I have described elsewhere (IEA, 1996), this 'blackboard structure' has proved more complex to implement than the textbooks would suggest, and there have been tensions between the aim of promoting competition — which is one of the statutory duties placed on both the Secretary of State and the Rail Regulator in the Railways Act — and achieving early privatization of railway operations. The purpose of this chapter is to describe how the structure has been modified as it has been implemented, the public-interest issues that have arisen as a consequence, and the likely future development of competition in the railway industry.

2. Moderation of Competition between Passenger Operators

Until 31 December 1996, I was under a statutory duty to take into account guidance from the Secretary of State. This duty, unique among regulators, was designed to ensure that regulatory decisions were consistent with the government's aim of early privatization of railway operations. Part of the guidance was that I should have regard to the government's policy that competition between franchisees should be limited, to provide the necessary certainty to allow the first round of franchising to proceed on a reasonable timescale. Without moderation of competition, it was feared, the risk of 'cherry-picking' by open-access operators would be so great that no private-sector operators would bid for the franchises.

Consistent with the transparent approach I have adopted to railway regulation from day one, I consulted in July 1994 on the extent to which, and the way in which, competition should be moderated (ORR, 1994a). In that consultation document, I stated clearly my belief that competition should improve efficiency and bring about benefits to passengers, and that if competition was moderated for the first generation of franchise passenger services, it might be difficult to introduce competition into the market at a later date. For those reasons, I was concerned that there should not be a total block on new competitive entry and, in particular that the competition between franchisees which resulted from the design of the franchise map should be preserved. I also looked for a framework which was predictable in its application, and which would allow a staged introduction of competition once private-sector operators were successfully installed in running the franchises.

Although much of the economic literature on access charges is written in the context of vertically integrated industries, the need to preserve cross-subsidy in order to minimize total subsidy payments which underpins the packaging of the initial franchises means that much of this literature is also relevant to railways. But while I considered ways in which the structure of access charges for franchised passenger services and open-access services might be developed to protect the financial position of the franchised operator, my conclusion was that the price mechanism alone could not balance the conflicting objectives of promoting competition while facilitating successful franchising. I looked, for example, at the framework of access deficit charges established in telecoms—but never implemented and subsequently abolished—and concluded that the same concerns expressed in that industry about uncertainty, complexity, and difficulties of calculation applied with equal or greater force to railways.

In the light of consultation, the policy I adopted (ORR, 1994b) was to adopt quantitative controls on the extent of new competitive entry. My overall competition policy objectives were, and remain:

- to use actual competition or the firm prospect of it in the provision of railway passenger services as a significant means of protecting the interests of passengers;
- to look to other means to protect passengers' interests where actual competition or the firm prospect of it is not available;
- to encourage the development of innovative services which enhance the use of the network, consistent with the competitive framework I have established; and
- to seek to establish a competitive environment which will promote efficiency and economy in the use of the network and which will promote the use of the network.

My decisions on moderation of competition have been implemented in the access agreements entered into between Railtrack and each of the train operators, which I approve under the provisions of the Railways Act. These agreements place a contractual restriction on Railtrack's ability to sell additional access rights to other existing or new operators. During the first stage of moderation of competition, which is expected to expire in 1999, operators are generally protected from competition on all point-to-point flows which exceed a specified materiality threshold (generally 0.2 per cent of each train operator's turnover). In some cases, protection is conditional, allowing other named existing operators to bid for additional rights, but, in most cases, new entry for scheduled passenger services is not permitted without the incumbent operator's agreement.

In the second stage of moderation of competition, which is expected to start in 1999 and expires automatically on 31 March 2002, the scope for new competitive entry will be increased. Operators will be able to nominate a revised list of protected flows for Stage II. Instead of entry being prohibited on those nominated flows approved by the Regulator as under Stage I, new entry will be permitted up to a threshold level (not exceeding 20 per cent of total revenue from protected flows). On existing competitive flows, and those nominated flows on which new entry occurs, there will be no subsequent restrictions on new entry. (Access rights for the new services will, of course, continue to require the Regulator's approval.)

Even where Railtrack has a contractual right to sell additional access rights, it would be open to me to refuse to approve such rights if I considered that to do so would be contrary to the public-interest objectives in the Railways Act. Developing competition involves a balance between the interests of the new entrant and the incumbent operator, and may also bring gains or losses to passengers. If a proposal for new access rights threatened the viability of existing services without bringing countervailing passenger benefits, I would be minded not to approve the new rights. But there is a clear danger in trying to 'pick winners', and to approve only new competitive entry which appears to be clearly in the interests of passengers. A key reason for promoting competition is that it operates as a 'discovery mechanism', and achieves results which far exceed those that result from a planned system. The second stage of moderation of competition has therefore been explicitly designed to leave it to the market to identify which of the nominated flows should, in practice, be opened up for competition.

It is too early to judge how far on-rail competition between passenger operators will develop. I do not, therefore, have any preconceptions about the nature of the competitive regime beyond 2002, although I have said that I expect changes to be incremental in nature. Again, there are potential lessons from other industries, where the introduction of competition has been phased both according to the size of customer and geographically. I also recognize that some operators may require protection from competition in the longer term in order to provide sufficient certainty to support investment in network enhancements or improved rolling-stock. For example, I have agreed that the main flows from London to stations on the West Coast Main Line should be protected from competition for the whole of the 15-year franchise period, provided the planned upgrade in services—involving both infrastructure enhancement and investment in a new fleet of tilting trains—is taken forward.

3. Horizontal Integration between Passenger Operators

Given the decision to moderate on-rail competition, it was all the more important to ensure that potential competition between franchisees should not be lost as a result of operators coming under common control. This created a potential tension between the duty of the Franchising Director to achieve best value for money in the award of initial franchises and my objective of preserving and ultimately increasing competitive opportunities. But the position was not straightforward for the Franchising Director either: successful completion of the franchising programme depended on maintaining a sufficiently broad field of potential bidders, so that the bidding process itself operated effectively. The Franchising Director also has a concern to ensure that, if any one of the franchisees gets into financial difficulties, there are other potential operators able to take on the franchise; he will also want to ensure a sufficiently broad range of potential bidders for the second round of franchising, starting in the year 2000.

In the case of the water industry, a special merger regime has been put in place to ensure that there are sufficient independent operators for the system of comparative competition to operate effectively. (The origins of this policy are described in Beesley (1992).) The underlying objective of the water regime, preserving management rivalry, also clearly applies in railways.

Although I share some competition functions in respect of railways with the Director General of Fair Trading (DGFT), application of the merger control provisions of the Fair Trading Act 1973 is wholly for the DGFT and the Secretary of State for Trade and Industry. In reaching decisions on individual merger proposals, however, the DGFT's established practice is to consult relevant sectoral regulators. Under the terms of the Railways Act, each franchise award constitutes a merger situation for the purposes of the Fair Trading Act.

Given the speed of the franchising process, many of the bidders have sought confidential guidance from the DGFT in advance of franchise award. In order that my advice to the DGFT on individual cases is based on consistent criteria, I published in March 1995 a document setting out my approach to mergers within the industry (ORR, 1996a). Where, as a result of the franchising process, two or more train operators potentially came under common ownership but do not share any routes in common, I have generally concluded that the effect on direct on-rail competition is limited, and that the merger would not be contrary to the public interest. Where there is an overlap, existing opportunities for on-rail competition will be lost as a result of the merger. The first issue I have considered, therefore, is whether lifting protection from competition on the common routes would be sufficient to restore existing competitive opportunities. I have lifted protection on a number of flows in the access agreements of Midland Main Line and Central Trains (both under the control of National Express) and in CrossCountry Trains' access agreement (following the acquisition by Virgin of that franchise and West Coast Trains).

On some parts of the network, capacity constraints limit the opportunities for open-access entry, so that lifting protection would not achieve the objective of restoring pre-existing competition. In such cases, I might also want to discuss with the Franchising Director whether additional protection to passengers — for example, in terms of increases in the minimum service levels or more extensive fares regulation — should be included in franchise agreements. However, any such provisions would need to be consistent with the statutory duties of the Franchising Director, which differ from mine, and would be enforced by him.

Despite — or perhaps because of — careful consideration of the possible public-interest detriments arising from train operators coming under common control, the degree of concentration of ownership resulting from the first round of franchising is relatively low. Although National Express controls five of the 25 franchises and Prism a further four, there are 13 different enterprises involved in franchising.

4. Horizontal Integration between Rail and Other Modes

Rail as a mode of transport — both for passengers and goods — is clearly in competition with other modes of transport. Indeed, a key question in considering the public-interest effects of mergers between train operators is how far this intermodal competition provides adequate protection to rail users or to what extent certain users are dependent on rail, at least in the short to medium term.[2]

For perhaps the majority of rail users, road transport offers the strongest competition to rail. Road transport offers the prospect of door-to-door service, at times to suit the passenger. For passengers, costs increase only minimally if additional people travel. But not all rail passengers have access to a car, and one of the competition issues raised by the initial franchising awards has been whether the involvement of

---

[2] The Franchising Director's policy on fare regulation, with comprehensive tariff-basket controls on commuters' fares into London, but more limited controls elsewhere, reflects a view that competition from other modes is not effective in protecting the interests of London commuters.

bus and coach companies is likely to enhance the public interest, by offering opportunities for better integration between modes,[3] or whether such mergers are against the public interest because of the loss of potential competition between modes.

Reaching a view on the public-interest implication of such cross-modal mergers depends critically on the identification of the relevant economic market. I have taken the view—as has the Office of Fair Trading (OFT) and Monopolies and Mergers Commission (MMC) in previous investigations—that rail and local bus services generally serve different markets. Although in some cases similar routes are served, the relative frequency of services, journey times, fares, and passenger numbers taken together suggest that the two modes appeal to different users. In such cases, common ownership of bus and rail services may bring positive public-interest benefits by providing opportunities for inter-modal integration which would not otherwise arise. Even here, however, the potential benefits of integration must not be overstated. It is open to train operators to provide their own dedicated bus or coach links — as has Sea Containers in respect of Great North Eastern Railways, while Stagecoach has put out to tender new bus links operating in conjunction with its South West Trains franchise. Many of the benefits of inter-modal integration may, therefore, be achievable through contracts rather than requiring joint ownership.

In some cases, local bus services may be in more direct competition with rail services. This possibility was reflected in the decision by the Secretary of State for Trade and Industry that a successful bid by Stagecoach for the ScotRail franchise would be referred to the Monopolies and Mergers Commission. In the event, that franchise was awarded to National Express.

An earlier franchised acquisition by National Express, Midland Main Line, was referred to the Monopolies and Mergers Commission because of the concern that the loss of competition between long-distance coach services and rail services from the East Midlands to London would be against the public interest. The issue of coach/rail competition was explored at some length in an earlier MMC report (MMC, 1994). That report concluded that, while coach services were regarded as inferior to rail services, reflected in a differential of some 30 per cent in relative fares levels, competition between them for the leisure market placed a constraint on the actions of both coach and rail operators. This conclusion was endorsed in the MMC's report on the Midland Main Line franchise award (MMC, 1996e).

---

[3] The need for such integration has been highlighted recently by the UK Round Table on Sustainable Development (Round Table, 1997).

That report highlighted two particular problems in judging the public-interest implications of railway mergers:
- the limited extent of information on cross-elasticities between rail and other modes; and
- the difficulty in adopting effective and proportionate structural remedies, particularly after a merger has taken place.

The second issue highlights the difficulty involved in trading off different aspects of the public interest, and the timing issues that arise in the UK system of merger control. The Franchising Director took the decision to award the Midland Main Line franchise to National Express on the basis that it offered best value for money, aware of the possibility of a MMC reference, but not able to take competition issues into account given his statutory duties. From the perspective simply of promoting competition, award to a different franchisee—so that long-distance coach operation and rail services were under different ownership—would have been the best outcome. But even in terms of the Regulator's public-interest objectives in Section 4 of the Railways Act, there was a need to balance the impact on the Franchising Director's budget and the service improvement offered by National Express, compared with what might be regarded by some as the more theoretical benefits from competition.

Whatever the *ex ante* view of the public interest might have been, in practice, the MMC was asked to consider the issues only after the franchise had been awarded. In those circumstances, requiring National Express to divest the rail franchise clearly appeared disproportionate, both in terms of the impact on National Express itself and in terms of the potential impact on the remainder of the franchising programme. But alternative structural remedies—such as requiring National Express to divest the specific overlapping coach routes—also raised questions of effectiveness. A key issue was whether barriers to entry in the coach market were sufficiently low that anti-competitive behaviour by National Express on the routes in question would be controlled by the threat of new entry.

The MMC concluded that the nature of National Express's activity—in particular, the extent to which it is able to offer network benefits similar to those enjoyed by rail users—meant that the potential for new entry could not be relied on to constrain its behaviour. But that very difficulty of entering the long-distance coach market meant that simple divestment of the routes would neither guarantee their provision by another operator nor, in the event of such entry, allow a new operator to offer the same service involving network benefits unless National Express was required to provide these to the new competitor. The MMC had sufficient doubts about the practicability of such a structural solution that it concluded that behavioural undertakings — in terms of limits on coach fare increases and controls on coach service levels — would be the most appropriate way of remedying the public-interest detriments of the merger.

5. Vertical Reintegration

Vertical separation in the railway industry was designed to achieve a number of objectives. For example, by separating network ownership from operating trains, the risk of anti-competitive behaviour by the network owner in downstream markets — which has been a perennial concern in telecoms — is avoided. Establishment of the ROSCOs was also designed to improve the prospects for competition: by reducing the capital requirements for train operators, the field for potential bidders for franchises was widened, making competition for the market more effective; and operation of an effective market in rolling-stock should also make it easier for on-rail competition to develop, both between existing franchisees and through the entry of open-access operators.

It is a condition of Railtrack's network licence that it cannot have a direct or indirect interest in the ownership of rolling-stock or the operation of trains without my approval. I attach great importance to financial transparency, and the avoidance of cross-subsidy in the relationship between the ownership and operation of infrastructure, the operation of trains, and other railway activities. This principle is also contained in European Community Directives. However, I recognize that there may be situations where vertical integration is in the public interest — one current example is on the Isle of Wight, where Island Line leases the network from Railtrack as well as operating the trains — and it may be that some schemes for developing the rail network would be more effectively taken forward if the promoter of the scheme had a direct interest in its use. But I would expect such situations to remain the exception rather than the rule.

The acquisition of one of the ROSCOs, Porterbrook Leasing Company Limited, by Stagecoach Holdings plc in 1996 raised difficult questions about the public-interest implications of such vertical reintegration, given the objectives underpinning the original industry structure. If either upstream (rolling-stock) or downstream (train-operation) markets were fully competitive, such vertical integration would be of limited concern. Indeed, there could in those circumstances be benefits from economies of scope and internalization of the risks which arise because of asymmetry of information between ROSCOs and train operators on the development of train services, and hence on the likely residual value of rolling-stock at the end of franchises. As described above, however, there are significant constraints placed on on-rail competition. Given the limited extent to which rolling-stock can be used on different parts of the network, and the absence of a 'pool' of surplus vehicles, the three ROSCOs could be regarded as being dominant in effectively three separate markets so far as existing rolling-stock is concerned, rather than vigorously competing across the whole industry. There does, however, appear to be more vigorous competition for new rolling-stock between the individual ROSCOs and new entrants, such as train manufacturers.

Against this background, acquisition of Porterbrook by Stagecoach therefore raised questions about the future state of competition in the market for provision of rolling-stock to train-operating companies, be they franchisees or open-access operators, in particular, those that may be competing with train-operating companies owned by Stagecoach; the consequent possibilities for the future state of competition in the market for the provision of passenger services, which might act to the detriment of passengers and have an adverse effect on the financial position of the Franchising Director; the impact on rolling-stock investment programmes; and the longer-term effects on industry structure of the precedent set by allowing vertical integration between ROSCOs and train-operating companies.

Although merger control functions are not exercised by sectoral regulators, there is now a well-established procedure for regulators to consult on mergers affecting the industry for which they are responsible, as a basis for providing advice to the DGFT before he makes his recommendation to the Secretary of State for Trade and Industry on whether the merger should be cleared or referred to the MMC, or whether undertakings should be sought in lieu of future reference. Accordingly, I issued a consultation paper exploring these concerns once the merger was announced (ORR, 1996b).

As part of its proposal for acquiring Porterbrook, Stagecoach offered a number of behavioural undertakings to establish Chinese Walls between its different operations and to commit itself, in its rolling-stock activities, to avoiding discrimination between Stagecoach-owned train operators and other train operators. In my consultation, I sought views on whether such undertakings would be adequate, or whether other measures should be sought, or the merger referred to the MMC for full examination.[4] Following this consultation, I provided confidential ad-

---

[4] Although clearly a key part of the railway industry, rolling-stock companies are not subject to licensing, so the option of modifying licence conditions to control possible anti-competitive behaviour was not available.

vice to the DGFT, who in turn recommended to the Secretary of State that modified undertakings should be accepted in lieu of a reference to the MMC. This recommendation was accepted and undertakings were subsequently agreed with Stagecoach. The undertakings seek to ensure that Porterbrook does not discriminate between Stagecoach-owned train operators and other operators when it comes to the supply of rolling-stock, and that ring-fences are established around the leasing and train-operating activities to prevent the exchange of confidential information about plans of other train operators. These undertakings also include monitoring provisions.

A particular issue which this merger highlighted was the extent to which the benefits of closer integration might be achieved through contractual arrangements rather than full merger. Indeed, one of the clear benefits of rail privatization has been the establishment of medium- and long-term contractual commitments between the parties—including commitments by the state to the Franchising Director, as to future subsidy levels—in place of the annual haggle over public expenditure which was a characteristic of nationalized industries.

6. Control of Anti-competitive Behaviour

Railway operators are all subject to the provisions of general competition law, including the monopoly provisions of the Fair Trading Act and the Competition Act. But in common with other regulated industries, opera-tors of railway facilities are also required to hold a licence which I monitor and enforce, and, subject to the procedural provisions in the Railways Act, may modify. In the case of railways, regulatory approval is also required for each individual contract of access to railways facilities (track, stations, and light maintenance depots) and any subsequent amendments; without such approval, agreements are void.

The access and licensing provisions of the Railways Act have three main purposes:

- safety and insurance, and to protect the interests of particular groups of users such as the disabled;
- to ensure that network benefits—the ability to obtain accurate and impartial information on all rail services, irrespective of operator, and to purchase through tickets for services covering more than one operator—are maintained; and
- to ensure that all operators and potential operators have equal access to the railway network and that the scope for anti-competi-tive behaviour is controlled.

In securing the third objective, I have sought to strike a balance between detailed approval of individual access agreements and more general provisions contained in licences. For example, now that the initial agreements for access to light maintenance depots are in place, I have sought to withdraw from detailed scrutiny of changes to those agreements. I have put in place, as provided for in the Railway Act, 'general approvals', which allow facility owners and beneficiaries to agree changes in access contracts which can then take effect without my prior approval.

My objective in doing this is not simply to reduce the burden of regulation, but more positively to promote development of the market in depot services, which has already seen a number of changes including contracting activities out to vehicle manufacturers. Although depot operators have a degree of geographical monopoly, there is clearly scope for a more competitive market to develop over time. However, until this happens, dependent users still risk exploitation, and need protection by the Regulator. My general approval does not override the obligation placed on depot operators in their licences not to discriminate unduly between depot users. Depot operators are also required to maintain separate accounts for their depot activities, and I have recently issued a detailed statement of the accounting information I require from them (ORR, 1996c).

Train operator licences also contain provisions to control exclusionary behaviour and, in the case of passenger train operators, predatory pricing. These provisions are not drawn as widely as the Fair Trading Condition recently introduced into telecom licences.[5] However, they cover some of the same ground as contained in Articles 85 and 86 of the Treaty of Rome, for example, where railway operators control what might be regarded as an essential facility. If a dominant operator acts in a way which excludes or limits competition, the procedure in the licence could lead to the particular action being prohibited. Given the intention of the new Government to incorporate the provisions of Articles 85 and 86 into UK competition law, further consideration will be needed about the circumstances in which use of licence provisions, rather than direct enforcement under general competition law, will be appropriate.

[5] The Condition allows the Regulator to investigate potential exclusionary behaviour or predatory pricing, and to issue a determination Notice. There is only a breach of the licence condition if the terms of that Notice are breached, whereas the telecom Condition contains a direct prohibition on anti-competitive behaviour. The definition of exclusionary behaviour is also limited to actions which unfairly 'exclude or limit competition between the licence holder and any other passenger service operator', and does not extend to distortion of competition in transport markets more generally.

7. Freight

Particular competition issues have arisen in respect of the rail freight market. Consistent with its overall restructuring programme, the government originally proposed to split British Rail's rail freight activities into six separate companies (three companies involved in domestic train load freight; Freightliner, mainly concentrating on container flows from deep sea ports; Railfreight Distribution, which includes international traffic; and Rail Express Systems, which operates services for the Royal Mail). In the event, while Freightliner was sold to a management buy-in team, the other five companies were sold to the same consortium, English, Welsh and Scottish Railway Holdings Ltd (EWS). Although open-access entry is unrestricted for freight traffic, the only services currently run by operators other than Freightliner and EWS are 'own-account' services operated by National Power and Direct Rail Services (a subsidiary of British Nuclear Fuels Limited). The result is that the majority of freight customers have little or no choice between rail freight operators.

While, for many types of freight, road competition constrains any market power that EWS might enjoy as the dominant rail freight operator, I have been concerned to ensure that it should not exploit its dominant position either by charging excessive prices to those of its customers who might be dependent on rail in the short or medium term, or by making it more difficult for new players to enter the market, for example, by refusing to sell surplus rolling-stock in the open market. I have, therefore, agreed with EWS licence modifications which will provide specific information on prices to final customers and on the disposition of its rolling-stock, as well as establishing a requirement not to cross-subsidize between EWS rail freight services, passenger charter services operated by Rail Express Systems, and any other activities undertaken by EWS.

As part of its strategy for developing rail freight, EWS has recently agreed a revised access contract with Railtrack, and submitted it to me for my approval. A single agreement replaces the hundred or so agreements under which EWS currently gains access to Railtrack's network, essentially with a different agreement for each flow. In respect of charging, the agreement envisages a fixed charge, equivalent to about three-quarters of the total track-access charges which EWS currently pays Railtrack, together with a low variable charge expressed in pounds per thousand gross tonne miles.

While I welcome moves to make it easier for the rail freight market to develop, I need to ensure that the provisions agreed between Railtrack and EWS do not make it more difficult for new operators to enter the market, for existing operators to compete, or for EWS to charge excessive prices to dependent users. Particular objectives have been:

- to protect dependent freight customers[6] from any abuse by Railtrack or freight operators of any monopoly position;
- to avoid distortion between freight customers in the final markets in which they compete;
- to promote competition between freight operators; and
- to ensure that rail freight is not put at a competitive disadvantage by complexity and uncertainty in arrangements for gaining access to the network.

As part of the process for reviewing this agreement, I consulted other operators and freight customers on whether existing provisions, both for approving modifications to access rights and in licences, are sufficient to guard against this (ORR, 1997*a*).

Analysis of the agreement suggested that there were potentially areas where approval of this agreement might enable the parties to behave in such a way as to be of regulatory concern in the future. For example:

- Railtrack may decide not to offer the same terms to other existing or new freight operators so that even if their operation were more efficient than that of EWS they would be less able to compete effectively for final customers;
- the low tonnage charge included in the proposed agreement could enable EWS to quote prices for new and existing traffic in a way which potentially excludes competition from other existing or potential freight operators; and
- protections for dependent rail freight customers which were previously available, either indirectly through the Regulator's scrutiny of individual access agreements or as a result of having a potentially greater choice of suppliers of railway services, are now limited. EWS may therefore be able to charge an excessive price to its dependent customers.

I sought views in particular on whether EWS's licence should be modified by including a provision prohibiting undue discrimination, on the same lines as the condition in Railtrack's network licence. I have now approved the access agreement, with modifications to protect the interests of other users, and published my provisional conclusions on the use of licence powers to deal with charging and competition issues (ORR, 1997*c*).

---

[6] In many segments of the rail freight market there is strong competition from road haulage. However, the Regulator considers that there are certain customers who do not have this choice and are therefore dependent on rail freight at least in the short and medium term.

8. The Future

The high-level aim of my office is 'to create a better railway for passengers and freight customers and better value for public funding authorities, through effective regulation in the public interest'. One of the supporting objectives is to 'ensure that where workable competitive structures can be achieved, and can benefit users, they are promoted and that monopoly is controlled to protect users and deliver benefits to them'. In this chapter, I have sought to explain how I have pursued this objective during the early stages of railway privatization.

There were no golden shares in railways, and a process of consolidation and reorganization has already started to take place, both through the initial franchising and sale processes and through subsequent acquisitions. The UK electricity industry shows how quickly ownership structures can change if mergers and takeovers are allowed to proceed. Even in that case, however, the extent of vertical reintegration has been limited, following the decision of the Secretary of State for Trade and Industry to block the mergers between National Power and Southern Electric and between PowerGen and Midlands Electricity. One of his reasons for doing so was a concern that significant reintegration would frustrate the development of consumer competition, which is due to be extended to all domestic users in 1998.

I expressed similar concerns in my consultation on the merger between Stagecoach and Porterbrook. While reintegration would be less of a concern if all parts of the railway industry were open to effective competition, early reintegration might prevent that effective competition ever emerging. It is for this reason, among others, that I have stated clearly (ORR, 1997b) that I will only support merger proposals in putting advice to the DGFT where I consider that a merger clearly operates in the public interest.

Developments in the UK railway industry will also be affected by developments in Europe. Already, some of the franchise awards have been considered under the European Community Merger Regulation; and although this prohibits member states from exercising competition functions under domestic legislation, the distinction between competition functions and effective ongoing regulation will need further clarification. The EU is also developing proposals for restructuring railways, with increasing emphasis on open access (EU, 1996), which will have an inevitable impact on the UK, even if only to reinforce the aims underlying the Railways Act.

I cannot forecast where the next merger or takeover might take place. My reaction to it will depend on the circumstances of the case. Nor can

I predict the extent to which on-rail competition will develop. However, I believe that the policies and criteria I have established in considering competition issues in the railway industry so far provide a sound basis for dealing with future cases, and demonstrate the importance I attach to competition. I believe it is in the interests of both rail users and operators for competition to continue to increase in the rail industry.

Bibliography

Areeda, P., and Turner, D. (1975), 'Predatory Pricing and Related Practices under Section 2 of the Sherman Act', *Harvard Law Review*, **88**, 637–733.

Armstrong, M. (1996*a*), 'Multiproduct Nonlinear Pricing', *Econometrica*, **64**, 51–75.

— (1996*b*), 'Network Interconnection', Discussion Paper no. 9625, University of Southampton, forthcoming in *The Economic Journal*.

— Vickers, J. (1996*a*), 'Multiproduct Price Regulation under Asymmetric Information', mimeo, University of Southampton.

— — (1996*b*), 'Regulatory Reform in Telecommunications in Central and Eastern Europe', *Economics of Transition*, **4**, 295–318.

— Cowan, S. G. B., and Vickers, J. S. (1994), *Regulatory Reform: Economic Analysis and British Experience*, Cambridge, MA, MIT Press.

— — — (1995), 'Nonlinear Pricing and Price Cap Regulation', *Journal of Public Economics*, **58**, 33–55.

— Doyle, C., and Vickers, J. S. (1996), 'The Access Pricing Problem: A Synthesis', *Journal of Industrial Economics*, **44**, 131–50.

Baumol, W. (1996), 'Predation and the Logic of the Average Variable Cost Test', *Journal of Law and Economics*, **39**, 49–72.

— Sidak, J. G. (1994), *Toward Competition in Local Telephony*, Cambridge, MA, MIT Press.

Becke, E. (1996), 'Factors Influencing Demand for Train Travel on the Reading–Gatwick Line', unpublished dissertation, University of Salford.

Beesley, M. E. (1992), 'Mergers and Water Regulation', in *Privatisation, Regulation and Deregulation*, London, Routledge.

— Littlechild, S. C. (1989), 'The Regulation of Privatized Monopolies in the United Kingdom', *RAND Journal of Economics*, **20**(3), 454–72.

British Gas (1989*a*), 'Gas Transportation Services', London, British Gas.

— (1989*b*), 'Schedules of Prices and Terms for the Supply of Gas', London, British Gas.

— Ofgas (1993), 'Gas Transportation and Storage: Joint Consultation Document', London, British Gas and Office of Gas Supply.

Byatt, I. (1997), 'Taking a View on Price Review. A Perspective on Economic Regulation in the Water Industry', *National Institute Economic Review*, January, 77–81

Cave, M., and Williamson, P. (1996), 'Entry, Competition and Regulation in UK Telecommunications', *Oxford Review of Economic Policy*, 12(4), 100–21.

Centre for Exploitation of Science and Technology (1994), *Waste Minimisation: A Route to Profit and Cleaner Production*, an interim report prepared by Neil Johnston, 2nd edn.

Council of Economic Advisers (1996), *Economic Report of the President*, Washington, DC, United States Government Printing Office.

Demsetz (1968), 'Why Regulate Utilities?', *Journal of Law and Economics*, 11, 55–66.

Department of Energy (1988), *Privatising Electricity*, Cm 322, London, HMSO.

DoE (1996), *Water: Increasing Customer Choice*, London, Department of the Environment.

Department of Transport (1992), *New Opportunities for the Railways: The Privatisation of British Rail*, White Paper, Cm 2012, London, HMSO.

Dilnot, A., and Helm, D. R. (1987), 'Energy Policy, Merit Goods and Social Security', *Fiscal Studies*, 8(3), 29–48.

Dixit, A. K., and Pindyck, R. S. (1994), *Investment under Uncertainty*, Princeton, Princeton University Press.

Doe, B. (1996), 'Tickets to Disaster', *Global Transport*, Autumn.

Economides, N. (1994), 'The Economics of Networks', New York University, Leonard N. Stern School of Business, Department of Economics, November.

Electricity Act (1989), Chapter 29, London, HMSO.

Energy Committee (1986), *Regulation of the Gas Industry*, HC15, HMSO.

EU (1996), *A Strategy for Revitalising the Community's Railway*, European Commission White Paper.

FERC (1996), '*Order 888*', Washington DC, Federal Energy Regulatory Commission.

Foreman-Peck, J., and Millward, R. (1994), *Public and Private Ownership of British Industry, 1820–1990*, Oxford, Clarendon Press.

Funk, C. (1992), 'How Can Natural Gas Markets Be Competitively Organized?', Économies et Sociétés, Série Économie de l'Énergie - EN, 5, 239-261.

Gas Act (1986), Chapter 44, London, HMSO.

—   (1995), Chapter 45, London, HMSO.

Gas Consumers Council (1996), *Annual Report 1995*, London, Gas Consumers Council.

Gillan, D. (1997), 'Supplying the New Railway Industry', *Modern Railways*, 426.

Gourvish, T. R. (1986), *British Railways 1948–73: A Business History*, Cambridge, Cambridge University Press.

Green, R. J., and Newbery, D. M. (1992), 'Competition in the British Electricity Spot Market', *Journal of Political Economy*, **100**(5), 929–53.

— — (1997), 'Competition in the Electricity Industry in England and Wales', *Oxford Review of Economic Policy*, **13**(1), 27–46.

Grout, P. (1996), 'Promoting the Superhighway', *Economic Policy*, **22**, 110–54.

Hancock, R., and Waddams Price, C. (1995), 'Competition in the British Domestic Gas Market: Efficiency and Equity', *Fiscal Studies*, **16**(3), 81–105.

— — (1997), 'The Competitive Market for Residential Gas Consumers, Evidence from the South West of England', Centre for Management under Regulation, University of Warwick, Research Paper 97/1.

Hansard Society (1997), *The Report of the Commission on the Regulation of Privatised Utilities*, London, The Hansard Society for Parliamentary Government.

Helm, D. R. (1994*a*), 'Regulating the Transition to the Competitive Electricity Market', in M. E. Beesley (ed.), *Regulating Utilities: The Way Forward*, IEA Readings 41, Institute of Economic Affairs in association with the London Business School.

— (1994*b*), 'British Utility Regulation: Theory, Practice, and Reform', *Oxford Review of Economic Policy*, **10**(3), 17–39.

— Rajah, N. (1994), 'Water Regulation: The Periodic Review', *Fiscal Studies*, **15**(2), 74–94.

HMSO (1996), *Transport. The Way Forward*, Cm 3234, London, HMSO.

House of Commons (1993), *British Energy Policy and the Market for Coal: Report*, HC 237, London, HMSO.

IEA (1996), *Regulating Utilities: A Time for Change?*, edited by M. Beesley, Institute for Economic Affairs.

Jenkinson, T. J., and Ljungqvist (1996), *Going Public*, Oxford, Oxford University Press.

— Mayer, C. P. (1994), 'The Costs of Privatisation in the UK and France', in M. Bishop, J. Kay, and C. P. Mayer, *Privatisation and Economic Performance*, Oxford, Oxford University Press.

— — (1997), 'Regulation, Diversification, and the Separate Listing of Utilities', in M. E. Beesley (ed.), forthcoming.

Katz, M. L., and Shapiro, C. (1994), 'Systems Competition and Network Effects', *Journal of Economic Perspectives*, **8**(2), 93–115.

Kay, J. (1995), 'Discussant's Comments', in M. Beesley (ed.), 'Utility Regulation: Challenge and Response', IEA Readings 42, London.

Klemperer, P. D., and Meyer, M. A. (1989), 'Supply Function Equilibria in Oligopoly under Uncertainty', *Econometrica*, **57**(6), 1243–77.

Laffont, J. J., and Tirole, J. (1990), 'Optimal Bypass and Cream Skimming', *American Economic Review*, **80**,1042–61.

— — (1993), *A Theory of Incentives in Procurement and Regulation*, Cambridge, MA, MIT Press.

— — (1994), 'Access Pricing and Competition', *European Economic Review*, **38**(9), 1673–710.

— — (1996), 'Creating Competition through Interconnection: Theory and Practice', *Journal of Regulatory Economics*, **10**, 227–56.

— Rey, P., and Tirole, J. (1996), 'Network Competition: I. Overview and Non-discriminatory Pricing', *RAND Journal of Economics*, forthcoming.

Littlechild, S. C. (1983), *Regulation of British Telecommunications' Profitability*, London, Department of Industry.

— (1986), *Economic Regulation of Privatised Water Authorities*, London, HMSO.

— (1988), 'Economic Regulation of Privatised Water Authorities and Some Further Reflections', *Oxford Review of Economic Policy*, **4**(2), 40–67.

— (1996), Introductory Comments on Professor C. Robinson, 'Profit, Discovery and the Role of Entry: The Case of Electricity', in M. E. Beesley (ed.), *Regulating Utilities: A Time for Change?*, IEA.

Lyons, B. R. (1996), 'Empirical Relevance of Efficient Contract Theory: Inter-firm Contracts', *Oxford Review of Economic Policy*, **12**(4), 27–52.

McCabe, K. A., Rassenti, S. J. and Smith, V. L. (1989), 'Designing 'Smart' Computer-Assisted Markets: An Experimental Auction for Gas Networks', *European Journal of Political Economy*, **5**(2/3),259–83.

McMaster, R., and Sawkins, J. W. (1993), 'The Water Industry in Scotland — Is Franchising Viable?', *Fiscal Studies*, **14**(4), 1–13.

Maddison, D., Pearce, D., *et al*. (1996), *The True Costs of Road Transport*, Earthscan.

Masten, S., and Crocker, K. (1985), 'Efficient Adaptation in Long Term Contracts: Take-or-Pay Provisions for Natural Gas', *American Economic Review*, **75**(5), 1083–93.

Mirrlees, J. (1976), 'Optimal Tax Theory: A Synthesis', *Journal of Public Economics*, **6**, 327–58.

MMC (1988), *Gas*, Cm500, Monopolies and Mergers Commission, London, HMSO.

MMC (1993a), *Gas: Volume 1 of Reports Under the Fair Trading Act 1973 on the Supply Within Great Britain of Gas Through Pipes to Tariff and Non-tariff Customers, and the Supply Within Great Britain of the Conveyance or Storage of Gas by Public Gas Supplies*, London, HMSO.

— (1993b), *Gas and British Gas plc*, Cmnd 2314–17, Monopolies and Mergers Commission, London, HMSO.

— (1994), *National Express Group PLC and Saltire Holdings Limited: A Report on the Merger Situation*, Monopolies and Mergers Commission, London, HMSO.

— (1995a), *South West Water Services Ltd: A Report on the Determination of Adjustment Factors and Infrastructure Charges for South West Water Services Ltd*, London, HMSO.

— (1995b), *Telephone Number Portability: A Report on the Reference Under Section 13 of the Telecommunications Act 1984*, London, HMSO.

— (1996a), *National Power Plc and Southern Electric Plc: A Report on the Proposed Merger*, Cm 3230, London, HMSO.

— (1996b), *PowerGen Plc and Midlands Electricity Plc: A Report on the Proposed Merger*, Cm 3231, London, HMSO.

— (1996c), *Severn Trent Plc and South West Water Plc*, Cm 3429, Monopolies and Mergers Commission, London, The Stationery Office.

— (1996d), *Wessex Water Plc and South West Water Plc*, Cm 3430, Monopolies and Mergers Commission, London, The Stationery Office.

— (1996e), *National Express Group plc and Midland Main Line Ltd: A Report on a Merger Situation*, London, Monopolies and Mergers Commission, The Stationery Office.

— (1997a), *Northern Ireland Electricity plc: A Report on the Reference under Article 15 of the Electricity (Northern Ireland) Order 1992*, London, The Stationery Office.

— (1997b), *BG plc*, Monopolies and Mergers Commission, London, The Stationery Office.

Morrison, S., and Winston, C. (1989), 'Enhancing the Performance of the Deregulated Air Transportation System', *Brookings Papers on Economic Activity*, Special Issue, 1–123.

Mueller, J., and Vogelsang, I. (1979), 'Staatliche Regulierung—Regulated Industry in den USA und Gemeinwohlbindung in wettbewerblichen Ausnahmebereichen in der Bundesrepublik Deutschland', Baden-Baden, Germany.

NGC (1996), *1996 Seven Year Statement for the years 1996/7 to 2002/3*, London, National Grid Company.

Newbery, D. M. (1994), 'The Impact of Sulfur Limits on Fuel Demand and Electricity Prices in Britain', *Energy Journal*, **15**(3), 19–41.

— (1995a), 'Competition and Regulation in the Electricity Industry', Proceedings of the OECD/World Bank Conference on Competition and Regulation in Network Infrastructure Industries, Paris.

— (1995b), 'Reforming Road Taxation', Basingstoke, Group Public Policy, The Automobile Association.

— Pollitt, M. G. (1997), 'Privatization and Restructuring in the CEGB 1986–94 — Was it Worth it?', *Journal of Industrial Economics*, September.

Offer (1994a), *Decision on a Monopolies and Mergers Commission Reference*, Birmingham, Office of Electricity Regulation, February.

— (1994b) *The Distribution Price Control: Proposals*, Birmingham, Office of Electricity Regulation, August.

— (1995), *The Distribution Price Control: Revised Proposals*, Birmingham, Office of Electricity Regulation, July.

— (1996), *Statement by the Director General of Electricity Supply About the Arrangements for Opening the Electricity Market in 1998*, Birmingham, Office of Electricity Regulation.

Offer NI (1996), *Price Control Reviews for Northern Ireland Electricity Plc: Director General's Proposals*, Belfast, Office of Electricity Regulation Northern Ireland.

Ofgas (1994a), News Release 16/94, 30 September, London, Office of Gas Supply.

— (1994b), 'Competition in the Non-domestic Market: A Consultation Document', London, Office of Gas Supply.

— (1995), 'Referral by the Gas Consumer Council Relating to Discounts for Customers Paying by Direct Debit: The Director General's Decision', London, Office of Gas Supply.

— (1996a), 'Investigation into Discounts for British Gas Supply's Tariff Customers Paying Promptly or by Direct Debit: The Director General's Decision', London, Office of Gas Supply.

— (1996b), 'Review of the Competitive Gas Supply Market Above 2,500 therms a Year', London, Office of Gas Supply.

— (1996c), '1997 Price Control Review: Supply at or below 2,500 therms a year — British Gas Trading', London, Office of Gas Supply.

— (1996d), '1997 Price Control Review: British Gas Transportation and Storage: The Director General's Final Proposals', London, Office of Gas Supply.

OFT (1991), 'The Gas Review, Report', London, Office of Fair Trading.

Oftel (1995*a*), *Pricing of Telecommunications Services From 1997: A Consultative Document*, London, Oftel.

— (1995*b*), *Universal Telecommunications Services: A Consultative Document*, London, Oftel.

— (1996*a*), *Promoting Competition in Service Provision over Telecommunications Networks: A Consultative Document*, London, Oftel.

— (1996*b*), *Pricing of Telecommunications Services From 1997: A Statement*, London, Oftel.

— (1996*c*), *Fair Trading in Mobile Service Provision: A Consultative Document*, London, Oftel.

— (1996*d*), *Promoting Competition in Service Provision over Telecommunications Networks: A Statement*, London, Oftel.

— (1996*e*), *Pricing of Telecommunications Services From 1997: A Consultative Document*, London, Oftel.

— (1996*f*), *Network Charges From 1997: A Consultative Document*, London, Oftel.

— (1996*g*), *Market Information Update*, London, Oftel.

— (1997), *Network Charges from 1997*, Consultative Document, London, Oftel.

Ofwat (1991), *Paying for Water: The Way Ahead*, Birmingham, Office of Water Services.

— (1995*a*), *1995–96 Report on Tariff Structure and Charges*, Birmingham, Office of Water Services.

— (1995*b*), *Competition in the Water Industry: Inset Appointments and their Regulation*, Birmingham, Office of Water Services.

— (1996*a*), *1995–96 Report on the Cost of Water Delivered and Sewage Collected*, Birmingham, Office of Water Services.

— (1996*b*), *The Regulation of Common Carriage Agreements in England and Wales: A Consultation Paper*, Birmingham, Office of Water Services.

— (1997*a*), *1997–98 Report on Tariff Structure and Charges*, Birmingham, Office of Water Services.

— (1997*b*), *Tariff Rebalancing and the Tariff Basket – A Consultation Paper*, Birmingham, Office of Water Services.

— (1997*c*), *Water Pricing: The Importance of Long Run Marginal Costs*, Birmingham, Office of Water Services.

Oil and Gas (Enterprise) Act (1982), London, HMSO.

OPRAF (1996), Passenger Rail Industry Overview, June, Office of Passenger Rail Franchising.

Ordover, J., and Saloner, G. (1989), 'Predation, Monopolization and Antitrust', in R. Schmalensee and R. Willig (eds) (1989).

ORR (1994*a*), *Competition for Railway Passenger Services: A Consultation Document*, Office of the Rail Regulator.

— (1994*b*), *Competition for Railway Passenger Services: A Policy Statement*, Office of the Rail Regulator.

— (1996*a*), *Change of Control of Passenger Train Operators: Criteria and Procedures*, Office of the Rail Regulator.

— (1996*b*), *Stagecoach Holdings PLC's proposed Acquisition of Porterbrook Leasing Company Ltd: Consultation Paper by the Rail Regulator*, Office of the Rail Regulator.

— (1996*c*), *Regulatory Accounting Information: Light Maintenance Depots*, Office of the Rail Regulator.

— (1997*a*), *Charging, Competition and Rail Freight Development Issues raised by the proposed EWS Track Access Agreement: A Consultation Document*, Office of the Rail Regulator.

— (1997*b*), *Regulatory Objectives for Passenger Train and Station Operators*, Office of the Rail Regulator.

— (1997*c*), *Charging, Competition and Rail Freight Development Issues Raised by the Proposed EWS Track Access Agreement: Provisional Conclusions*, Office of the Rail Regulator.

Pethick, F. (1996), 'Competition in the Water and Sewerage Industries', *Utility Finance*, February, 18–19.

Pool Statistical Digest (1996), London, Electricity Pool of England and Wales.

Price, C. (1989), 'An Industrial Gas Tariff', University of Leicester, Department of Economics Discussion Paper No. 97.

Ramsey, F. (1927), 'A Contribution to the Theory of Taxation', *Economic Journal*, **37**, 47–61.

Round Table (1997), *Making Connections*, UK Round Table on Sustainable Development.

Sappington, D. E. (1994), 'Principles of Regulatory Policy Design', mimeo, Washington, DC, World Bank.

Schmalensee, R., and Willig, R. (eds) (1989), *Handbook of Industrial Organization*, Amsterdam, North–Holland.

Schweppe, F., Caramanis, C., Tabors, R. D. and Bohn, R. E. (1988), *Spot Pricing of Electricity*, Kluwer Academic Publishers.

Sharkey, W. W., and Sibley, D. S. (1993), 'Optimal Non-linear Pricing with Regulatory Preference over Customer Type', *Journal of Public Economics*, **50**, 197–229.

Sherman, R. (1989), *The Regulation of Monopoly*, Cambridge, Cambridge University Press.

Shleifer, A. (1985), 'A Theory of Yardstick Competition', *Rand Journal of Economics*, **16**, 319–27.

Thackray, J. (1995), *New Bills for Old: The Dilemmas of Water and Sewerage Charges*, Discussion Paper 12, London, Centre for the Study of Regulated Industries.

Tirole, J. (1988), *The Theory of Industrial Organization*, Cambridge, MA, MIT Press.

Varian, H. (1989), 'Price Discrimination', in R. Schmalensee and R. Willig (eds) (1989).

Vickers, J. S. (1994), *Concepts of Competition*, Oxford, Clarendon Press.

— Yarrow, G. (1988), *Privatisation. An Economic Analysis*, Cambridge, MA, MIT Press.

Waddams Price, C. (1996), 'Social Equity and the Provision of Electricity', mimeo, Centre for Management under Regulation, University of Warwick.

Waterson, M. (1996), 'Vertical Integration and Vertical Restraints', in T. J. Jenkinson (ed.) *Readings in Microeconomics*, Oxford, Oxford University Press.

Whish, R. (1993), *Competition Law*, 3rd edn, London, Butterworths.

Williamson, O. E. (1976), 'Franchise Bidding for Natural Monopoly — In General and With Respect to CATV', *Bell Journal of Economics*, 7, 73–107.

— (1985), *The Economic Institutions of Capitalism*, New York, Free Press.

Willig, R. D. (1978), 'Pareto-superior Nonlinear Outlay Schedules', *Bell Journal of Economics*, 9, 56–69.

Wilson, R. (1993), *Nonlinear Pricing*, Oxford, Oxford University Press.

Winsor, T. (1997), 'Railtrack's Investment Programme', *Modern Railways*, 489.

Winston, C. (1993), 'Economic Deregulation: Days of Reckoning for Microeconomists', *Journal of Economic Literature*, 31, 1263–89.

World Bank (1994). *World Development Report 1994: Infrastructure for Development*, New York, Oxford University Press.

Zupan, M. (1989), 'The Efficiency of Franchise Bidding Schemes in the Case of Cable Television', *Journal of Law and Economics*, 32.

Index

abstraction licences 245
access pricing principles 34–8
  gas industry 114–17
  rail industry 249
  telecommunications 148–53, 158
ACP (anti-competitive practices) powers 18
Acts of Parliament (UK)
  Competition Act (1980) 1
  Competition and Service (Utilities) Act (1992) 236, 238
  Energy Act (1983) 1
  Fair Trading Act (1973) 238, 251
  Gas Act (1995) 108, 110
  Oil and Gas (Enterprise) Act (1982) 1
  Railways Act (1993) 178–80, 190n, 248, 257
  Transport Act (1974) 176
  Water Industry Act (1991) 238
AdTranz 184
Aire and Calder project 243
airline industry 49, 61n
  landing rights auctions 76
Anglian Water Services 168, 239n, 241
anti-competitive practices (ACP) powers 18
Areeda–Turner rule 32

BG Trading, see Centrica
BG Transco 111, 115–17
bottleneck facilities 51–2
British Coal 88
British Energy 195
British Gas 108–31
  company split 6–7, 111
  stranded contracts problem 12–13
British Rail (BR) 178–80, 184–5
British Rail Engineering Ltd 183
British Telecom (BT) 139–47
  call charges 154n

  equipment aspects 219–27
  proposed merger with MCI 229
Burkhardt, Ed 179n, 187, 191
bus industry 186
  railway bidding by 187–8, 253
Buxted Chicken 168, 241

cable TV companies 140–1
Cellnet 145, 146
Central Electricity Generating Board (CEGB) 193
Central Trains 252
Centrica 7, 111, 113
CfDs (contracts for differences) 79
Channel Tunnel 70n
Cheadle Waterworks Company 235
Chiltern Railways 184
Cholderton 161n
Clear Communications 66
coal
  clean-coal stations 98
  coal contracts 95
  coal market collapse (UK) 90, 103
common carriage 51n, 168–70, 172–3, 243–4
comparative (yardstick) competition 162–3, 236–8
compensation issues 68
Competition Act (1980) 1
competition law (UK) 244, 258
Competition and Service (Utilities) Act (1992) 236
Concert 229
congestion pricing 46n, 47
contract carriage 55
contracting out 164
contracts for differences (CfDs) 79
CrossCountry Trains 252
cross-subsidies 6, 8, 14–15
  BT equipment and 221

cross-subsidies (*cont.*)
  entry barriers and 74
  prohibiting 31–2

'dash for gas' 103, 110
dead-weight losses 84
Demsetz–Chadwick auction 71n
derivative markets 11–12
Director General
  of Electricity Supply (DGES) 5, 20, 79,
    94–5, 105–6
  of Fair Trading 251
  of Gas Supply 109, 111, 112, 127–31
  of Telecommunications 18
  of Water Services 161, 171–2, 234, 236
Direct Rail Services 187, 259
Drakelow C (coal station) 98n
Drax 98

Eastern Electricity 8, 17
Eastern Group 8, 11, 91, 195, 197
ECPR, *see* efficient component pricing
    rule
Edison Mission Energy 11n
EFA (electricity forward agreement) 11
efficient component pricing rule (ECPR)
    34–8, 53, 54
  gas industry 115
  telecommunications 151, 153n, 158
Electricité de France 89n, 104
electricity industry 7, 18–19, 77–107
  derivative markets 11
  DGES 5, 20, 79, 94–5, 105–6
  electricity forward agreement 11
  England and Wales 77–107, 193–205
  Europe and USA 2
  natural monopoly or competitive? 45
  'pooling' 42, 56
  pre-privatization 9
  regulator's perspective 193–212
  Scotland 205–10
  smart markets 59n
  transitionary processes 20
Energy Act (UK, 1983) 1
Energy Act (USA, 1992) 2
Energy Group 8, 100, 195, 197
English Welsh & Scottish Railways (EWS)
    187, 259–60
entry restrictions (theory of) 71–4
equal access 139, 145

European utility policy 2
EWS (English Welsh & Scottish Rail-
    ways) 187, 259–60

Fair Trading Act (1973) 238, 251
Federal Energy Regulatory Commis-
    sion 2
Fife Energy 207
FirstBus 186
First Hydro 11n
flexibility mechanism 12n
forward markets 11–12
franchise competition 5, 50–1
  electricity industry 95–7
  rail industry 180–4, 189–91
  water industry 163–4
Freightliner 259

Gas Act (1995) 108, 110
gas industry 108–31
  BG company split 6–7, 111
  Chile 74
  development of competition 117–21
  European Union directives 13
  Germany 64
  Hong Kong 64
  interruptible contracts 51–2
  pipeline access charges 114–17
  regulator's role 121–3, 127–31
  regulatory reform 18
  spot markets 11–12
  tariff structure 123–7
gas-turbine plant 200–1, 207
General Utilities 163, 166, 238
golden shares 5
  NZ telecommunications and 66
Great North Eastern Railways 186n, 253
Great Western Trains 186

Hanson plc 94
Herfindahl index 195
  in England & Wales 195–6, 204–5
  in Scotland 206, 208–9
High Marnham (coal station) 98n
Hyder 5, 8
Hydro-Electric 205–10

India Telecom 70
inset appointments 165–70, 236
  large-user tariffs and 171–2, 240

inset appointments (*cont.*)
  sewerage industry 239–41
InterCity 177, 179
International Petroleum Exchange 11
inverse elasticity rule 26
Ionica 140*n*, 159
Ironbridge (coal station) 98*n*
Island Line (IOW) 255

Lang, Ian 99
large-user tariffs 171–2
  Ofwat on 167, 240, 241–2
Littlechild, Stephen 5, 20, 79, 94–5, 105–6, 164
  regulator's perspective 193–212
London Underground 184
long-term contracts 9, 45
Lyonnaise des Eaux 238

McKinnon, James 111
Magnox Electric 195
ManWeb 8, 100
Mercury 1, 139–47, 153
Mercury One-2-One 146
mergers, *see* MMC (Monopolies and Mergers Commission)
metering systems 15–16
  electricity industry 95–6
  water industry 236
Mid Kent Water 163, 166, 238
Midland Main Line 188, 252, 253–4
Midlands Electricity 94, 99, 261
Mission Energy 197
MMC (Monopolies and Mergers Commission) 16–17
  on bus/rail takeovers 188
  electricity reports 99, 101–2
  gas reports 109–11, 124
  proposal to reform 244
  rail reports 253–7
  water reports 163
  on water/sewerage companies 238
mobile telecommunications 145–6
MOTO (Mercury One-2-One) 146

National Express 188, 252, 253–4
National Grid Company 7, 193, 197
National Power 11, 77–8, 97–101, 193–205
  bidding strategy 82
  output levels 89, 202

rail freight operations 187, 259
  Southern Electric and 261
  voluntary undertakings 17
National Rivers Authority 160
natural monopoly 43–9
  in telecommunications 134–7
  in water industry 162
network externality 137–8, 137*n*
Network South Central 190*n*
Network SouthEast 179
New Zealand Telecom 66
node pricing 46–8
Northern Electricity 94
Northern Ireland Electricity 17*n*
North West Water 8
Norweb 8
nuclear power industry 104
  Nuclear Electric 78, 88, 193–205
  Scottish Nuclear 205–10
number portability 138–9, 144–5

Offer 18, 66, 79
Ofgas 18, 109, 117, 128
Ofrail 18
OFREG 17*n*
Oftel 133*n*, 139, 142–7, 157–9
  regulator's perspective 213–33
  theoretical aspects 152–3
Ofwat 161, 165, 237
  on common carriage 168, 170
  Customer Services Committees 237
  inset applications 239–41
  on large-user tariffs 167, 240, 241
Oil and Gas (Enterprise) Act (1982) 1
Orange 146

PacifiCorp 8, 11, 100
pollution
  carbon monoxide emissions 103, 104
  sulphur emissions 104
pooling 55–8
Porterbrook Leasing Company 183, 255–7
PowerGen 11, 78, 97–101, 193–205
  Midlands Electricity and 261
  output levels 89, 202
  voluntary undertakings 17
price capping 17
  electricity industry 90–1
  gas industry 121–3

price capping (*cont.*)
  global price caps 29–31
  rail industry 185
pricing structure 23–39
  congestion pricing 46*n*, 47
  deregulation and 38–9
  ECPR, *see* efficient component pricing
    rule
  gas industry 123–7
  global price caps 29–31
  price discrimination 32–3
  pricing discretion 29–33
  railway services 194–5
  Ramsey pricing 25–9, 35–8, 150, 151
  tariff baskets 161, 166–7
  in telecommunications 215–16
  two-part pricing 26
Prism 252
Private Finance Initiative (PFI) 164*n*
Privatising Electricity (White Paper, 1988)
    77, 193
Public Service Obligation (PSO) 176, 177*n*

Rail Express Systems 259
Railfreight Distribution 259
rail industry 7, 175–92
  regulator's perspective 247–62
Railtrack 7, 183, 189–92
  rail freight and 259–60
Railways Act (1993) 178–80, 190*n*, 248,
    257
Ramsey pricing 25–9
  access pricing 35–8
  telecommunications 150, 151
Ratcliffe 98
Regional Railways 179
Regulator(s), *see* Director General
resale of capacity 55
road networks 60–1, 69–70, 76, 177*n*
Rooke, Denis 108, 129
Royal Commission on Environmental
    Pollution 191
Rugeley B (coal station) 98*n*

SAUR 163, 166, 238
scheduling systems 68–70
ScotRail franchise 188*n*, 253
Scottish electricity industry 205–10

Scottish Nuclear 205–10
ScottishPower 5, 8, 94, 100, 205–10
Sea Containers 253
Severn Trent Water 238, 239*n*, 245
sewerage, *see* water/sewerage industry
Sizewell B 194
smart markets 47*n*, 48–9, 75
  in electricity industry 59*n*
social security policy 15
  welfare weights 27
Southern Electricity 94, 99, 261
South Western Electricity (SWEB) 91
South West Trains 183, 253
South West Water 15, 163, 238
spot markets 11–12, 44–9
Spottiswoode, Clare 111, 112
Stagecoach 183, 253, 255–7
stranded assets 10, 13, 68
stranded contracts 7, 12
  British Gas 12–13
super-elasticities of demand 35*n*
SWALEC 8

tariff-basket controls 161, 166–7
telecommunication industry 132–59
  ACP powers 18
  Chile 69
  Eastern Europe 132*n*
  Ghana 70
  India 70
  Nebraska (USA) 66
  New Zealand 66
  theoretical aspects 60, 147–57
  UK regulator's perspective 213–33
  United States 2, 132*n*
Telecoms Act (USA, 1996) 2
television 134
  cable TV 140–1
Trafalgar House 94
transition processes 20–1
Transport Act (1974) 176
Transport. The Way Forward (White Pa-
    per, 1996) 177*n*

unbundling 64, 65
  gas industry 123
United States of America 2, 66
United Utilities 5, 8

VAT issues 15
vertical integration 8–9
  pros and cons 11
  restructuring 65
Virgin Rail Group 183, 252
Vodafone 145, 146

Water Industry Act (1991) 238
water/sewerage industry 160–74
  geographical effects 14–15
  regulator's perspective 234–46

welfare weights 27
Welsh Water 8
Wessex Water 238
West Burton (coal station) 98n
West Coast Main Line 183, 250
West Highland Line 178
wheeling $vs.$ poolco 41
Wintershall 64n
Wisconsin Central 187

yardstick competition 162–3, 236–8